Just the Facts!

Dozens of Garden Charts
Thousands of Gardening Answers

The Editors of Garden Way Publishing

A Garden Way Publishing Book

STOREY

Storey Communications, Inc.
Schoolhouse Road
Pownal, Vermont 05261

Edited by Kathleen Bond Borie and Gwen W. Steege

Cover design by Meredith Maker

Text design and production by Nancy Bellnier, Mass Media

Production Assistance by Meredith Maker

Garden Way Publishing was founded in 1973 as part of the Garden Way Incorporated Group of Companies, dedicated to bringing gardening information and equipment to as many people as possible. Today the name "Garden Way Publishing" is licensed to Storey Communications, Inc., in Pownal, Vermont. For a complete list of Garden Way Publishing titles call 1-800-827-8673. Garden Way Incorporated manufactures products in Troy, New York, under the Troy-Bilt® brand including garden tillers, chipper/shredders, mulching mowers, sicklebar mowers, and tractors. For information on any Garden Way Incorporated product, please call 1-800-345-4454.

Printed in the United States by Courier

10   9   8   7   6   5   4

Library of Congress Cataloging-in-Publication Data

Just the facts : dozens of garden charts – thousands of gardening answers / edited by Kathleen Bond Borie and Gwen Steege.

       p.   cm.

     "A Garden Way Publishing book."

     Includes bibliographical references and index.

     ISBN 0-88266-867-6

     1. Gardening—Charts, diagrams, etc.   2. Gardening—Miscellanea.   3. Plants, Ornamental—Charts, diagrams, etc.   4. Plants, Ornamental—Miscellanea.   I. Borie, Kathleen Bond.   II. Steege, Gwen, 1940–   .   III. Garden Way Publishing.

     SB450.96.C48   1993

     635'.0212—dc20
                                        92-56146
                                          CIP

SOURCES OF CHARTS

The charts in this book appeared originally in the following Garden Way Publishing and Storey Publishing books and Country Wisdom Bulletins. (To order, write Storey Communications, Inc., P.O. Box 445, Pownal, VT 05261, or call 1-800-441-5700.)

The Able Gardener by Kathleen Yeomans, R. N. (1992, 304 pages)

A-to-Z Hints for the Vegetable Gardener from the 10,000 members of the Men's Garden Clubs of America (1976, 128 pages)

Bugs, Slugs and Other Thugs by Rhonda Massingham Hart (1991, 224 pages)

Building a Healthy Lawn by Stuart Franklin (1988, 176 pages)

Carrots Love Tomatoes by Louise Riotte (1975, 228 pages)

Creating a Wildflower Meadow by Henry W. Art. (Country Wisdom Bulletin #A-102, 1988, 32 pages)

Down-to-Earth Vegetable Gardening Know-How for the '90s by Dick Raymond (1991, 194 pages)

Fertilizers for Free by Charles Siegchrist (Country Wisdom Bulletin #A-44, 1980, 32 pages)

The Flower Arranger's Garden by Patricia R. Barrett (Country Wisdom Bulletin #A-103, 1988, 32 pages)

Flowers That Last Forever by Betty E. M. Jacobs (1988, 232 pages)

Fruits and Berries for the Home Garden by Lewis Hill (1992, 280 pages)

Fruits and Vegetables: 1001 Gardening Questions Answered by The Editors of Garden Way Publishing (1990, 160 pages)

Gardening Answers by The Editors of Garden Way Publishing (Country Wisdom Bulletin #A-49, 1981, 32 pages)

A Garden of Wildflowers by Henry W. Art (1986, 304 pages)

Growing and Using Herbs Successfully by Betty E. M. Jacobs (1976, revised 1981, 240 pages)

The Harvest Gardener by Susan McClure (1992, 304 pages)

Herbal Treasures by Phyllis Shaudys (1990, 320 pages)

Joy of Gardening by Dick Raymond (1982, 384 pages)

Landscaping with Annuals by Ann Reilly (Country Wisdom Bulletin #A-108, 1988, 32 pages)

Landscaping with Bulbs by Ann Reilly (Country Wisdom Bulletin #A-99, 1987, 32 pages)

Lawns and Landscapes: 1001 Gardening Questions Answered by The Editors of Garden Way Publishing (1989, 160 pages)

Let It Rot! by Stu Campbell (1975, revised 1990; 160 pages)

The Mulch Book by Stu Campbell (1991, 128 pages)

Perennials: 1001 Gardening Questions Answered by The Editors of Garden Way Publishing (1989, 160 pages)

Planning & Planting Your Dwarf Fruit Orchard by The Editors of Garden Way Publishing (Country Wisdom Bulletin #A-133, 1992, 32 pages)

The Pleasure of Herbs by Phyllis Shaudys (1986, 288 pages)

Pruning Trees, Shrubs, and Vines by The Editors of Garden Way Publishing (Country Wisdom Bulletin #A-54, 1980, 32 pages)

Pruning Simplified by Lewis Hill (1979, 224 pages)

Roses Love Garlic by Louise Riotte (1983, 240 pages)

Saving Seeds by Marc Rogers (1990, 192 pages)

Secrets of Plant Propagation by Lewis Hill (1985, 168 pages)

Starting Seeds Indoors by Ann Reilly (Country Wisdom Bulletin #A-104, 1988, 32 pages)

Successful Small Food Gardens by Louise Riotte (1993, 200 pages)

Sunspaces by Peter Clegg & Derry Watkins (1987, 208 pages)

Tips for the Lazy Gardener by Linda Tilgner (1985, 128 pages)

Contents

A Word about This Book

One of gardening's appeals is its mystery.

No matter how experienced the gardener, each year's garden offers discoveries and

new challenges. Learning to garden is therefore a process of accumulating information,

some of it from books by other gardeners and some from the garden itself.

At times, however, a quick reference is more valuable than a lengthy explanation.

How many times have you wished you could get right to the facts —just the facts?

In this book, we have drawn from a wide variety of sources to provide a collection of lists, charts,

and maps that will help you quickly and easily find the basic information you need.

For in-depth explanations, refer to the sources cited with each chart.

We hope this book will serve as another useful gardening tool

to make your garden more successful and more enjoyable.

PART I:
GARDENING TECHNIQUES

WEATHER

USDA Hardiness Zone Map/4

Average Frost Dates/5

USDA Hardiness Zone Map

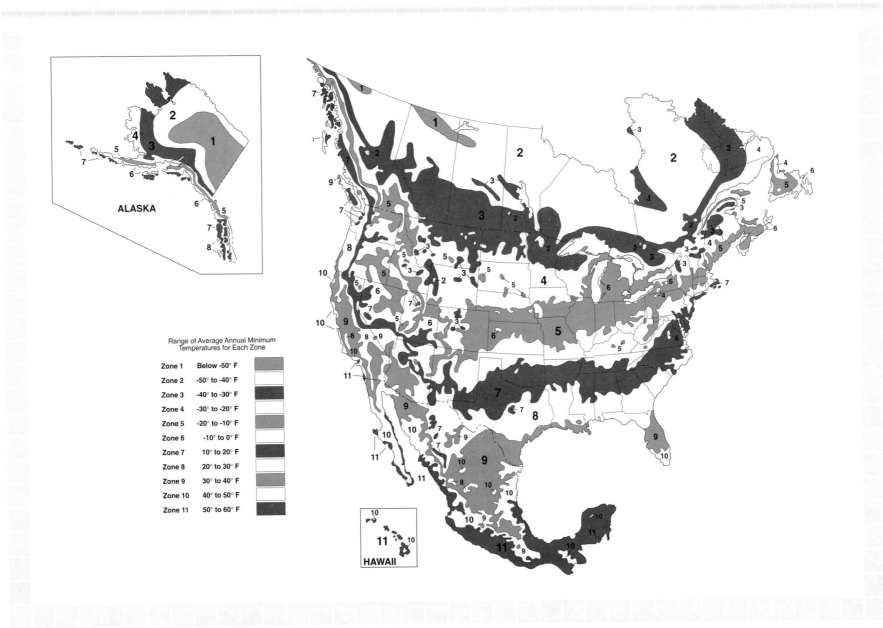

Range of Average Annual Minimum
Temperatures for Each Zone

Zone 1	Below -50° F
Zone 2	-50° to -40° F
Zone 3	-40° to -30° F
Zone 4	-30° to -20° F
Zone 5	-20° to -10° F
Zone 6	-10° to 0° F
Zone 7	10° to 20° F
Zone 8	20° to 30° F
Zone 9	30° to 40° F
Zone 10	40° to 50° F
Zone 11	50° to 60° F

ALASKA

HAWAII

Source: *Fertilizers for Free*, Editors of Garden Way Publishing

Average Frost Dates in the U.S.

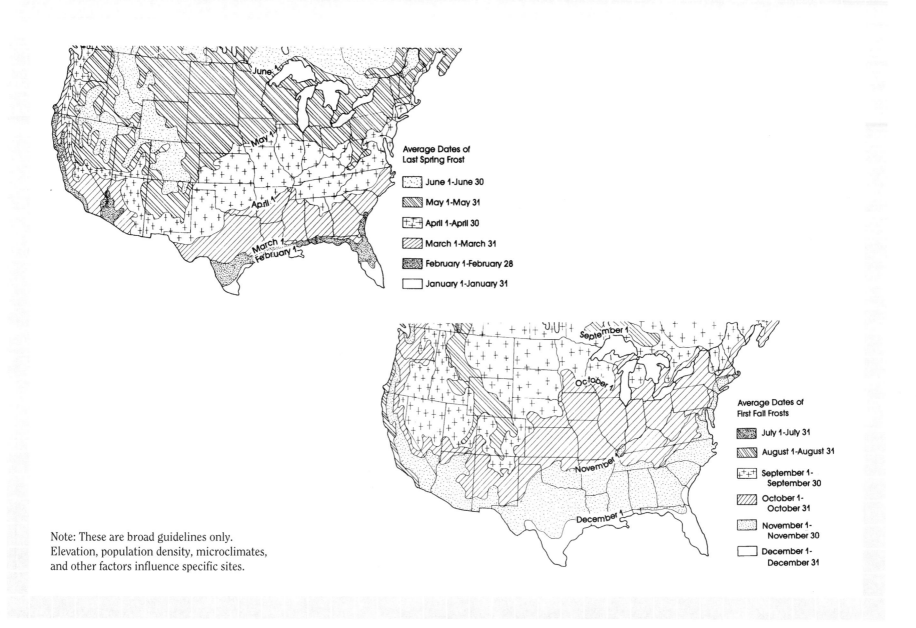

Average Dates of Last Spring Frost

- June 1-June 30
- May 1-May 31
- April 1-April 30
- March 1-March 31
- February 1-February 28
- January 1-January 31

Average Dates of First Fall Frosts

- July 1-July 31
- August 1-August 31
- September 1-September 30
- October 1-October 31
- November 1-November 30
- December 1-December 31

Note: These are broad guidelines only. Elevation, population density, microclimates, and other factors influence specific sites.

Source: *Down-to-Earth Gardening Know-How for the '90s,* Dick Raymond

Soil pH

The pH Scale

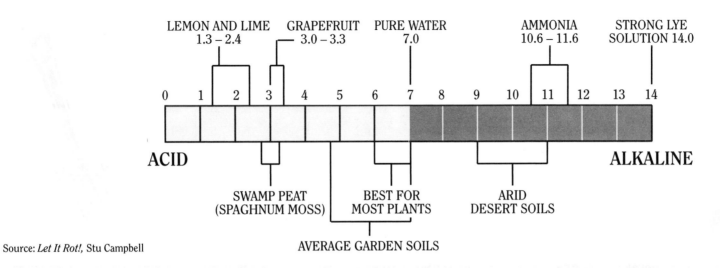

Source: *Let It Rot!*, Stu Campbell

How to Raise pH Value 1 Unit

Soil	Ground Limestone, Marl, or Oyster Shells (Lbs. Per 100 Sq. Ft.)	Burnt Lime (Lbs. Per 100 Sq. Ft.)	Hydrated Lime (Lbs. Per 100 Sq. Ft.)
Light sandy soil	3	2	2½
Sandy loams	4½	2½	3⅓
Loams	6¾	3¾	5
Silt loams and clay loams	8	4½	6

Note: For soils low in organic matter, reduce the above amounts by 25%; for soils high in organic matter, increase by 100%.
Source: *Successful Small Food Gardens*, Louise Riotte

How to Lower pH Value 1 Unit

Soil	Sulphur (Lbs. Per 100 Sq. Ft.)	Aluminum Sulphate (Lbs. Per 100 Sq. Ft.)	Iron Sulphate (Lbs. Per 100 Sq. Ft.)
Light sandy soil	½	2½	3
Silt loams and clay loams	2	6½	7½

Source: *Fertilizers for Free*, Charles Siegchrist

pH Preferences of Some Common Crops

Alfalfa	6.0–8.0	Chives	6.0–7.0	Lettuce	6.0–7.0	Raspberry, red	5.5–7.0
Apple	5.0–6.5	Clover, red	6.0–7.5	Millet	5.0–6.5	Rhubarb	5.5–7.0
Artichoke (Jerusalem)	6.5–7.5	Corn	5.5–7.5	Mushroom	6.5–7.5	Rutabaga	5.5–7.0
Asparagus	6.0–8.0	Cotton, upland	5.0–6.0	Mustard	6.0–7.5	Sage	5.5–6.5
Avocado	6.0–8.0	Cowpea	5.0–6.5	Oats	5.0–7.5	Salsify	6.0–7.5
Barley	6.5–7.8	Crabapple	6.0–7.5	Okra	6.0–7.5	Shallot	5.5–7.0
Bean, lima	6.0–7.0	Cranberry	4.2–5.0	Olive	5.5–6.5	Sorghum	5.5–7.5
Bean, pole	6.0–7.5	Cucumber	5.5–7.0	Onion	6.0–7.0	Soybean	6.0–7.0
Beet, sugar	6.5–8.0	Currant, red	5.5–7.0	Orange	6.0–7.5	Spinach	6.0–7.5
Beet, table	6.0–7.5	Eggplant	5.5–6.5	Parsley	5.0–7.0	Squash, crookneck	6.0–7.5
Blackberry	5.0–6.0	Endive	5.8–7.0	Parsnip	5.5–7.0	Squash, Hubbard	5.5–7.0
Blueberry	4.0–5.5	Garlic	5.5–8.0	Pea	6.0–7.5	Strawberry	5.0–6.5
Broccoli	6.0–7.0	Gooseberry	5.0–6.5	Peach	6.0–7.5	Swiss chard	6.0–7.5
Broom sedge	4.5–6.0	Grape	5.5–7.0	Peanut	5.3–6.6	Thyme	5.5–7.0
Brussels sprout	6.0–7.5	Grapefruit	6.0–7.5	Pear	6.0–7.5	Timothy	5.5–6.5
Buckwheat	5.5–7.0	Hazelnut	6.0–7.0	Pecan	6.4–8 0	Tomato	5.5–7.5
Cabbage	6.0–7.5	Hickory nut	6.0–7.0	Pepper	5.5–7.0	Turnip	5.5–6.8
Cantaloupe	6.0–7.5	Horseradish	6.0–7.0	Pineapple	5.0–6.0	Vetch	5.2–7.0
Carrot	5.5–7.0	Kale	6.0–7.5	Plum	6.0–8.0	Walnut	6.0–8.0
Cashew	5.0–6.0	Kohlrabi	6.0–7.5	Potato	4.8–6.5	Watercress	6.0–8.0
Cauliflower	5.5–7.5	Kumquat	5.5–6.5	Potato, sweet	5.2–6.0	Watermelon	5.5–6.5
Celery	5.8–7.0	Leek	6.0–8.0	Pumpkin	5.5–7.5	Wheat	5.5–7.5
Cherry, sour	6.0–7.0	Lemon	6.0–7.0	Quince	6.0–7.5		
Cherry, sweet	6.0–7.5	Lentil	5.5–7.0	Radish	6.0–7.0		
Chicory	5.0–6.5	Lespedeza	4.5–6.5	Raspberry, black	5.0–6.5	*(Courtesy of Sudbury Laboratories, Inc.)*	

Source: *Successful Small Food Gardens,* Louise Riotte

Optimum pH Range for Vegetable Crops

	5.0	5.5	6.0	6.5	7.0	7.5	8.0
Asparagus							
Beets							
Cabbage							
Muskmelons							
Peas							
Spinach							
Summer Squash							
Celery							
Chives							
Endive							
Rhubarb							
Horseradish							
Lettuce							
Onions							
Radishes							
Cauliflower							
Sweet Corn							
Pumpkins							
Tomatoes							
Snap Beans							
Lima beans							
Carrots							
Cucumbers							
Parsnips							
Peppers							
Rutabagas							
Winter Squash							
Eggplant							
Watermelons							
Potatoes							

Source: *Down-to-Earth Gardening Know-How for the '90s,* Dick Raymond

pH Preferences of Lawn Grasses

Bentgrass	5.5–6.5
Bermudagrass	5.0–7.0
Bluegrass, annual	5.0–7.5
Bluegrass, Canada	5.5–7.5
Bluegrass, Kentucky	6.0–7.5
Bluegrass, roughstock	5.5–7.5
Buffalograss	6.0–8.5
Carpetgrass	4.5–7.0
Centipedegrass	4.0–6.0
Clover, white	5.5–7.0
Fescue, chewings	5.5–7.5
Fescue, creeping red	5.5–7.5
Fescue, tall	5.5–7.5
Gramagrass	6.0–8.5
Redtop	5.0–7.5
Ryegrass	5.5–8.0
St. Augustine grass	6.0–8.0
Wheatgrass	6.0–8.5
Zoysia	4.5–7.5

(Courtesy of Sudbury Laboratories, Inc.)

Source: *Successful Small Food Gardens,* Louise Riotte

FERTILIZERS

Know Your Plant Food Elements

ELEMENT	SYMBOL	FUNCTION IN PLANT	DEFICIENCY SYMPTOMS	EXCESS SYMPTOMS	SOURCES
PRIMARY PLANT FOOD ELEMENTS					
Nitrogen	N	Gives dark green color to plant. Increases growth of leaf and stem. Influences crispness and quality of leaf crops. Stimulates rapid early growth.	Light green to yellow leaves. Stunted growth.	Dark green. Excessive growth. Retarded maturity. Loss of buds or fruit.	Manure, blood meal, fish emulsion
Phosphorus	P	Stimulates early formation and growth of roots. Gives plants a rapid and vigorous start. Is important in formation of seed. Gives hardiness to fall-seeded grasses and grains.	Red or purple leaves. Cell division retardation.	Possible tie up of other essential elements.	Superphosphate, rock phosphate, bone meal
Potash	K	Increases vigor of plants and resistance to disease. Stimulates production of strong, stiff stalks. Promotes production of sugar, starches, oils. Increases plumpness of grains and seed. Improves quality of crop yield.	Reduced vigor. Susceptibility to diseases. Thin skin and small fruit.	Coarse, poor colored fruit. Reduced absorption of Mg and Ca.	Muriate or sulphate of potash, greensand, wood ashes, seaweed
SECONDARY PLANT FOOD ELEMENTS					
Magnesium	Mg	Aids photosynthesis. Key element in chlorophyll.	Loss of yield. Chlorosis of old leaves.	Reduced absorption of Ca and K.	Magnesium sulphate (epsom salts). Dolomite is 1/3 Mg.
Sulphur	S	Helps to build proteins.	Looks like nitrogen deficiency.	Sulphur burn from too low pH.	Sulphur, superphosphate
Calcium	Ca	Part of cell walls. Part of enzymes.	Stops growing point of plants.	Reduces the intake of K and Mg.	Limestone, basic slag, gypsum, oyster shells

continued

ELEMENT	SYMBOL	FUNCTION IN PLANT	DEFICIENCY SYMPTOMS	EXCESS SYMPTOMS	SOURCES
MINOR (OR MICRO) ELEMENTS					
Zinc	Zn	Aids in cell division. In enzymes and auxins.	Small, thin, yellow leaves. Low yields.	None known.	Zinc sulphate
Iron	Fe	A catalyst. In the enzyme system. Hemoglobin in legumes.	Yellowing of leaves, the veins remaining green.	None known.	Iron sulphate (copperas), chelated iron
Manganese	Mn	In enzyme system.	Mottled chlorosis of the leaves. Stunted growth.	Small dead areas in the leaves with yellow borders around them.	Manganese sulphate (tecmangam)
Copper	Cu	Enzyme activator	Multiple budding. Gum pockets.	Prevents the uptake of iron. Causes stunting of roots.	Copper sulphate, neutral copper
Molybdenum	Mo	Helps in the utilization of N.	Symptoms in plants vary greatly.	Poisonous to livestock.	Sodium molybdate
Boron	B	Affects absorption of other elements. Affects germination of pollen tube.	Small leaves. Heart rot and corkiness. Multiple buds.	Leaves turn yellowish red.	Borax
ELEMENTS FROM AIR AND WATER					
Carbon	C	Keystone of all organic substances.	None known.	None known.	Air (carbon dioxide)
Oxygen	O	Respiration	White areas at lead veins. High nitrates.	None known.	Air and water
Hydrogen	H	Necessary in all plant functions.	Wilting.	Drowning.	Water

Source: *Down-to-Earth Vegetable Gardening Know-How,* Dick Raymond

ORGANIC FERTILIZERS

FERTILIZER	NUTRIENTS	APPLICATION RATE	USES
Blood meal	N 15% P 1.3% K 7%	Up to 3 lbs. per 100 sq. ft. (more will burn plants)	Readily available nitrogen. Speeds decomposition of compost.
Bonemeal	N 3% P 20% K 0% Ca 24-30%	Up to 5 lbs. per 100 sq. ft.	Raises pH. Excellent source of phosphorus. Good for fruit, bulbs, flowers.
Cow manure	N 2% P 1% K 1%	40 lbs. per 50-100 sq. ft.	If fresh, will burn plants. Because slow releasing, a valuable soil additive.
Cottonseed meal	N 6% P 3% K 2%	2-5 lbs. per 100 sq. ft.	Acidifies soil. Lasts 4-6 months.
Fish emulsion, Fish meal	N 5-8% P 4-6% K 0-1%	Meal: Up to 5 lbs. per 100 sq. ft. Emulsion: 20:1	In early spring, as a foliar spray. Lasts 6-8 months.
Gypsum	Ca 23-57% S 17%	Up to 4 lbs. per 100 sq. ft.	When both calcium and sulfur are needed and soil pH is high. Helps loosen clay soils.
Kelp meal, Liquid seaweed	N 1% P 0% K 12% Trace minerals	Meal: Up to 1 lb. per 100 sq. ft. Liquid, dilute 25:1	Contains natural growth hormones. Use sparingly. Lasts 6 months.
Sulfur	S 100%	1 lb. per 100 sq. ft. to lower pH 1 point. As fungicide, 3 tablespoons per 1 gallon of water.	Lowers pH in alkaline soils. Increases crop protein. Ties up excess magnesium.

NUTRIENT SYMBOLS: N Nitrogen   Ca Calcium
                   P Phosphorus   S   Sulfur
                   K Potash

Source: *The Able Gardener,* Kathleen Yeomans, R.N.

APPROXIMATE COMPOSITION OF NATURAL FERTILIZER MATERIALS

MATERIAL	PERCENT NITROGEN (N)	PERCENT PHOSPHORIC ACID (P)	PERCENT POTASH (K)
BULKY ORGANIC MATERIALS			
Alfalfa hay	2.5	.5	2.0
Bean straw	1.2	.3	1.2
Grain straw	.6	.2	1.0
Olive pomaces	1.2	.8	.5
Peanut hulls	1.5	–	.8
Peat	2.3	.4	.8
Sawdust	.2	–	.2
Seaweed (kelp)	.6	–	1.3
Timothy hay	1.0	.2	1.5
Winery pomaces	1.5	1.5	.8
MANURES			
Bat guano	10.0	4.5	2.0
Cow manure, dried	1.3	.9	.8
Cow manure, fresh	.5	.2	.5
Hen manure, dried, w/litter	2.8	2.8	1.5
Hen manure, fresh	1.1	.9	.5
Horse manure, fresh	.6	.3	.5
Pig, fresh	.6	.5	.4
Sheep manure, dried	1.4	1.0	3.0
Sheep manure, fresh	.9	.5	.8

MATERIAL	PERCENT NITROGEN (N)	PERCENT PHOSPHORIC ACID (P)	PERCENT POTASH (K)
ROCK POWDERS			
Basic slag	–	8.0 - 17.0	–
Greensand (Glauconite)	–	1.4	4.0 - 9.5
Hybro-tite	–	.002	4.5
Rock phosphate (apatite)	–	38.0 - 40.0	–
VEGETATIVE & ANIMAL CONCENTRATES			
Bonemeal, steamed	2.0	22.0	–
Castor pomace	6.0	1.9	.5
Cocoa shell meal	2.5	1.5	2.5
Cottonseed meal	6.0	3.0	1.0
Dried blood meal	13.0	1.5	.8
Fish meal	10.0	6.0	–
Fish scrap	5.0	3.0	–
Garbage tankage	1.5	2.0	.7
Hoof & horn meal	12.0	2.0	–
Sewerage sludge	2.0	1.4	.8
Sewerage sludge, activated	6.0	3.0	.1
Soybean meal	7.0	1.0	.1
Tankage, animal	9.0	6.0	–
Tankage, processed	7.0	1.0	.1
Tobacco dust and stems	1.5	.5	5.0
Wood ashes	–	1.8	5.0

Source: *Down-to-Earth Vegetable Gardening Know-How,* Dick Raymond

Amount of Fertilizer To Use for Each 2% of Nitrogen Needed

MATERIAL	NITROGEN (%)	APPLY PER 100 SQ. FT.	APPLY PER ACRE
Bloodmeal	15.0	10 oz.	265 lbs.
Felt wastes	14.0	12 oz.	285 lbs.
Hoofmeal/Horndust	12.5	13 oz.	320 lbs.
Guano	12.0	14 oz.	335 lbs.
Animal tankage	8.0	1¼ lbs.	500 lbs.
Cottonseed meal	8.0	1¼ lbs.	500 lbs.
Fish scraps	8.0	1¼ lbs.	500 lbs.
Milorganite (activated sludge)	6.0	1⅝ lbs.	665 lbs.
Castor pomace	5.5	1¾ lbs.	725 lbs.
Bonemeal	4.0	2½ lbs.	1,000 lbs.
Peanut shells	3.6	2¾ lbs.	1,100 lbs.
Tobacco stems or powder	3.3	3 lbs.	1,200 lbs.
Cowpea/Vetch/ Alfalfa hay	3.0	3⅝ lbs.	1,450 lbs.
Cocoa shells	2.7	3¾ lbs.	1,500 lbs.

Note: Most of these nitrogen sources also supply varying amounts of phosphorus or potash. For example, bonemeal contains 24 percent phosphorus.

(Courtesy of Sudbury Laboratories, Inc.)

Source: *Successful Small Food Gardens,* Louise Riotte

Conversion Rates of Fertilizers (per square feet)

AREA IN SQUARE FEET	POUNDS OF FERTILIZER TO APPLY, WHERE AMOUNT TO BE APPLIED PER ACRE IS:		
	100 LBS.	400 LBS.	800 LBS.
100	.25	1	2
500	1.25	5	10
1,000	2.50	10	20
1,500	3.75	15	30
2,000	5.00	20	40

These charts will help to adapt fertilizer recommendations for large acreage to a small garden. For small amounts of fertilizer it is easier to measure by volume than by weight. To convert charts that call for pounds, you can figure one pound of common garden fertilizer is equivalent to two cupfuls.

Source: *Down-to-Earth Vegetable Gardening Know-How,* Dick Raymond

RATES OF APPLICATION OF DIFFERENT FERTILIZER FORMULAS

FERTILIZER FORMULA	1,000 SQ. FT.	10 FT. SINGLE ROW	10 FT. WIDE ROW	SINGLE PLANT
5-10-5	40 lbs.	2 cups	6 cups	3 tbsp.
8-32-16	25 lbs.	1½ cups	4½ cups	2 tbsp.
10-6-4	20 lbs.	1 cup	3 cups	1½ tbsp.
12-12-12	17 lbs.	1 cup	3 cups	1½ tbsp.

Source: *Down-to-Earth Vegetable Gardening Know-How,* Dick Raymond

RECOMMENDED TIMES FOR APPLYING FERTILIZER AS SIDE-DRESSING

CROP	TIME OF APPLICATION	CROP	TIME OF APPLICATION	CROP	TIME OF APPLICATION
Asparagus	Before growth starts in spring, and after harvesting to promote fern growth	Cucumbers	At "stand up" stage just before they start to run	Peppers	When plants start to blossom
Beans*	No need to side-dress	Eggplant	When plants start to blossom	Potatoes	At last hilling, before plants start to blossom
Beets*	No need to side-dress	Kale	Four weeks after planting	Spinach*	No need to side-dress
Broccoli	Three weeks after transplanting	Lettuce*	No need to side-dress	Squash	At "stand up" stage just before they start to run
Cabbage	Three weeks after transplanting	Muskmelon	At "stand up" stage just before they start to run	Tomatoes	When plants start to blossom
Carrots*	No need to side-dress	Onions	Four weeks and six weeks after planting	Turnips*	No need to side-dress
Cauliflower	Three weeks after transplanting	Peas*	No need to side-dress	Watermelon	At "stand up" stage just before they start to run

* Assuming fertilizer has been added to the rows before planting.

Source: *Down-to-Earth Gardening Know-How for the '90s,* Dick Raymond

COMPOST

MATERIALS FOR YOUR COMPOST PILE

Alfalfa meal and hay (the meal will activate the pile)	Corn stalks (shred or chop)	Hay (mixed grasses or salt marsh hay)	Peat moss
Algae (pond weeds)	Cottonseed hulls	Hedge clippings	Phosphate rock
Apple pomace (cider press waste)	Cotton waste ("gin trash")	Hops (brewery waste)	Pine needles (use sparingly; they are acidic and break down slowly)
Ashes (wood, not coal. Sprinkle lightly between layers, don't add ashes in big clumps)	Cowpeas	Kelp (seaweed)	Potash rock
Banana skins (as well as all fruit and vegetable peels, stalks, and foliage)	Cucumber vines (unless they are diseased or insect-infected)	Leaf mold	Potato wastes (skins, etc.; watch out for insect-infested vines)
Bean shells and stalks	Dog food (dry dog food is a nitrogen/protein activator)	Leaves	Rhubarb leaves
Bird cage cleanings	Dolomite	Lettuce	Rice hulls
Broccoli stalks (shred, cut, or pound soft with a mallet)	Earthworms	Lime (agricultural)	Shells (ground clam, crab, lobster, mussel, and oyster)
Buckwheat hulls or straw	Eelgrass	Limestone (ground)	Sod and soil removed from other areas
Cabbage stalks and leaves	Eggshells (grind or crush)	Milk (sour)	Soybean straw
Cocoa hulls	Fish scraps (bury in the center of the pile)	Muck	Sphagnum moss
Cat litter (prophyllite, alfalfa pellets, or vermiculite before the cat has used it. Alfalfa pellets will help activate the pile)	Flowers	Melon wastes (vines, leaves, and rinds, unless diseased or infested)	Sugar cane residue (bagasse)
Citrus wastes and rinds	Grape pomace (winery waste)	Oat straw	Tea leaves
Clover	Granite dust	Olive residues	Vetch
Coffee wastes and grounds	Grass clippings (let dry first and use in thin layers between other materials; a thick mass will be a mess)	Pea pods and vines	Weeds (even with seeds, which will be killed as the pile heats up)
Corn cobs (shred or chop)	Greensand	Peanut hulls	Wheat straw

Source: *Down-to-Earth Gardening Know-How for the '90s,* Dick Raymond

COMPOSTING SYSTEMS AT A GLANCE

TYPE	ADVANTAGES	DISADVANTAGES
Slow outdoor pile	Easy to start and add to; low maintenance.	Can take a year or more to decompose; nutrients are lost to leaching; can be odorous and attract animals and flies.
Hot outdoor pile	Fast decomposition; weed seeds and pathogens are killed; more nutrient-rich because less leaching of nutrients; less likely to attract animals and flies.	Requires lots of effort to turn and aerate and manage the process; works best when you have lots of material to add right away, as opposed to a little bit at a time.
Bins and boxes	Neat appearance; holds heat more easily than a pile; deters animals; lid keeps rain off compost; if turned, decomposition can be quite rapid.	Costs you time to build the bins or money to buy them.
Tumblers	Self-contained and not messy; can produce quick compost; relatively easy to aerate by turning the tumbler; odor not usually a problem; no nutrient leaching into ground.	Tumblers are costly; volume is relatively small; works better if material is added all at once.
Pit composting	Quick and easy; no maintenance; no investment in materials.	Only takes care of small amounts of organic matter.
Sheet composting	Can handle large amounts of organic matter; no containers required; good way to improve soil in large areas.	Requires effort to till material into the soil; takes several months to decompose.
Plastic bag or garbage can	Easy to do year-round; can be done in a small space; can be done indoors; requires no back labor.	Is mostly anaerobic, so smell can be a problem; can attract fruit flies; need to include plenty of leaves or other high carbon material to avoid a slimy mess.
Worm composter	Easy; no odor; can be done indoors; can be added to continuously; so nutrient-rich it can be used as a fertilizer; good way to compost food waste.	Requires some care when adding materials and removing castings; need to protect worms from temperature extremes; can attract fruit flies.

Source: *Let It Rot!,* Stu Campbell

NATURAL ACTIVATORS FOR COMPOST PILES

Alfalfa meal (The best activator. Sold as "Litter Green" kitty litter or pelletized as rabbit food. Sometimes sold in 50-pound bags at feed stores. Try a place that sells feed for horses.)	Existing compost	Blood meal	Cottonseed meal	Fish meal	Horn meal
	Soil	Bonemeal	Dry dog food	Hoof meal	Manure

Source: *Down-to-Earth Gardening Know-How for the '90s,* Dick Raymond

COMPOST TROUBLE-SHOOTING CHART

SYMPTOM	POSSIBLE CAUSE	SOLUTION
Unpleasant odor from pile	Not enough oxygen due to compaction	Aerate.
	Not enough oxygen due to overwatering	Add carbon materials such as cornstalks, leaves, or wood chips to soak up excess water. Also improve aeration.
	If odor of ammonia, too much nitrogen	Add carbon materials and aerate.
Pile not heating up	Lack of nitrogen	Mix in a nitrogen source such as fresh grass clippings, fresh manure, or blood meal. If you can't mix the materials easily, try making holes in the pile and pouring in the nitrogen materials.
	Not enough moisture	Stick a garden hose down into the pile in several locations and water. Or poke holes into the pile with a rod and pour water down the holes using a watering can.
	Pile needs to be turned.	Use a pitchfork to bring materials from the outside of the pile into the center.
	Compost may be finished.	If it looks dark and crumbly and smells earthy instead of moldy or rotten, it's probably ready.
Compost is damp and warm only in the center.	Pile is too small.	Gather more materials and rebuild a larger pile.

Source: *Let It Rot!,* Stu Campbell

CARBON TO NITROGEN RATIO OF SOME COMPOST INGREDIENTS

To get some organic material to compost properly, you should mix materials so that the mixture is about thirty parts of carbon to one part of nitrogen. There is nothing precise about this, but gardeners should be aware that a mixture with too much carbon, such as a pile of leaves, will not heat up, while a mixture with too much nitrogen will manufacture ammonia – and the nitrogen will be wasted.

In the following list, the figure given is the amount of carbon per one part of nitrogen:

Straw	150-500	Pine needles	60-110	Grass clippings	25	Animal droppings	15
Ground corn cobs	50-100	Oak leaves	50	Manure with bedding	25	Leguminous plants	15
Sawdust	150-500	Young weeds	30	Vegetable trimmings	25		

Source: *Fertilizers for Free,* Charles Siegchrist

GREEN MANURES AND MULCH MATERIALS

Green Manures

COMMON NAME		LEGUME	SOIL PREFERENCE	LIME REQMTS (Low, Med., High)	ADAPTED TO SOILS OF LOW FERTILITY	RELATIVE LONGEVITY OF SEED	SEEDING RATE (lbs. per acre)	SEEDING RATE (lbs. per 1000 sq. ft.)	DEPTH TO COVER SEED
Barley		No	Loams	L		Long	100	2½	¾
Beans	Mung	Yes	Widely Adaptable	L	•	Short	70	2	1
	Soy	Yes	Loams	M		Short	90	2½	1½
	Velvet	Yes	Loams	L	•	Short	120	4	2
Beggar Weed		Yes	Sandy Loams	L	•		15	½	½
Brome Grass, Field		No	Widely Adaptable	L		Long	30	1	½
Buckwheat		No	Widely Adaptable	L	•		50	1½	¾
Bur Clover		Yes	Heavy Loams	M		Long	30	1	½
Chess or Cheat Grass		No	Loams	L		Long	40	1	¾
Clover	Alsike	Yes	Heavy Loams	M		Long	8	¼	½
	Crimson	Yes	Loams	M	•	Medium	30	1	½
	Subterranean	Yes	Loams	M		Medium	30	1	½
Corn		No	Widely Adaptable	L		Medium	90	2½	1
Cow-Pea		Yes	Sandy Loams	L	•	Short	90	2½	1½
Crotalaria		Yes	Light Loams	L	•	Long	15	½	¾
Fenugreek		Yes	Loams	L	•	Long	35	1	½
Guar		Yes	Widely Adaptable	L	•	Long	40	1½	1
Indigo, Hairy		Yes	Sandy Loams	L	•	Short	10	½	½
Kale, Scotch		No	Widely Adaptable	H	•	Long	14	¼	½
Lespedeza	Common	Yes	Loams	L	•	Short	25	1	½
	Korean	Yes	Loams	L	•	Short	25	1	½
	Sericea	Yes	Loams	L	•	Medium	25	1	½
Lupine	Blue	Yes	Sandy Loams	L		Short	100	2½	1
	White	Yes	Sandy Loams	L		Short	120	2	1
	Yellow	Yes	Sandy Loams	L		Short	80	2	1

AREAS FOR WHICH BEST ADAPTED					WHEN TO SOW*	WHEN TO TURN UNDER*	COMMENTS
NE & NC States	S & SE States	Gulf Cst & FL	NW States	SW States			
•			•	•	Sp F	Su Sp	Not good on sandy or acid soils. Sow spring varieties in north, winter varieties in milder climates.
	•	•		•	Sp or Su	Su or F	Warm weather crops. Do not sow until ground is warm and weather is settled.
•	•	•	•	•	Sp or Su	Su or F	
		•			Sp or Su	Su or F	
		•			Sp or ESu	Su or F	Seeding rate is for scarified seed. Treble the amount if unhulled seed is used.
•					F Sp	Sp F	Good winter cover. Easy to establish. Hardier than rye. More heat tolerant.
•			•		LSp & Su	Su or F	Quick growing. Plant only after ground is warm.
	•	•	•	•	F	Sp	Not winter hardy north. One of best winter crops where mild winters prevail.
			•		F	Sp	
•		•	•	•	Sp F	F Sp	Less sensitive to soil acidity and poorly drained soils than most clovers.
•	•	•	•	•	F Sp	Sp F	Not winter hardy north. A good winter annual from New Jersey southward.
•	•	•	•	•	F	Sp	
•	•	•	•	•	Sp or Su	Su or F	Do not sow until ground is warm.
	•	•		•	LSp or ESu	Su or F	Withstands drought & moderate shade well. Don't sow until weather is warm & settled.
	•	•		•	Sp or Su	Su or F	Does well on acid soils. Resistant to root knot nematode. Sow scarified seed.
			•		F	Sp	
				•	Sp or ESu	Su or F	Thrives on warm soils. Do not plant too early.
	•	•		•	Sp or ESu	Su or F	
•	•	•	•	•	Su or F	Sp	Can be eaten after serving as winter cover. In Northern areas interplant with winter rye for protection. Except in deep south, plant in summer for good growth before frost.
	•				ESp	Su or F	Good on acid soils of low fertility.
	•				ESp	Su or F	Good on acid soils of low fertility.
	•			•	ESp	Su or F	Easy to establish on hard, badly eroded soils.
		•			Sp F	Su Sp	Good on sour and acid soils.
•		•			Sp F	Su Sp	Good on sour and acid soils. Less popular than yellow and blue lupine.
•		•			Sp F	Su Sp	Good on sour and acid soils.

continued

Green Manures (continued)

Common Name		Legume	Soil Preference	Lime Reqmts (Low, Med., High)	Adapted to Soils of Low Fertility	Relative Longevity of Seed	Seeding Rate (lbs. per acre)	Seeding Rate (lbs. per 1000 sq. ft.)	Depth to Cover Seed
Millet		No	Sandy Loams	L		Long	30	1	½
Mustard, White		No	Loams				8	¼	¼
Oats		No	Widely Adaptable	L		Long	100	2½	1
Pea	Field	Yes	Heavy Loams	M		Short	90	2½	1½
	Rough	Yes	Sandy Loams	L	•	Medium	60	1½	1
	Tangier	Yes		M		Medium	80	2½	1
Rape		No	Loams	L			8	¼	¼
Rescue Grass		No	Widely Adaptable	L		Long	35	1	¾
Rye, Spring		No	Widely Adaptable	L		Long	90	2	¾
Rye, Winter		No	Widely Adaptable	L		Long	90	2	¾
Rye-Grass, Italian		No	Widely Adaptable	L		Long	35	1	¾
Sesbania		Yes	Widely Adaptable	L	•	Long	25	1	¾
Sorghum		No	Light Loams			Long	90	2½	¾
Sudan Grass		No	Widely Adaptable	L		Long	35	1	¾
Sunflower		No	Widely Adaptable	L			20	¾	¾
Sweet Clover	Common White	Yes	Heavy Loams	H		Long	15	½	½
	Annual (Hubam)	Yes	Loams	H		Long	15	½	½
	Yellow	Yes	Loams	H		Long	15	½	½
	Yellow Annual	Yes	Loams	H		Long	15	½	½
Vetch	Common	Yes	Widely Adaptable	L		Medium	60	1½	¾
	Hairy	Yes	Widely Adaptable	L	•	Long	60	1½	¾
	Hungarian	Yes	Heavy Loams	L		Long	60	1½	¾
	Purple	Yes	Loams	L		Long		1½	¾
	Woolly Pod	Yes	Widely Adaptable	L		Long	60	1½	¾
Wheat, Winter		No	Loams	L		Long	100	2½	¾

Source: *Down-to-Earth Vegetable Gardening Know-How,* Dick Raymond

AREAS FOR WHICH BEST ADAPTED							
NE & NC States	S & SE States	Gulf Cst & FL	NW States	SW States	WHEN TO SOW*	WHEN TO TURN UNDER*	COMMENTS
●					LSp or Su	Su or F	Sow only after ground is warm, a week or 10 days after normal corn planting time. Fast growing
●					Sp	Su	
●	●	●	●	●	Sp / F	Su or F / Sp	Winter oats (sown in fall) are suitable only where mild winters prevail.
●	●	●	●		ESp / F	Su / Sp	Sow in fall only where winters are mild. Distinctly a cool weather crop.
	●				F	Sp	
●			●		Sp	Su	
●				●	Sp or Su	Su or F	
		●		●			Adapted to mild winters and humid climates.
●	●				Sp	Su	
●	●				F	Sp	One of the most important winter cover crops. Can be sown late.
●	●	●	●	●	F / Sp	Sp / Su	An important winter cover crop where winters are mild. In severe climates sow in spring or summer.
	●	●		●	Sp or Su	Su or F	Quick grower. Better adapted to wet soils & will grow at higher altitudes than crutalaria.
●	●			●	LSp or Su	Su or F	Don't sow until ground is warm & weather is settled. More drought resistant than corn.
●	●	●	●	●	LSp or Su	Su or F	Rapid grower. Do not sow until ground is warm & weather is settled.
●	●	●	●	●	Sp or Su	Su or F	Intolerant of acid soils.
●	●						Quite winter hardy. Best results are from fall sowing.
●			●				A true annual. Best results from spring sowings.
●	●	●	●	●			Stands dry conditions better than common white sweet clover.
●	●	●	●	●	Sp / F	F / Sp	Most useful south of the cotton belt as winter cover. North not winter hardy. Makes short summer growth.
●	●	●	●	●	Sp / F	F / Sp	Not winter hardy where severe cold is experienced. Needs reasonably fertile soil.
●	●	●	●	●	Sp / F	F / Sp	The most winter hardy vetch. Best sown in fall mixed with winter rye or winter wheat.
●	●		●	●	Sp / F	F / Sp	Next to the hairy vetch the most winter hardy of the vetches. Not winter hardy where winters are severe. Needs fairly fertile soil.
●	●			●	Sp / F	F / Sp	Least hardy of the vetches. Suited for winter cover in mild climates only.
●	●	●		●	Sp / F	F / Sp	
●			●		F	Sp	

*KEY: Su = Summer   ESp = Early Spring
Sp = Spring   ESu = Early Summer
F = Fall   LSp = Late Spring

MULCH MATERIALS

MATERIAL	APPEARANCE	INSULATION VALUE	RELATIVE COST	THICKNESS	WEED CONTROL	WATER PENETRATION	SOIL MOISTURE RETENTION	DECOMPOSITION SPEED	COMMENTS
Aluminum foil	Poor	Fair; reflects sun's heat	Very high	1 layer	Good	Poor, unless perforated	Excellent	No decomposition	Aphids shy away from foil-mulched plants. Should be removed and recycled.
Asphalt	Poor	Fair	High	½ -1 in.	Fair	Fair	Fair-good	Decomposes in about 1 year	Complicated for home gardener to apply.
Bark, mixed	Good	Good	Moderate	2-3 in.	Good	Good	Good	Slow unless composted before use	Must be replaced only every two years. Can be stringy, difficult to manage.
Bark, redwood	Excellent	Good	High	2-3 in.	Fair	Fair; repels water in some places	Fair	Very slow; add nitrogen to application	Earthworms avoid redwood. May act as an insect repellent.
Buckwheat hulls	Good	Good	High	1-1½ in.	Good; may sprout	Excellent	Fair	Slow	Easy to handle. May be blown around in high wind or splashed by rain.
Burlap	Poor	Fair	Moderate	1 layer or more	Poor	Excellent	Fair	Slow	Excellent for preventing erosion on slopes. New grass grows right through it.
Cocoa hulls	Good-excellent	Good; absorbs heat from sun	High in most areas	1 in.	Good	Good unless allowed to mat	Good	Slow; adds nitrogen to soil	Sawdust can be added to improve texture and increase water retention. May develop mold. Has chocolatey smell.
Coffee grounds	Good	Fair	Low but not plentiful	Never more than 1 in.	Good	Fair; may cake	Good	Fairly rapid	Use carefully. May prevent ventilation. Best used in container gardens.

continued

MATERIAL	APPEARANCE	INSULATION VALUE	RELATIVE COST	THICKNESS	WEED CONTROL	WATER PENETRATION	SOIL MOISTURE RETENTION	DECOMPOSITION SPEED	COMMENTS
Compost	Fair	Good	High; supply usually limited	1-3 in.	Good	Good if well rotted	Good	Rapid; adds nutrients	Partially decomposed compost is an excellent feeding mulch.
Cork, ground	Fair-good	Excellent	High	1-2 in.	Good	Good	Good	Very slow; has little effect on soil nitrogen	Odorless. Stays in place nicely once it has been soaked.
Corncobs, ground	Good	Good	Low in Midwest	2-3 in.	Excellent	Fair; should be well soaked before applying	Excellent	Nitrogen fertilizer should be added	Avoid close contact with stems of plants because of heat generation.
Cottonseed hulls	Good	Good	Low in the South	1-2 in.	Good	Good	Good	Fairly rapid	Will blow in wind. Has fertilizer value similar to cottonseed meal.
Cranberry vines	Good	Fair	Low in some areas	3-4 in., 2 in. if chopped	Fair-good	Good	Good	Fairly rapid	Excellent winter cover mulch. Pea vines have similar characteristics.
Evergreen boughs	Poor	Good; recommended for wind protection	Low	1 to several layers	Fair	Good	Fair	Slow	Good for erosion control. Should be removed from perennials in spring.
Felt paper (tar paper)	Poor	Good; absorbs heat from sun	High	1 layer	Excellent	Poor, unless perforated	Good	Extremely slow if at all	Difficult to manage, tears. Must be carefully weighted and removed each fall.
Fiberglass	Poor	Excellent	High	3½-6 in.	Excellent	Fair; will get soggy and mat	Good	No decomposition	Unpleasant to handle. Totally fireproof. Mats are better than building insulation.

continued

MATERIAL	APPEARANCE	INSULATION VALUE	RELATIVE COST	THICKNESS	WEED CONTROL	WATER PENETRATION	SOIL MOISTURE RETENTION	DECOMPOSITION SPEED	COMMENTS
Grass clippings	Poor if not dried. Can have unpleasant odor.	Good	Low	1 in. maximum	Fair	Good if not matted	Fair	Rapid; green grass adds nitrogen	Can be mixed with peat moss. After drying can be spread thinly around young plants. Could contain herbicides. If very fresh, could heat up enough to damage plants.
Geotextiles	Poor, without a cover mulch	Poor	High	Single layer	Good	Fair	Good	Rapid with exposure to sunlight; slower with use of cover mulch	Use of a cover mulch highly recommended.
Green ground covers (cover crops)	Fair	Good once there is a heavy sod	Low	Allow to grow to full height	Good	Good	Good	Decomposing legumes and cover crops are rich in nitrogen	Should be harvested or tilled directly into the soil.
Growing green mulch	Excellent	Fair	Moderate	1 layer	Fair	Good	Good	Will live from one year to the next	Includes myrtle, pachysandra, etc. Use where you are not going to walk.
Hay	Poor unless chopped	Good	Low, if spoiled	6-8 in., 2-3 in. if chopped	Good	Good	Good	Rapid; adds nitrogen	Second- or third-growth hay that has not gone to seed is ideal.
Hops, spent	Fair	Fair; heats up when wet	Low where available	1-3 in.	Good	Good	Good	Slow; rich in nitrogen and other nutrients	Avoid close contact with trunks and stems because of heating.
Landscape fabric	Poor	Good	High	1 layer	Good	Good	Good	Slow; can last several years	Use in permanent beds. Cover with attractive top mulch.

continued

MATERIAL	APPEARANCE	INSULATION VALUE	RELATIVE COST	THICKNESS	WEED CONTROL	WATER PENETRATION	SOIL MOISTURE RETENTION	DECOMPOSITION SPEED	COMMENTS
Leaf mold	Fair	Good	Low	1½ in.	Fair-good	Fair; prevents percolation if too thick	Good	Rapid	An excellent feeding mulch. Use like compost.
Leaves	Fair	Good	Low	4-6 in.	Good	Fair; likely to mat	Good	Fairly slow; adds nitrogen	Contributes many valuable nutrients. Can be chopped and mixed with other things.
Manure	Poor-Fair	Good	Moderate-high	As thick as supply allows	Fair	Fair-good	Good	Rapid; adds nitrogen; packaged mixes may have harmful salts	Should be at least partially rotted. Supplies many nutrients.
Muck	Poor	Fair	Moderate	1-2 in.	Fair	Good, but will splash and wash away	Fair	Rapid	Very fertile. Can be mixed with other materials to improve texture.
Newspaper	Poor	Good	Low	2 layers	Excellent	Fair	Good	Lasts 1 season	Cover with hay or other top mulch to hold in place. Use between rows and on paths.
Oak leaf mulch	Good	Good	Low	2-4 in.	Good	Good	Good	Slow	Recommended for acid-soil plants. Has only slight influence on soil pH.
Oyster shells, ground	Good	Fair	High	1-2 in.	Fair	Good	Good	Slow	Works like lime. Will raise soil pH.
Paper	Poor; can be covered with soil	Fair	Low, but specialized mulch paper is expensive	1-several layers	Good	Poor unless perforated	Good	Slow, unless designed to be biodegradable	Can be shredded and used effectively.

continued

MATERIAL	APPEARANCE	INSULATION VALUE	RELATIVE COST	THICKNESS	WEED CONTROL	WATER PENETRATION	SOIL MOISTURE RETENTION	DECOMPOSITION SPEED	COMMENTS
Paper pulp	Poor	Fair	Moderate	½ in.	Fair	Fair	Good	Rapid, nitrogen-rich as side-dressing	Requires special equipment. Useful in deep-planting operations. Good way to recycle.
Peanut hulls	Good	Good	Low where plentiful	1-2 in.	Good	Good	Good	Rapid; adds nitrogen	Can be mixed with other material for superior appearance. Might splash in rain.
Peat moss	Good	Good	Moderate-high	1 in.	Good	Poor; absorbs much water	Poor; draws moisture from soil	Very slow	Adds little or no nutrients to soil. Valuable only as a soil conditioner.
Pine needles	Good-excellent	Good	Low	1-1½ in.	Good	Excellent	Good	Slow; very little earthworm activity	Often used with acid-soil plants, cut can be used elsewhere.
Plastic	Poor, but can be covered	Fair; some colors absorb heat	Moderate-high	1-6 mil.	Excellent	Poor unless perforated	Excellent	No decomposition	Contributes nothing to the soil. Must be handled twice a year. Various colors available. Can use black plastic to warm soil before planting heat-loving crops.
Poultry litter	Poor	Fair	Low-moderate	½ in.	Fair	Good	Fair	Very rapid; adds nitrogen	Should not be used unless mixed with dry material. Excellent fertilizer.
Pyrophyllite	Fair	Fair	High	1-3 in.	Fair	Good	Fair	Extremely slow	Should be considered a permanent mulch.
Salt hay	Good	Good	Moderate, unless you gather it yourself	3-6 in.	Good; contains no seed	Good, does not mat	Good	Slow	Can be used year after year. Is pest-free. Good for winter protection.
Sawdust	Fair-good	Good	Low	1-1½ in.	Good	Fair	Fair	Slow unless weathered; robs soil nitrogen	Has high carbon content. Does not sour soil. Very little earthworm activity.

continued

MATERIAL	APPEARANCE	INSULATION VALUE	RELATIVE COST	THICKNESS	WEED CONTROL	WATER PENETRATION	SOIL MOISTURE RETENTION	DECOMPOSITION SPEED	COMMENTS
Seaweed (kelp)	Poor	Good; recommended as a winter mulch	Low in coastal areas	4-6 in.	Excellent	Fair	Good	Slow; adds nitrogen and potash	Provides sodium, boron, and other trace elements. Excellent for sheet composting.
Stone	Excellent	Good; dark stone retains heat, light stone reflects	High	2-4 in.	Fair, except shale	Good	Fair	Extremely slow	Should be considered permanent mulch. Contributes some trace elements through leaching.
Straw	Fair, unless chopped	Good	Low-moderate	6-8 in., 1-2 in. if chopped	Good; avoid oat straw for weed control	Good	Good	Fairly slow; nitrogen fertilizer is helpful	Should be seed-free if possible. Straw is highly flammable.
Sugarcane (bagasse)	Poor-fair	Good	Moderate	2-3 in.	Good	Good	Good	Rapid due to sugar content	Needs to be replenished often. Has fairly low pH. Mix with lime.
Vermiculite	Excellent	Excellent	High	½ in.	Good	Good	Good	Extremely slow	Totally sterile. Recommended for hothouse use. Will blow and splash outdoors.
Walnut shells	Excellent	Good	Low where plentiful	1-2 in.	Good	Good	Good	Very slow	Will furnish good trace elements. Resists fire.
Wood chips	Good	Good	Moderate	2-4 in.	Good	Good	Good	Fairly slow; little effect on soil nitrogen	May contain carpenter ants, but does not retain tree diseases.
Wood shavings	Fair	Fair	Low	2-3 in.	Fair	Good	Fair	Very rapid; will use up soil nitrogen.	Hardwood shavings are better than pine or spruce Chips or sawdust make better mulch.

Source: *The Mulch Book,* Stu Campbell

COMPANION PLANTING

Insect-Deterrent Plants

PLANT	INSECT DETERRED	PLANT	INSECT DETERRED
Asters	Most insects	Mole Plant	Deters moles and mice if planted here and there
Basil	Repels flies and mosquitoes	Nasturtium	Deters aphids, squash bugs, striped pumpkin beetles
Borage	Deters tomato worm – improves growth and flavor of tomatoes	Onion family	Deters most pests
Calendula	Most insects	Petunia	Protects beans
Catnip	Deters flea beetle	Pot Marigold	Deters asparagus beetles, tomato worms, and general garden pests
Celery	White cabbage butterfly	Peppermint	Planted among cabbages, it repels the white cabbage butterfly
Chrysanthemum	Deters most insects	Radish	Especially deters cucumber beetle
Dead Nettle	Deters potato bug – improves growth and flavor of potatoes	Rosemary	Deters cabbage moth, bean beetle, and carrot fly
Eggplant	Deters Colorado potato beetle	Rue	Deters Japanese beetle
Flax	Deters potato bug	Sage	Deters cabbage moth, carrot fly
Garlic	Deters Japanese beetle, other insects and blight	Salsify	Repels carrot fly
Geranium	Most insects	Southernwood	Deters cabbage moth
Horseradish	Plant at corners of potato patch to deter potato bug	Summer Savory	Deters bean beetles
Henbit	General insect repellent	Tansy	Deters flying insects, Japanese beetles, striped cucumber beetles, squash bugs, ants
Hyssop	Deters cabbage moth	Tomato	Asparagus beetle
Marigold	The workhorse of the pest deterrents. Plant throughout garden to discourage Mexican bean beetles, nematodes, and other insects	Thyme	Deters cabbage worm
Mint	Deters white cabbage moth and ants	Wormwood	Carrot fly, white cabbage butterfly, black flea beetle

Source: *Gardening Answers,* Editors of Garden Way Publishing

Companion Planting Guide

FRUIT/VEGETABLE	FRIENDS	ENEMIES
Asparagus	Tomatoes, nasturtiums, parsley, basil	Onions, garlic, gladiolus
Beans	Potatoes, beets (bush beans only), carrots, peas, cauliflower, cabbage (bush), eggplant, cucumbers, corn, radishes (pole), summer savory, celery (bush), strawberries, rosemary, petunia, parsnips (bush), sunflower (bush)	Beets and cabbage family (pole beans only), onion family (both), kohlrabi, sunflower (pole), gladiolus, fennel
Beets	Bush beans, cabbage, lettuce, onions, kohlrabi, lima beans	Pole beans
Broccoli	Onion family, herbs. See "Cabbage."	See "Cabbage."
Brussels Sprouts	Carrots, herbs	See "Cabbage."
Cabbage	Beets, carrots, beans (bush), lettuce, spinach, onions, cucumbers, kale, potatoes, celery, herbs (aromatic), dill, sage (repels cabbage butterflies), rosemary, mint*, chamomile, nasturtiums	Strawberries, tomatoes, pole beans
Cantaloupes	Corn	None
Carrots	Beans, peas, tomatoes, onions, leeks, Brussels sprouts, peppers, cabbage, leaf lettuce, red radishes, chives, rosemary, sage	Dill, celery, parsnips
Cauliflower	See "Cabbage."	See "Cabbage."
Celery	Cabbage, cauliflower, leeks, tomatoes, bush beans, peas	Carrots, parsnips
Corn	Beans, peas, early potatoes, cucumbers, cantaloupes, squash, cabbage, parsley, pumpkin	None
Cucumbers	Beans, peas, corn, tomatoes, cabbage, lettuce, radishes, sunflowers, dill, nasturtiums	Potatoes, aromatic herbs, sage
Eggplant	Beans, peppers	None
Kale	Cabbage, herbs (aromatic)	None
Kohlrabi	Beets, lettuce, onions	Tomatoes, pole beans
Leeks	Celery, carrots, celeriac, onions	Peas, beans
Lettuce	Beets, carrots, radishes (leaf), kohlrabi, strawberries, cabbage, onion family (aids lettuce), basil, cucumbers	None
Lima Beans	Beets, radishes	None

continued

FRUIT/VEGETABLE	FRIENDS	ENEMIES
Onion Family (including garlic)	Beets, tomatoes, broccoli, peppers, kohlrabi, lettuce, cabbage, leeks, summer savory, carrots, strawberries, chamomile, parsnips, turnips	Beans, peas, asparagus
Parsley	Asparagus, tomatoes, corn	None
Parsnips	Bush beans, peppers, potatoes, peas, radishes, onions, garlic	Carrots, celery, caraway
Peas	Radishes, carrots, cucumbers, corn, beans, turnips, celery, potatoes	Onion family, gladiolus
Peppers	Tomatoes, eggplant, onions, carrots, parsnips	None
Potatoes	Beans, cabbage, corn, peas, marigolds, horseradish (planted at corners), eggplant (as a lure for Colorado potato beetle), parsnips	Pumpkin, squash, cucumbers, turnips, rutabagas, tomatoes, sunflowers, raspberry
Pumpkin	Corn, eggplant, radishes	Potatoes
Radishes	Peas, pole beans, leaf lettuce, nasturtiums, cucumbers, carrots, lima beans, chervil, parsnips	None
Soybeans	Grows with anything, helps everything	None
Spinach	Cabbage, strawberries	None
Squash	Corn, nasturtiums	Potatoes
Strawberries	Lettuce (as a border), spinach, beans, onions, borage	Cabbage
Tomatoes	Asparagus, peppers, celery, onions, carrots, cucumbers, basil, parsley, mint*, chives, marigolds, nasturtiums	Dill, potatoes, cabbage, kohlrabi, fennel
Turnips and Rutabagas	Peas and most vegetables, including onion family	Potatoes

* Mint is handy to have around – but it's a notorious spreader. To contain roots, grow it in a large flower pot sunk to ground level. Locate under an outdoor faucet if you can, as mint will welcome the occasional drippings.

Source: *A-to-Z Hints for the Vegetable Gardener,* Men's Garden Clubs of America

COMPANIONABLE HERBS

HERBS	COMPANIONS	HERBS	COMPANIONS
Basil	Companion to tomatoes, dislikes rue. Repels flies and mosquitoes.	Mint	Companion to cabbage and tomatoes; deters white cabbage moth.
Borage	Companion to tomatoes, squash, and strawberries; deters tomato worm.	Mole plant	Deters moles and mice if planted around garden.
Caraway	Plant here and there; loosens soil.	Nasturtium	Companion to radishes, cabbage, and cucurbits; plant under fruit trees. Deters aphids, squash bugs, striped pumpkin beetles.
Catnip	Plant in borders; deters flea beetle.	Petunia	Companion to beans.
Chamomile	Companion to cabbages and onions.	Pot Marigold	Companion to tomatoes but plant elsewhere too. Deters tomato worm, asparagus beetles, and other pests.
Chervil	Companion to radishes.	Rosemary	Companion to cabbage bean carrots, and sage; deters cabbage moth, bean beetles, and carrot fly.
Chives	Companion to carrots.	Rue	Companion to roses and raspberries; deters Japanese beetles. Dislikes sweet basil.
Dead Nettle	Companion to potatoes; deters potato bug.	Sage	Plant with rosemary cabbage and carrots; dislikes cucumbers. Deters cabbage moth, carrot fly.
Dill	Companion to cabbage; dislikes carrots.	Southernwood	Companion to cabbage; deters cabbage moth.
Fennel	Most plants dislike it; plant away from gardens.	Sowthistle	In moderate amounts this weed can help tomatoes, onions, and corn.
Flax	Companion to carrots, potatoes; deters potato bug.	Summer Savory	Companion to beans and onions; deters bean beetles.
Garlic	Plant near roses and raspberries; deters Japanese beetle.	Tansy	Plant under fruit trees; companion to roses and raspberries. Deters flying insects, Japanese beetles, striped cucumber beetles, squash bugs, and ants.
Horseradish	Plant at corners of potato patch; deters potato bug.	Thyme	Companion to cabbage; deters cabbage worm.
Henbit	General insect repellent.	Wormwood	As a border it keeps animals from the garden.
Hyssop	Companion to cabbage and grapes; deters cabbage moth. Dislikes radishes.	Yarrow	Plant along borders, paths, and near aromatic herbs; enhances production of essential oils.
Marigolds	Plant throughout garden; it discourages Mexican bean beetles, nematodes, and other insects. The workhorse of companion plants.		

Source: *Tips for the Lazy Gardener*, Linda Tilgner

PRUNING

SHRUBS TO BE PRUNED AFTER BLOOMING

The best time to prune these shrubs that bloom on year-old wood is just after the blossoms have faded. Then the shrub will grow new branches and form the buds that will bloom the following year.

Akebia	Chionanthus (white fringe)	Jasminum (jasmine)	Rhododendron
Amelanchier (shadblow)	Cornus (dogwood, without berries)	Kalmia (laurel)	Ribes (flowering currant)
Azalea	Cotinus coggyria (smoke tree)	Kerria japonica (Japanese rose)	Rosa
Benzoin (spice bush)	Crataegus oxyacantha (English hawthorne)	Kolwitzia amabilis (beautybush)	Spirea (bridal wreath)
Berberis (barberry)	Cydonia (Japanese quince)	Lonicera fragrantissima (bush honeysuckle)	Spirea thunbergii
Buddleia alternifolia (butterfly bush)	Cytisus (broom)	Magnolia	Spirea van Houtei
Calycanthus floridus (sweet shrub, (strawberry shrub)	Daphne (garland flower)	Philadelphus (mock-orange)	Syringa (lilac)
Caragana (Siberian pea)	Deutzia	Physocarpus (ninebark)	Tamarix (spring-flowering)
Celastrus (bittersweet)	Exochorda (pearlbush)	Pieris (andromeda)	Viburnum carlesi, V. lantana (snowball)
Cercis (Judas tree, redbud)	Forsythia (goldenbell)	Potentilla (cinquefoil)	Viburnum opulus (highbush cranberry)
Chaenomeles (flowering quince)	Hydrangea hortensia	Prunus (flowering almond, cherry, plum)	Weigela

continued

SHRUBS TO BE PRUNED BEFORE THE BUDS SHOW GREEN			
Shrubs that form flowers on wood grown the same season should be pruned when the plant is dormant			
Abelia x *grandiflora*	*Cephalanthus* (buttonbush)	*Hypericum* (St. Johnswort)	*Salix* (willow)
Abelia schumannii	*Clethra* (sweet pepper bush)	*Indigofera* (indigo)	*Salvia greggii* (autumn sage)
Acanthopanax (five-leaved aralia)	*Cytisus nigricans* (broom)	*Kerria*	*Sambucus canadensis* (American elder)
Althea, shrubby (Rose of Sharon)	*Diervilla sessilifolia* (bush honeysuckle)	*Lagerstroemia* (crape myrtle)	*Sorbaria* (false spirea)
Amorpha (indigo bush)	*Euonymus kiautschovica* (spreading euonymus)	*Lespedeza* (bush clover)	*Spiraea* (all summer-blooming spirea)
Aralia elata (Japanese angelica)	*Fatsia japonica* (Japanese fatsia)	*Ligustrum* (privet)	*Staphylea* (bladdernut)
Artemisia (sagebrush, southernwood, wormwood)	*Franklinia alatamaha* (Franklin tree)	*Lilac japonica* (tree lilac)	*Stephanandra*
Baccharis (groundsel shrub)	*Garrya* (silk-tassel)	*Lonicera* (berried honeysuckle)	*Symphoricarpos* (coralberry, snowberry)
Berberis (barberry)	*Hamamelis virginiana* (witch hazel)	*Lycium* (matrimony vine)	*Tamarix odessana* (late-flowering tamarisk)
Buddleia (butterfly bush, except for B. alternifolia)	*Hibiscus*	*Rhamnus frangula* (alder, buckthorn)	*Viburnum* (berry-bearing)
Callicarpa (beautyberry)	*Holodiscus discolor* (ocean-spray)	*Rhus* (sumac, smoke tree)	*Vitex* (chaste tree)
Caryopteris (bluebeard)	*Hydrangea arborescens* 'Grandiflora'	*Roses* (garden bush varieties)	
Ceanothus	*Hydrangea paniculata* 'Grandiflora'	*Rubus odoratus* (flowering raspberry)	

Sources: *Pruning Trees, Shrubs and Vines*, Editors of Garden Way Publishing; *Pruning Simplified*, Lewis Hill

Pruning Guide for Selected Fruit Trees and Shrubs

TYPE OF TREE	WHEN	HOW
Apple	Winter or early spring	Train tree for low head. Prune moderately. Keep tree open with main branches well spaced around tree. Avoid sharp V-shaped crotches.
Blackberry	After bearing and summer	Remove at ground canes that bore last crop. In summer cut back new shoots 3½ feet high.
Raspberry	After bearing and in fall	Remove at the ground canes which bore last crop. Remove weak new canes and thin to no closer than 6 inches apart. In fall head back canes 4 or 5 feet.
Cherry	Winter or early spring	Prune moderately, cut back slightly the most vigorous shoots.
Currant	Early spring	Remove old unfruitful growth. Encourage new shoots.
Gooseberry	Early spring	Same as currant. Cut back new shoots at 12 inches high and side shoots to two buds.
Grape	Late winter or early early spring, before sap starts	Requires heavy pruning of old wood to encourage new bearing wood. Remove all old branches back to main vine. Cut back the previous year's new growth to four buds.
Peach	Early spring	Prune vigorously – remove one-half of the previous year's growth, keep tree headed low, and well thinned-out.
Plum	Early spring	Remove dead and diseased branches, keep tree shaped up by cutting back rank growth. Prune moderately.
Quince	Early spring	Cut back young trees to form low, open head. Little pruning of older trees required except to remove dead and weak growth.

TYPE OF SHRUB	WHEN	HOW
Barberry	Early spring	Little pruning required except to remove a few old branches occasionally to encourage new growth. Head back as necessary to keep plant in shape.
Butterfly Bush	Early spring	Cut out all dead wood. Remove some old branches and head-in as necessary to keep plant properly shaped.
Clematis	Depends on flowering time	Spring-blooming types should be cut back after bloom, if shaping is desired. Early-summer-blooming types should be cut back 6-8" to a pair of strong buds in March, if shaping is desired. Summer-and-fall-blooming types should be cut back to 12" from ground every March.
Crabapple	Early spring	Prune moderately. Cut out dead and broken branches and suckers.

continued

TYPE OF SHRUB	WHEN	HOW
Deutzias	After flowering	Remove a few older branches and all dead wood. Do not let growth get too dense.
Dogwood, Flowering	After flowering	Remove dead wood only.
Dogwood, Other	Spring	Varieties grown for colored twigs should have the old growth removed to encourage bright-colored new shoots.
Elderberry	After fruiting	Prune severely. Remove one-half of season's growth.
Forsythia	After flowering	Remove a few older branches at the ground each year and head back new growth as necessary.
Honeysuckle, Bush	After fruiting	Cut out some old branches. Keep bush open.
Hydrangea	Early spring	Hills of Snow variety: cut back to ground. Others: remove dead and weak growth, cut old flowering stems back to two buds.
Laurel, Mountain	After flowering	Prune very little. Remove a few old branches at the ground from weak, leggy plants to induce growth from the roots.
Lilac	After flowering	Remove diseased and scaly growth, cut off old flower heads, and cut out surplus sucker growth.
Mock-Orange	After flowering	Cut out dead wood and a few old branches to thin out plant.
Rhododendron	After flowering	Treat same as Laurel, Mountain.
Roses, Climbing	After flowering	Cut out about one-half of old growth at the ground and retain the vigorous new shoots from the root for next year's flowers. Head back as necessary.
Roses: Tea, Hybrid, Perpetual	Spring after frosts	Cut away all dead and weak growth and shorten all remaining branches or canes to seven or eight buds.
Rose of Sharon	When buds start	Cut out all winter killed growth back to live wood.
Snowberry	Early spring	Thin out some old branches and cut back last season's growth of that part remaining to three buds.
Trumpet Vine	Early spring	Prune side branches severely to the main stem.
Weigela	After flowering	Prune lightly, remove all dead, weak growth and head in as necessary. Cut out a few old branches at the ground to induce new growth.
Wisteria	Spring	Cut back the new growth to the spurs at the axils of the leaves. This can be repeated in midsummer.
Viburnum	Early spring	Prune lightly. Remove all dead, weak and a few of the old branches.
Virginia Creeper	Spring	Clip young plants freely. Older plants require little pruning except to remove dead growth and some thinning.

Source: *Pruning Trees, Shrubs and Vines,* Editors of Garden Way Publishing

PRUNING ORNAMENTAL TREES

BOTANICAL NAME	COMMON NAME	SPECIAL REMARKS	BOTANICAL NAME	COMMON NAME	SPECIAL REMARKS
Amelanchier	shadbush	Prune only to shape, as either bush or tree	*Koelreuteria paniculata*	golden rain tree	Prune to shape when young
Carpinus betulus	European hornbeam	Prune to tree form	*Laburnum anagyroides*	golden-chain	Prune after blooming
Carpinus orientalis	Oriental hornbeam	Prune to tree form	*Magnolia*	magnolia	Prune just after blooming
Cassia fistula	golden-shower, senna	Cut back season's growth to short spurs after blooming	*Malus*	flowering crab apple	Prune to shape, renew old wood if necessary
Cercis	redbud	Prune after blooming if necessary	*Myrica cerifera*	wax myrtle	Prune to remove winter injury, or to shape, in late winter
Cornus florida	flowering dogwood	Prune as little as possible, heals slowly	*Myrica pensylvanica*	bayberry	Prune to remove suckers, winter injury
Cornus Kousa	Kousa dogwood	See *Cornus florida*	*Oxydendrum arboreum*	sourwood	Needs pruning early
Cotinus obovatus	American smoke tree	Prune to grow as bush or small tree, cut off fading flowers	*Prunus*	flowering almond, apricot, cherry, peach, plum	Prune to shape in late winter
Crataegus	hawthorn	Prune to shape in late winter, renew branches if necessary	*Rhamnus davurica*	buckthorn	Prune to shape in late winter
Elaeagnus	Russian olive	Prune only to control size if necessary, in late winter	*Sorbus*	mountain ash	Prune to tree form, in late winter
Euonymus atropurpurea	burning bush	Prune in late winter, only if necessary	*Symplocos paniculata*	sweetleaf	Prune to shape, renew old branches
Franklinia alatamaha	Franklin tree	Prune to tree form	*Syringa reticulata*	Japanese tree lilac	Prune right after blooming, if necessary
Halesia monticola	silver-bell	Needs pruning rarely	*Viburnum*	cranberry bush, nannyberry, black haw	Prune in late winter only, as necessary
Hydrangea paniculata 'Grandiflora'	peegee hydrangea	Prune in late winter			

Source: *Pruning Simplified*, Lewis Hill

PART II:
GARDEN AND LANDSCAPE PLANTS

SEEDS

CHARACTERISTICS OF COMMON VEGETABLES SAVED FOR SEED

VEGETABLE	PLANT TYPE	SEED VIABILITY* (YEARS)	HOW POLLINATED	NEED ISOLATION IF YOU ARE COLLECTING & SAVING SEED
Asparagus	Perennial	3	Insect	Yes
Bean	Annual	3	Self	Limited
Beet	Biennial	4	Wind	Yes
Broccoli	Annual	5	Insect	Yes
Brussels Sprouts	Biennial	5	Insect	Yes
Cabbage	Biennial	5	Insect	Yes
Carrot	Biennial	3	Insect	Yes
Cauliflower	Biennial	5	Insect	Yes
Celeriac	Biennial	5	Insect	Yes
Celery	Biennial	5	Insect	Yes
Chinese Cabbage	Annual	5	Insect	Yes
Chive	Perennial	2	Insect	Yes
Corn, Sweet	Annual	1-2	Wind	Yes
Cowpea	Annual	3	Self	Limited
Cucumber	Annual	5	Insect	Yes
Eggplant	Annual	5	Self	Limited
Jerusalem Artichoke	Perennial			No
Kale	Biennial	5	Insect	Yes
Kohlrabi	Biennial	5	Insect	Yes
Leek	Biennial	3	Insect	Yes
Lettuce	Annual	5	Self	Limited
Lima Bean	Annual	3	Self	Limited

* As reported by authorities. Ideal storage techniques can significantly prolong seed viability.

continued

VEGETABLE	PLANT TYPE	SEED VIABILITY* (YEARS)	HOW POLLINATED	NEED ISOLATION IF YOU ARE COLLECTING & SAVING SEED
Muskmelon	Annual	5	Insect	Yes
New Zealand Spinach	Annual	5	Wind	Yes
Okra	Annual	2	Self	Limited
Onion	Biennial	1-2	Insect	Yes
Parsley	Biennial	2	Insect	Yes
Parsnip	Biennial	1-2	Insect	Yes
Pea	Annual	3	Self	Limited
Peanut	Annual	1-2	Self	Limited
Pepper	Annual	4	Self	Limited
Popcorn	Annual	1-2	Wind	Yes
Potato	Annual		Self	No
Pumpkin	Annual	5	Insect	Yes
Radish	Annual	5	Insect	Yes
Rutabaga	Biennial	5	Insect	Yes
Salsify	Biennial	2	Self	No
Soybean	Annual	3	Self	Limited
Spinach	Annual	5	Wind	Yes
Squash, Summer	Annual	5	Insect	Yes
Squash, Winter	Annual	5	Insect	Yes
Swiss Chard	Biennial	4	Wind	Yes
Tomato	Annual	4	Self	Limited
Turnip	Annual	5	Insect	Yes
Watermelon	Annual	5	Insect	Yes

* As reported by authorities. Ideal storage techniques can significantly prolong seed viability.

Source: *Saving Seeds*, Marc Rogers

Optimal Germination Temperatures for Seeds

CROP	IDEAL TEMPERATURE (DEGREES F)	MINIMUM TEMPERATURE (DEGREES F)	CROP	IDEAL TEMPERATURE (DEGREES F)	MINIMUM TEMPERATURE (DEGREES F)
Asparagus	75		Muskmelon	90	75
Basil	70		Okra	95	70
Bean	80		Onion	75	50**
Beet	85	50	Oregano, Greek	60	
Cabbage	85	45	Parsley	75	50
Carrot	80	45	Parsnip	65	50 (not over 85)
Cauliflower	80	45	Pea	75	40 (not over 85)
Celery*	70	60 (not over 85)	Pepper	85	65
Swiss Chard	85	50	Pumpkin	95	70
Chervil	55		Radish	85	45
Chives	70	60	Sage	70	
Corn	85	60	Sorrel	70	
Cucumber	95	60**	Spinach	70	45 (not over 85)
Dill	70		Squash	95	70
Eggplant	85	75**	Summer savory	70	
Fennel	70		Tomato	85	60
Lettuce	75	40 (not over 85)	Turnip	85	60**
Lovage	65		Watermelon	95	70**

*   Best with a 10°F drop at night
** Germinates at over 100°F

Source: *The Harvest Gardener,* Susan McClure

SEEDS THAT REQUIRE SPECIAL TREATMENT

COMMON NAME	BOTANICAL NAME	TREATMENT	COMMON NAME	BOTANICAL NAME	TREATMENT
African daisy	*Arctotis* species/hybrids	sow early	Blanket flower	*Gaillardia* x *grandiflora*	light
Angelica	*Angelica archangelica*	stratify ASAP	Blazing star	*Mentzelia lindleyi*	sow early
Anise	*Pimpinella anisum*	resent transplant	Bleeding-heart	*Dicentra spectabilis*	stratify
Annual phlox	*Phlox drummondii*	cool/resent transplant/ sow early	Blue lace flower	*Trachymene coerulea*	resent transplant
Asparagus	*Asparagus officinalis*	soak	Borage	*Borago officinalis*	dark/resent transplant/sow early
Baby's-breath	*Gypsophila* species	sow early	Broccoli, Brussels sprouts, cabbage, cauliflower, Chinese cabbage, collards, kale, kohlrabi, mustard, turnip	*Brassica* species	sow early
Baby-blue-eyes	*Nemophila menziesii*	sow early/cool	Browallia	*Browallia speciosa*	light
Bachelor's-button, cornflower	*Centaurea cyanus*	sow early/dark	Burning bush	*Kochia scoparia*	ASAP
Balloon flower	*Platycodon grandiflorus*	light	Butterfly flower, poor-man's orchid	*Schizanthus* x *wisetonensis*	dark
Basket-of-gold	*Alyssum montanum*	light	California poppy	*Eschscholzia californica*	sow early/ cool/resent transplant
Beard-tongue	*Penstemon* hybrids	cool	Candytuft	*Iberis sempervirens*	cool
Beet, Swiss chard	*Beta vulgaris*	sow early	Cape marigold	*Dimorphotheca sinuata*	ASAP
Begonia	*Begonia* species	light	Caraway	*Carum carvi*	resent transplant
Bellflower	*Campanula* species	light	Carrot	*Daucus carota*	resent transplant
Bells-of-Ireland	*Moluccella laevis*	sow early/light/cool	Carrot	*Daucus carota* var. *sativus*	sow early

continued

COMMON NAME	BOTANICAL NAME	TREATMENT	COMMON NAME	BOTANICAL NAME	TREATMENT
Chamomile	*Matricaria recutita*	cool/sow early	Fennel	*Foeniculum* species	resent transplant/dark
Chervil	*Anthriscus cerefolium*	resent transplant/sow early	Flax	*Linum* species	resent transplant
Chinese primrose	*Primula sinensis*	dark	Flossflower	*Ageratum houstonianum*	light
Christmas rose	*Helleborus niger*	stratify	Flowering tobacco	*Nicotiana alata*	light
Coleus	*Coleus* x *hybridus*	light	Forget-me-not	*Myosotis* species	dark
Columbine	*Aguilegia* species/hybrids	light/stratify	Garden cress	*Lepidium sativum*	sow early
Coralbells	*Heuchera sanguinea*	cool	Gas plant	*Dictamnus albus*	stratify/cool
Coriander	*Coriandrum sativum*	sow early/resent transplant/dark	Globeflower	*Trollius europaeus*	stratify
Corn	*Zea mays*	resent transplant	Impatiens	*Impatiens wallerana*	light
Cranesbill	*Geranium sanguineum*	ASAP	Larkspur	*Consolida ambigua*	dark/sow early
Creeping zinnia	*Sanvitalia procumbens*	resent transplant/light	Lavender	*Lavandula angustifolia*	stratify
Daylily	*Hemerocallis* hybrids	stratify	Leek	*Allium ampeloprasum*	sow early
Delphinium	*Delphinium* species	ASAP/dark	Leopard's-bane	*Doronicum cordatum*	light
Dill	*Anethum graveolens*	sow early/resent transplant/light	Lettuce	*Lactuca sativa*	light/sow early
False rock cress, purple rock cress	*Aubrieta deltoidea*	cool	Lilyturf	*Liriope muscari*	soak
Love-in-a-mist	*Nigella damascena*	resent transplant	Lupine	*Lupinus* species	resent transplant/soak/scarify

continued

COMMON NAME	BOTANICAL NAME	TREATMENT	COMMON NAME	BOTANICAL NAME	TREATMENT
Mallow	*Hibiscus* species	scarify/soak	Ornamental pepper	*Capsicum annuum*	light
Maltese-cross	*Lychnis chalcedonica*	light	Ornamental cabbage	*Brassica oleracea* 'Acephala'	stratify/light
Marjoram	*Origanum majorana*	sow early	Painted-tongue	*Salpiglossis sinuata*	dark
Matricaria, feverfew	*Chrysanthemum parthenium*	light	Parsley	*Petroselinum crispum*	sow early/soak/resent transplant
Mexican sunflower	*Tithonia rotundifloia*	light	Parsnip	*Pastinaca sativa*	resent transplant/soak/sow early
Midsummer aster, fleabane	*Erigeron* species	cool	Pea	*Pisum sativum*	sow early/resent transplant
Reseda odorata	*Mignonette*	light/sow early/resent transplant	Perennial pea	*Lathyrus latifolius*	soak/cool
Morning-glory and other closely related plants	*Ipomoea* species	soak/scarify	Perennial and sweet pea	*Lathyrus* species	scarify
Mustard, rutabaga, turnip	*Brassica* species	resent transplant	Periwinkle	*Catharanthus roseus*	dark
Nasturtium	*Tropaeolum majur*	resent transplant/dark	Petunia	*Petunia* x *hybrida*	light
Nemesia	*Nemesia strumosa*	dark	Phlox	*Phlox* species	dark
Okra	*Abelmoschus esculentus*	soak	Phlox	*Phlox paniculata*	stratify
Onion	*Allium cepa*	sow early	Poppy	*Papaver* species	resent transplant/cool
Oriental poppy	*Papaver orientale*	light	Poppy	*Papaver* species (except *P. orientale*)	dark

continued

COMMON NAME	BOTANICAL NAME	TREATMENT	COMMON NAME	BOTANICAL NAME	TREATMENT
Pot marigold	*Calendula officinalis*	dark	Swiss chard, beet	*Beta vulgaris*	resent transplant
Primrose	*Primula* species	stratify	Tahoka daisy	*Machaeranthera tanacetifolia*	sow early/ stratify
Primrose	*Primula* species (except P. sinensis)	light	Thrift, sea pink	*Armeria maritima*	soak
Pyrethrum, painted daisy	*Chrysanthemum coccineum*	ASAP	Thyme, mother of thyme	*Thymus* species	cool
Radish	*Raphanus sativus*	resent transplant/ sow early	Tickseed	*Coreopsis grandiflora*	light
Rock cress, wall cress	*Arabis* species	light	Transvaal daisy	*Gerbera jamesonii* hybrids	light/ASAP
Rocket	*Eruca vesicaria*	sow early/resent transplant	Treasure flower	*Gazania rigens*	dark
Rosemary	*Rosmarinus officinalis*	cool	Tree mallow	*Lavatera* hybrids	resent transplant
Salvia (red-flowered varieties)	*Salvia* species	light	Verbena	*Verbena* species	dark
Savory	*Satureja* species	light	Viola, violet, pansy	*Viola* species	stratify/dark
Scarlet sage	*Salvia splendens*	ASAP	Wake-robin	*Trillium ovatum*	stratify
Sesame	*Sesamum indicum*	resent transplant	Wallflower	*Cheiranthus cheiri*	cool
Shasta daisy	*Chrysanthemum* x *superbum*	light	Wild blue indigo, false indigo	*Baptisia australis*	scarify
Snapdragon	*Antirrhinum majus*	light	Yarrow	*Achillea* species	light
Spinach	*Spinacia oleracea*	resent transplant/ sow early			
Stock	*Matthiola* species	light			
Strawflower	*Helichrysum bracteatum*	light			
Sweet pea	*Lathyrus odoratus*	cool/soak/dark			
Sweet alyssum	*Lobularia maritima*	sow early/light			

KEY: Light = Need light to germinate
Dark = Need darkness to germinate
Soak = Require soaking before sowing
Stratify = Require stratification (cold treatment) before sowing
Scarify = Require scarification (nicking or filing) before sowing
Cool = Need cool temperature (55°F) to germinate
ASAP = Seeds are not long lived and should be sown as soon soil can be worked

Source: *Starting Seeds Indoors,* Editors of Garden Way Publishing

VEGETABLES

CUSTOMIZED CHART FOR PLANNING AND PLANTING

ANNUAL VEGETABLE	AMOUNT TO PLANT PER PERSON	FEET OF ROW PER PERSON		PLANTS/FT AFTER THINNING* OR TRANSPLANTS/FT		DISTANCE BETWEEN PLANTS	WIDTH OF WIDE ROW	DEPTH TO PLANT SEEDS	DAYS TO GERMINATE	YOUR NOTES			SUCCESSION CROP & DATE	COMMENTS
		SINGLE ROW	WIDE ROW	SINGLE ROW	WIDE ROW					VARIETIES PLANTED	DATE PLANTED	DATE OF FIRST HARVEST		
HARDY CROPS (Plant when ground can be worked, 20-40 days before the last frost.)														
Broccoli	5-10 plants	8-12'	4-6'	1	5	12-14" stagger planting 2-1-2	16'	¼"	6-9				No – smaller heads will form after first central head is harvested.	Best started from transplants; seeds require 80-100 days to harvest.
Brussels Sprouts	5-10 plants	8-12'	4-6'	1	5	12-14" stagger planting 2-1-2	16"	¼"	6-9				No	Best started from transplants; requires 100+ days from seed. Pick off lower leaves after sprouts form.
Cabbage	5-10 plants	8-12'	3-6'	1	5	12-14" stagger planting 2-1-2	16"	¼"	6-9				No – cut first head and smaller heads will form.	Transplants best.
Garlic	5 bulbs	2'	1'	3-4	36	3-4"	20"	2"	(bulb)					Start harvesting when small. Use tops and bulbs.
Kale	¼ pkt.	5-10'	3-6'	3*	9	6-8"	16"	¼"	6-9				Midsummer	Will survive frost, snow.
Kohlrabi	¼ pkt.	3-5'	1-3'	3-4*	24*	3-4"	16"	¼"	6-9				Late summer	Best at 3" in diameter. Substitute for water chestnuts in stir-fry.
Onion Sets	1 lb.	10-15'	3-6'	6	49	2-3"	20"	1"					Follow early harvest with additional sets.	Use fresh from greentails to maturity. Harvest for storage after tops fall over.
Onion Plants	1 bunch	10-15'	3-6'	6	36	3-4"	20"	1"					No	
Peas	¼ lb.	15-25'	6-12'	6-7	24	2-4"	16-36"	1"	7-10				Follow with fall crops such as seeded cauliflower, turnips, kohlrabi, broccoli.	Does well in spring. Doesn't like hot weather. Sugar Snap varieties require 5-6' fence or poles.

* These are plants started by sprinkling seeds in the row and then thinning by hand or by dragging a garden rake through the row. Peas and beans are easier to seed by hand and do not need thinning. The numbers per row are approximate for all small seeds. Remember, they do need room to grow.

Note: Copy these pages for year-to-year record keeping.

continued

ANNUAL VEGETABLE	AMOUNT TO PLANT PER PERSON	FEET OF ROW PER PERSON		PLANTS/FT AFTER THINNING* OR TRANSPLANTS/FT		DISTANCE BETWEEN PLANTS	WIDTH OF WIDE ROW	DEPTH TO PLANT SEEDS	DAYS TO GERMINATE	YOUR NOTES			SUCCESSION CROP & DATE	COMMENTS
		SINGLE ROW	WIDE ROW	SINGLE ROW	WIDE ROW					VARIETIES PLANTED	DATE PLANTED	DATE OF FIRST HARVEST		
HARDY CROPS (continued)														
Radish	½ pkt.	5-10'	2-4'	10*	140*	1-2"	16"	¼"	3-5				Plant at two-week intervals.	Plant with other seeds to mark rows.
Rutabaga	½ pkt.	5-10'	2-5'	2-3	10-12	6-8"	16"	½"	6-10				No	Good for winter storage.
Shallots	5 bulbs	2'	1'	3-4	24	4-5"	20"						Follow with second crop of lettuce.	Onionlike; used in French sauces or fresh.
Spinach	½ pkt.	5-10'	2-5'	4-5*	20*	3-5"	16"	¼"	7-12				Plant and harvest early. Follow with most tender crops.	Likes cool weather. Goes to seed quickly in warm weather.
Turnip	¼ oz.	10-15'	2-5'	3-5*	10-12*	6-8"	16"	¼"	7-12				Follow early harvest with fall salad greens or peas.	Good for winter storage.
SEMI-HARDY CROPS (Plant 10-30 days before last frost.)														
Beets	½ pkt.	5-10'	3-6'	6-8*	30*	2-4"	16"	½"	7-12				Midsummer	Beet greens removed during thinning can be cooked like other greens.
Carrots	½ pkt.	5-10'	3-6'	7*	50*	1-2"	16"	¼"	12-18				Midsummer	Darkest green foliage indicates the largest carrots.
Cauliflower	3-5 plants	5-10'	3-6'	1-2	9	8-10" stagger planting	20"	¼"	6-9				Late summer	Start as transplants in spring. Seed in early summer for fall crops.
Lettuce	½ pkt.	5-10'	2-4'	Head, 2-3; Leaf, 5-6	Head, 9*; Leaf, 20*	Head, 8-10" stagger planting; Leaf, 4-5"	16"	¼ "	5-10				Early and late summer	3" spacing for leaf lettuce, 8" for head lettuce. Cut, don't pull, for second and third harvest.

* These are plants started by sprinkling seeds in the row and then thinning by hand or by dragging a garden rake through the row. Peas and beans are easier to seed by hand and do not need thinning. The numbers per row are approximate for all small seeds. Remember, they do need room to grow.

Note: Copy these pages for year-to-year record keeping.

continued

| ANNUAL VEGETABLE | AMOUNT TO PLANT PER PERSON | FEET OF ROW PER PERSON | | PLANTS/FT AFTER THINNING* OR TRANSPLANTS/FT | | DISTANCE BETWEEN PLANTS | WIDTH OF WIDE ROW | DEPTH TO PLANT SEEDS | DAYS TO GERMINATE | YOUR NOTES | | | SUCCESSION CROP & DATE | COMMENTS |
		SINGLE ROW	WIDE ROW	SINGLE ROW	WIDE ROW					VARIETIES PLANTED	DATE PLANTED	DATE OF FIRST HARVEST		
SEMI-HARDY CROPS (continued)														
Swiss Chard	¼ pkt.	5-10'	2-4'	5-6*	20*	4-6"	16"	½-1"	7-10				Cut in all seasons.	Cut and serve when plants are 8-10" tall.
TENDER VEGETABLES (Plant on the average last frost date.)														
Snap Beans (bush)	½ lb.	25-50'	10-15'	6-8	20	3-4"	20"	1"	5-10				Try second crop of beans, beets, or carrots.	Pick young, before individual beans are visible in the pod.
Snap Beans (pole)	¼ lb.	15-25'	No	4-6	4-6	4-6 seeds per pole; 6" apart in a row.	6"	1"	7-14				Try second crop of beans, beets, or carrots.	Pick young, before individual beans are visible in the pod.
Lima Beans	¼ lb.	10-15'	8-10'	5-8*	16*	3-6"	16"	1-1½"	5-9				No	Plant after ground warms up. Bear continuously all season.
Cantaloupe	½ pkt.	2-3 hills	2-3 hills	3-6 per hill	No	4-6' between hills 4-6' between rows	4 times diam. of seed	4-10					No	Plant 5-6 seeds per hill. Later thin to best 3-4 plants.
Sweet Corn	½ lb.	25-50'	No	4-6	No	8-12" between plants 30-36" between rows	1"	5-12					Plant seed at 2-week intervals to stretch harvest.	Pick immediately before serving to prevent natural sugars in the ear from turning to starch.
Cucumber	2-3 hills	8-16'	No	4-5 per hill	No	4-6' between hills 4-6' between rows	½-1"	7-10					No	Plant 5-6 seeds per hill. Later thin to best 3-4 plants.
Eggplant	2-3 plants	4-6'	3-4'	1	6	12" stagger planting	16"	½"	10-14				No	Transplants are a good idea in the North.
Peppers	2-3 plants	4-6'	3-4'	1	6	12" stagger planting	16"	½"	7-10				No	Transplants in the North. Likes poor soil. Leave green peppers on plant for red peppers.

* These are plants started by sprinkling seeds in the row and then thinning by hand or by dragging a garden rake through the row. Peas and beans are easier to seed by hand and do not need thinning. The numbers per row are approximate for all small seeds. Remember, they do need room to grow.

Note: Copy these pages for year-to-year record keeping.

continued

ANNUAL VEGETABLE	AMOUNT TO PLANT PER PERSON	FEET OF ROW PER PERSON		PLANTS/FT AFTER THINNING* OR TRANSPLANTS/FT		DISTANCE BETWEEN PLANTS	WIDTH OF WIDE ROW	DEPTH TO PLANT SEEDS	DAYS TO GERMINATE	YOUR NOTES			SUCCESSION CROP & DATE	COMMENTS
		SINGLE ROW	WIDE ROW	SINGLE ROW	WIDE ROW					VARIETIES PLANTED	DATE PLANTED	DATE OF FIRST HARVEST		
TENDER VEGETABLES (continued)														
Pumpkins	2-3 hills	12-18'	No	4-5 per hill	No	5-8' between hills 6-10' between rows		1"	7-10				No	Needs space to sprawl. Grow as a barrier around corn to keep raccoons out.
Squash (zucchini and summer)	2-3 hills	5-10'	No	4-6 seeds in each hill	No	3-4' between hills 3-4' between rows		½-1"	7-10				No	For extra-early crop, start some indoors and transplant.
Squash (winter)	2-3 hills	12-18'	No	4-6 seeds in each hill	No	5-8' between hills 6-10' between rows		1"	7-10				No	Needs space to sprawl. Grow as a barrier around corn to keep raccoons out.
Tomato	3-5 plants	10-15'	No		No	18-36"		¼"	7-10				No	Start indoors. Transplant after danger of frost passes.
Watermelon	3-5 hills	25-40'	No		No	5-8' between hills 6-10' between rows		½-1"	4-14				No	Start indoors. Grow under plastic tunnels for head start in the North.
SOUTHERN FAVORITES														
Collards	¼ pkt.	4-6'	3-4'	1*	5-6*	10-12" stagger planting	20"	¼"	6-9				Can follow early crop like lettuce.	A fall crop in the South. Flavor improves after light frost. Sometimes planted spring and fall.
Mustard Greens	¼ pkt.	3-5'	1-3'	8-12*	24*	4-5"	16"	¼"	5-8				Can follow early crop like lettuce.	Often a fall crop in the South.
Okra	2 plants	3-5'	No	1-2	No	10-12"	16"	½"	4-14				No	Likes hot weather. Harvest when pods are 4" long or less.

* These are plants started by sprinkling seeds in the row and then thinning by hand or by dragging a garden rake through the row. Peas and beans are easier to seed by hand and do not need thinning. The numbers per row are approximate for all small seeds. Remember, they do need room to grow.

Note: Copy these pages for year-to-year record keeping.

Source: *Down-to-Earth Gardening Know-How for the '90s*, Dick Raymond

Natural Controls for Vegetable Pests

GARDEN PESTS	SUSCEPTIBLE PLANTS/ DAMAGE	HOMEMADE REMEDIES/CULTURAL CONTROLS/ TRAPS & BARRIERS	BIOLOGICAL CONTROLS	NATURAL INSECTICIDES
Aphid	Wide range of plants; sucks sap and causes yellowing of leaves and loss of plant vigor; some transmit viral diseases	Soapy water sprays; aluminum foil place on ground under young plants reflects the sky and confuses insects; as a lure, use yellow containers of soapy water, commercial yellow sticky traps, or a board painted yellow and coated with a sticky solution such as Tanglefoot; cover plants with Reemay or other row cover	Ladybugs; spiders; syrphid flies; lacewings	Safer's soap; nicotine; pyrethrum; sabadilla; summer horticultural spray oil
Asparagus Beetle [1]	Asparagus; chews tips and foliage	Remove garden plants after harvest; shake beetles into can of soapy water; use row cover early in season; dust plants with rock phosphate or bone meal		Pyrethrum, rotenone
Cabbage Looper	Crucifers, greens, beans, peas, potatoes, tomatoes; chews leaves	Sprinkle worms with flour or salt; cover plants with Reemay or other row cover to prevent moths from laying eggs; resistant varieties, timed planting [2]	Trichogramma wasps: *Bacillus thuringiensis*	Rotenone; pyrethrum/ diatomaceous earth blend; sabadilla
Cabbage Maggot [1]	Brassicas, parsnips, radishes, turnips; tunnels in stems just below ground. Seedlings wilt and die	Apply lime or wood ashes to soil. Timed planting [2]	Beneficial nematodes	
Carrot Rust Fly [1]	Carrots, celery, parsley, parsnips; maggots tunnel into roots, stunting plants	Sprinkle wood ashes around base of plant; rotate crops; timed planting [2]		
Colorado Potato Beetle	Potatoes, tomatoes, peppers, eggplant; chews leaves and terminal growth	Hand pick beetles and larvae; remove orange egg masses from undersides of leaves; spray with mixture of basil leaves and water; 1'-thick layer of clean hay or straw mulch kee[s beetles from climbing to the stems; cover with Reemay or other row cover; resistant varieties; timed planting [2]	Ladybugs; M-One (*Bacillus thuringiensis* var. San Diego), nematodes	Rotenone; sabadilla
Corn Earworm [1]	Corn; feeds on foliage and kernels. Opens plants to disease and other insects	Just after silk has browned, apply 10-20 drops of mineral oil containing rotenone with eye dropper to silk tassles or spray mineral oil on tassles. In fall, remove debris and cultivate thoroughly	Trichogramma wasps, *Bacillus thuringiensis*[3], beneficial nematodes	Rotenone
Cutworm	All plants; some chew through plant stems near soil line, others eat buds, leaves, fruits, roots	Place collar of newspaper around stem when transplanting into garden; keep garden clear of weeds and grass in fall to discourage egg-laying; sprinkle wood ashes around plants	Braconid wasps; tachinid flies; beneficial nematodes; *Bacillus thuringiensis*[3]	Diatomaceous earth
European Corn Borer	Corn and many other crops; chews leaves and tassles, bores into stems	Plow under stalks in fall or early spring before adults emerge; keep grass and weeds down; timed planting [2]	Ladybugs; braconid wasps; tachinid flies; *Bacillus thuringiensis*[3]	Ryania; rotenone; sabadilla

continued

GARDEN PESTS	SUSCEPTIBLE PLANTS/ DAMAGE	HOMEMADE REMEDIES/CULTURAL CONTROLS/ TRAPS & BARRIERS	BIOLOGICAL CONTROLS	NATURAL INSECTICIDES
Flea Beetle	Crucifers, tomatoes, eggplant, peppers; eats holes in leaves; causes wilting and retards plant growth	Frequent cultivation disturbs eggs; remove garden plants after harvest; beetles don't like shade so plant susceptible plants near shade-giving crops; sprinkle wood ashes on plants; use garlic or hot pepper sprays; cover with Reemay or other row cover; plant resistant varieties; timed planting [2]	Beneficial nematodes	Diatomaceous earth; rotenone; pyrethrum; sabadilla
Harlequin Bug	Cabbage family, collards, kohlrabi, mustard, radish, turnip; sucks plant sap causing blotchy leaves, wilting, and eventual death	Hand pick; keep weeds down; resistant varieties		Liquid rotenone/pyrethrum; sabadilla
Hornworm	Tomatoes, peppers, eggplant, potato; devours leaves and fruits	Hand pick; sprinkle dried hot peppers on plants; Four-o'clocks as trap crop; timed planting [2]	*Bacillus thuringiensis* [3] ; trichogramma wasps; braconid wasps	Rotenone
Japanese Beetle	Grubs feed mostly on grass roots; adults feed on a variety of plants, skeletonizing leaves and chewing flowers	Hand pick; dispose of any diseased fruit on ground; grubs are discouraged by high soil pH; larkspur foliage is toxic to beetles; geraniums repel beetles; smartweed planted around periphery of garden is a repellent; place commercial traps with floral and sex lures at periphery of garden; timed planting [2]	*Bacillus popilliae* (milky spore) infects grubs (most effective when applied on a neighborhood-wide basis); beneficial nematodes	Sabadilla, liquid rotenone/pyrethrum controls adult beetles
Leafhopper	Potatoes, beans, celery, eggplant, rhubarb, beets, roses; feeds on foliage, causing stunted, crinkled, curled leaves; some transmit viruses	Insect prefers open areas so shelter susceptible plants; cover with Reemay or other row cover, especially for a month beginning when plants are few inches high; resistant varieties		Diatomaceous earth; Safer's Soap; liquid rotenone/pyrethrum; summer horticultural spray oil
Leaf Miner	Many crops; larvae tunnel inside leaves, stunting growth	Destroy infected leaves; cultivate well in fall; cover with Reemay or other row cover; timed planting [2]		
Mexican Bean Beetle	Beans; skeletonizes leaves; plants become shredded and dried out, and die	Destroy eggs; hand pick beetles; clean plant debris after harvest to limit egg-laying habitat; earlier plantings are less susceptible; grow nasturtiums, marigolds, savory, or garlic nearby; resistant varieties	Ladybugs; Pediobius wasps kill larvae	Liquid rotenone/ pyrethrum; rotenone dust; sabadilla; summer horticultural spray oil

continued

GARDEN PESTS	SUSCEPTIBLE PLANTS/ DAMAGE	HOMEMADE REMEDIES/CULTURAL CONTROLS/ TRAPS & BARRIERS	BIOLOGICAL CONTROLS	NATURAL INSECTICIDES
Onion Maggot[1]	Onion; tunnels into bulbs, making them inedible	Pull up and destroy infested plants; spread onions throughout the garden rather than in one bed		
Slug	Many plants; eats foliage and fruits	Hand pick; sprinkle slugs with salt; protective borders of sand, lime, or ashes; mulch with wood shavings or oak leaves; trap with saucers of stale beer set out in the garden; lay boards, newspapers, and other debris on ground as traps; copper bands; plastic traps		Diatomaceous earth
Spider Mite	Many plants; sucks plant sap causing blotchy yellow leaves and leaf drop	Spray cold water or solution of wheat flour, buttermilk and water on leaves; soapy water sprays; dormant oil sprays	Ladybugs; lacewings	Liquid rotenone/ pyrethrum; Safer's Soap; summer horticultural spray oil
Squash Bug	Squash and other vine crops; sucks plant sap, injecting toxin that causes plant wilting and death	Hand pick; likes moist protected areas so keep garden free of debris and other hiding places; trellises raise vines out of bugs' reach; grow marigolds, radishes, tansy, or nasturtiums nearby; dust with wood ashes and lime; cover with Reemay or other row cover; resistant varieties; timed planting [2]	Tachinid flies	Sabadilla; rotenone dust; liquid rotenone/ pyrethrum
Squash Vine Borer	Squash and other vine crops; bores into stems causing wilting of runners or entire plant	Wrap strips of nylon stocking around stems to discourage adults from climbing stems to lay eggs, or pile up soil in a mound as high as the blossoms and add soil as plants grow; cover with Reemay or other row cover; resistant varieties; timed planting [2]	Trichogramma wasps	Rotenone; sabadilla; diatomaceous earth
Striped Cucumber Beetle	Cucumbers and other vine plants; larvae feed on underground stems and roots; adults feed on entire plants; can spread disease	Hand pick; heavy mulching; interplant with catnip, tansy, or radishes; cover plants with Reemay or other row cover; resistant varieties; dust with wood ashes or rock phosphate; grow plants on trellises; timed planting [2]	Braconid wasps, tachinid flies, beneficial nematodes	Liquid rotenone/ pyrethrum; sabadilla
Tarnished Plant Bug	Beans, celery, chard, lettuce, strawberries; sucks plant sap from stems, buds, and fruits; injects toxin that deforms flowers, blackens terminal shoots, dwarfs and pits fruit	Remove plant debris after harvest; white sticky traps		Sabadilla dust; liquid rotenone/ pyrethrum
Thrips	Onions, beans, cukes, melons, tomatoes, many flowers; suck sap and scar fruits and leaves; transmit viruses	Keep garden free of weeds and debris; aluminum foil mulch keeps thrips off low-growing crops; soapy water sprays; yellow sticky traps	Green lacewings	Liquid rotenone/ pyrethrum; Safer's Soap; tobacco and sulfur dusts

continued

GARDEN PESTS	SUSCEPTIBLE PLANTS/ DAMAGE	HOMEMADE REMEDIES/CULTURAL CONTROLS/ TRAPS & BARRIERS	BIOLOGICAL CONTROLS	NATURAL INSECTICIDES
Weevils (many types) [1]	Many vegetables; puncture holes in leaves, stems, and fruits, sometimes defoliating plant	Hill up soil around stems of sweet potato vines; rotate crops; remove plant debris; timed planting [2]	Beneficial nemotodes	Diatomaceous earth, rotenone
Wireworm	Potatoes, beans, lettuce, carrots, cabbage, corn, onion, beets, turnips; chews roots, seeds and tubers	Cultivate to expose worms and discourage egg laying; plant green manure crop such as clover; bury halved potatoes cut side down in soil to trap worms (discard potatoes after 2 days)	Beneficial nemotodes	Tobacco dust or tobacco tea

[1] This information from *1001: Fruits and Vegetables* and *Bugs, Slugs and Other Thugs*, Storey Communications
[2] Timed planting means timing the planting of crops to take into account the life cycle of insect pests and when they cause the most damage in your region.
[3] Sold under several trade names, such as Dipel and Thuricide

Sources: Gardener's Supply, with additional information from *Fruits and Vegetables: 1001 Gardening Questions Answered,* Editors of Garden Way Publishing and *Bugs, Slugs and Other Thugs,* Rhonda Massingham Hart; reprinted with permission from Gardener's Supply, Burlington, VT

NATURAL CONTROLS FOR VEGETABLE DISEASES

DISEASE	DESCRIPTION	DAMAGE	PLANTS AFFECTED	CONTROLS
Anthracnose	Fungus disease that overwinters on infected seed, plant debris, or in soil	Appears as dark brown circular sunken spots on pods or fruit. The centers of the spots may ooze pink spores. Reddish discoloration of the leaf veins. Leaves may wither and fall early. High humidity, high rainfall, and high temperatures encourage spread	Beans, cantaloupe, cucumbers, melons, peppers, and tomatoes	If anthracnose is a problem, don't save your own seed for planting. Use western-grown seed because the disease is not a problem there. Rotate crops. Avoid working in the garden when it is wet because this encourages disease spread. Spray or dust with copper
Bacterial Blight	Usually spread by infected seeds	Brown and water-soaked spots on the leaves and pods. Infected areas often turn yellow, then brown, and finally die. Spots on the pods enlarge and often exhibit reddish markings	Beans, peas	If bacterial blight is a problem, don't save your own seed for planting. Rotate crops and clean up old debris. Avoid working in the garden when it is wet because this encourages disease spread
Bacterial Wilt	Wilt organisms live within cucumber beetles and are transmitted to the vine crop through their feces. The bacteria clog the water and nutrient transport system of the plant.	First appears as wilting of a few leaves or a small portion of the vine. The rest ot the vine wilts within a week or so. When the vine is cut, a white substance oozes from the stem. This disease is most severe east of the Mississippi River	All vine crops	Pull out and destroy infected plants before the disease spreads. Control cucumber beetles with rotenone or sabadilla
Blackleg	A fungus disease that is carried on seed and lives in the soil	Lower stem blackens and is completely girdled. Young plants yellow, wilt, and die	Broccoli, Brussels sprouts, cabbage, cauliflower	Rotate crops. Clean up plant debris
Blossom End Rot	Caused by environmental factors, not a pathogen. Most likely to occur when plants have been grown under favorable conditions during first part of the season and are then subjected to drought when fruit begins developing. Can also occur after prolonged wet conditions	Blossom end of fruit becomes dry, sunken, leathery, and brown-black, or light-colored and papery in peppers. Half of each fruit may be affected	Tomatoes, peppers, watermelons, squash	Maintain even soil moisture. Mulch and cultivate only shallowly during drought. Fertilize properly based on a soil test. Add lime if needed
Clubroot	A fungal slime mold that lives in the soil and enters the plant through the roots	Roots become enlarged and swollen (clubbed), often cracking or rotting. Young plants are killed, while older, larger plants have reduced yields. The above ground portion of the plant yellows and wilts during the day, but recovers at night	Brassicas	Use a 4-year rotation plan because spores can survive in the soil a long time. The disease thrives in acid soil, so keep the pH above 6.0
Damping Off	Fungus disease that lives in soil	Base of the stem near the soil is pinched and bent over causing seedling to die	Many	Plant in well-drained soil. Use sterile potting mix for indoor growing

continued

DISEASE	DESCRIPTION	DAMAGE	PLANTS AFFECTED	CONTROLS
Downy Mildew	Fungus disease that overwinters in crop residues and spreads through infected seeds	Lettuce and spinach have pale spots on the leaves with furry, whitish growth on the underside. Lima beans have white, felt-like growths on the pods, with a possible reddish discoloration around the white areas. Most common to eastern US because high humidity and cool temperatures promote spread	Beans, brassicas, cantaloupes, cucumbers, lettuce, onions, spinach, all vine crops	Plant resistant varieties. Pull up and destroy infected plants and all crop residues. Rotate crops yearly. Avoid wetting tops of plants when watering. Spray or dust with copper
Early Blight	Fungus disease that overwinters in plant debris	Leaves develop dark brown spots that have a series of concentric rings within each one, giving it a target-like appearance. Spots usually appear on the older leaves first. Under favorable conditions, especially in warm, wet weather, the disease spreads rapidly over the entire plant. Serious infections cause reduced yields and defoliation of the plant	Potatoes, tomatoes	Plant healthy seed potatoes and tomato seedlings. Rotate crops. Remove plant debris. Spray or dust with copper
Fusarium Wilt/ Verticillium Wilt	Fungal infections of vascular tissues. Fungus lives in the soil and infects plants through the roots	Leaves and stems turn yellowish. Plants wilt and have a brown discoloration inside the stems. Plant growth is stunted, and yields are reduced. Fungus develops during hot, dry weather	Potatoes, tomatoes, eggplants, peppers, okra, melons	Plant resistant varieties. Rotate crops. Practice 4-year rotation for okra
Late Blight	Fungus disease that overwinters in plant debris.	First appears as wet-soaked or light spots on leaves. Spots turn black, and a white fungal growth may be seen on the underside of the leaf. The disease spreads rapidly under cool, wet condition, causing all the above-ground parts of the plant to become soft and blighted. At this stage, there is a strong odor	Tomatoes, potatoes	Plant resistant varieties. Plant clean seed potatoes. Rotate crops. Don't follow either tomatoes or potatoes by each other. Clean up all crop debris. Spray or dust with copper
Leaf Spot	Fungus disease that overwinters on seeds or infected crop debris	Plant leaves are dotted with small, tannish spots with purplish borders. The disease may cause leaves to drop later in the season and is most troublesome east of the Rocky Mountains	Beets, chard, tomatoes	Rotate crops. Remove crop residues. Spray or dust with sulfur; use copper on tomatoes
Mosaic	Virus that overwinters in perennial weeds. In the spring, it is transmitted by aphids to vine crops and other host plants	Leaves become mottled, plants are stunted, and yields are greatly reduced. Infected fruit is mottled, bumpy, and misshapen	Beans, cucumbers, melons, peppers, squash, tomatoes	Plant healthy seed. Plant mosaic-resistant varieties. Pull and destroy infected plants. Keep weeds out. Control aphids with insecticidal soap, nicotine or pyrethrum sprays, or horticultural spray oil

continued

DISEASE	DESCRIPTION	DAMAGE	PLANTS AFFECTED	CONTROLS
Neck Rot	Fungus disease that usually attacks onions in storage and overwinters in infected bulbs	Onions have brownish, dry rot areas around the neck. Eventually, the entire bulb may rot	Onions	Allow onions to mature completely in the field before harvesting. Cure and store them properly. Don't try to store bulbs that have been bruised or damaged. Sweet varieties tend to be more susceptible
Powdery Mildew	Fungus disease that lives in soil and plant debris. Encouraged by dry, hot weather	White or brown mealy growth on leaves and young stems (especially on the upper surface and occasionally on fruit). Plants may yellow, wither, and die	Many	Plant resistant varieties. Allow ample space between plants for good air circulation. Rotate crops and cut weeds. Destroy crop residue. Spray or dust with sulfur
Root Rot	Fungus disease that lives in the soil	Yellowish, unhealthy-looking plants, often with withering of lower stem. Plants do not respond to water and fertilizer. Roots covered with mold	Beans, carrots, corn, peas	Rotate crops yearly. Plant in well-drained soil. Raise beds if the soil is too wet. Remove and destroy affected plants. Control harmful nematodes with beneficial nematodes
Rust	Fungus disease that overwinters on infected plant residue	Numerous, tiny, rust-colored spots appear on leaves. Leaves turn yellow and die. High humidity and wet weather encourage spread	Asparagus, beans	Plant resistant varieties. Cut and burn infected ferns, and remove all crop residue. Spray or dust with sulfur or copper
Scab	Fungus disease that overwinters on seed, infected crop debris, and in soil	Dark, sunken spots on fruit. In severe cases, these will be like small craters over the entire fruit. There may be ooze or a fungus growth from infected areas. Cool, wet weather encourages spread	Cucumbers, melons, squash, potatoes	Plant resistant varieties. Rotate crops. Remove plant debris. Spray or dust with copper
Smut (Corn)	Fungus disease that overwinters on crop debris and in the soil	First appears as whitish-gray galls on the ear or other part of the plant. As galls mature, they turn black and finally burst, releasing thousands of spores. Warm, dry weather encourages spread	Corn	Plant resistant varieties. Remove and destroy smut galls before they break open. Remove all crop debris. Rotate crops. Don't compost diseased plants
Sunscald	Caused by too much exposure to sun, especially during hot, dry weather	Large, irregular, white areas on fruit that may appear paperlike. White or reddish spots may develop on leaves. Affected areas often covered with dark molds. Occurs commonly on plants that have lost foliage due to disease	Tomatoes, peppers	Use varieties with more foliage. Control defoliating diseases. Fertilize and water properly
Viruses	Viruses live in soil, plant debris, and living plant tissue. Can be spread by insects, nematodes, on pruning tools, on your hands	Symptoms include yellowing, stunting, spotting, mottling, mosaic pattern, streaking	Many	Use resistant varieties. Control weeds, insects, and nematodes. Sterilize pruners, and wash hands after handling infected plants or tobacco
Yellow (Aster)	Caused by mycoplasmas that overwinter in weeds and other perennial plants. Spread by leafhoppers	Plants are yellow and stunted. Yields are reduced	Celery, lettuce, spinach	Keep weeds cut. Plant lettuce in sheltered areas because leafhoppers prefer open spaces. Control leafhoppers with diatomaceous earth, insecticidal soap, liquid rotenone/pyrethrum, or horticultural spray oil

Sources: *Joy of Gardening,* Dick Raymond; *Down-to-Earth Vegetable Gardening Know-How,* Dick Raymond; *The Able Gardener,* Kathleen Yeomans, R.N.

Garden Problem Guide

SYMPTOMS	POSSIBLE CAUSES	POSSIBLE CURES
Dying young plants	Fertilizer burn Disease (damping-off)	Mix fertilizer thoroughly with soil. Treat seed; don't overwater.
Stunted plants (pale to yellow)	Low soil fertility Low soil pH (too acid) Poor soil drainage Shallow or compacted soil Insects or diseases Nematodes	Soil test for fertilizer recommendations. Soil test for lime recommendations. Drain and add organic matter. Plow deeper. Identify and use control measures. Soil test for treatment recommendations.
Stunted plants (purplish color)	Low temperature Lack of phosphorus	Plant at recommended time. Add phosphorus fertilizer.
Holes in leaves	Insects Hail	Identify and use control measures. Be thankful it was not worse.
Spots, molds, or darkened areas on leaves and stems	Disease Chemical burn Fertilizer burn	Identify, spray, or dust, use resistant varieties. Use recommended chemical at recommended rate. Keep fertilizer off plants.
Wilting plants	Dry soil Excess water in soil Nematodes Disease	Irrigate if possible. Drain. Soil test for treatment recommendations. Use resistant varieties if possible.
Weak, spindly plants	Too much shade Too much water Plants too thick Too much nitrogen	Remove shade or move plants to sunny spot. Drain or avoid overwatering. Seed at recommended rate. Avoid excess fertilization.
Failure to set fruit	High temperature Low temperature Too much nitrogen Insects	Follow recommended planting time. Follow recommended planting time. Avoid excess fertilization. Identify and use control measures.
Tomato leaf curl	Heavy pruning in hot weather Disease	Don't. Identify and use control measures.
Dry brown to black rot on blossom end of tomato	Low soil calcium Extremely dry soil	Add lime. Irrigate.
Misshapen tomatoes ("catfacing")	Cool weather during blooming	Plant at recommended time.
Abnormal leaves and growth	Herbicide damage Virus disease	Don't use a sprayer that has previously applied an herbicide. Remove infected plants to prevent spreading. Control insects that transmit viruses.

Source: *Down-to-Earth Gardening Know-How for the '90s,* Dick Raymond

Herbs

Herb Growth and Use Chart

HERB	BOTANICAL NAME	LIFE CYCLE	AVERAGE HEIGHT	GROWING	SPECIFIC NEEDS (assume full sun unless otherwise noted)	BASIC USES
Ambrosia	*Chenopodium botrys*	HA	18"	Sow inside or outside; SS		Fragrant fresh or dried arrangements and wreaths
Angelica	*Angelica archangelica*	BI	4'	Sow outside in fall; SS	Moist, rich soil; part shade OK	Culinary, medicinal, potpourri fixative
Anise	*Pimpinella anisum*	A	24"	Sow outside		Culinary, medicinal, cosmetic
Artemisia (Silver)	(Ornamental Silver Mound, King, Queen)	P	6-24"	Root divisions		Fresh or dried wreaths and arrangements
Basil	*Oscimum basilicum* and family	A	18"	Sow indoors in late spring; sensitive to cold	Rich soil; Bush B. best for pot culture	Culinary, potpourri, fly deterrent, cosmetics
Bay, Sweet	*Laurus nobilis*	TP (in pots)	2-6'	Stem cuttings	Pot culture in cold climates	Culinary, potpourri, cosmetics
Bergamot	*Monarda didyma* (Bee balm)	P	36"	Root divisions	Part shade	Tea, potpourri, cosmetics
Borage	*Borago officinalis*	A	30"	Sow inside for early start	Rich soil; part shade OK	Cucumber flavor for salads, candied petals, medicinal
Calendula	*Calendula officinalis*	A	24"	Sow inside for early start	Sow in peat pots	Culinary, food coloring, medicinal, cosmetic
Chamomile (Annual)	*Matricaria recutita*	A	18"	Sow inside; SS		Tea, medicinal, dye, potpourri
Chamomile (Perennial)	*Chamaemelum nobile* ("German" C.)	P	6"	Sow inside; SS		Hair rinse, ground cover
Caraway	*Carum carvi* ("Roman" C.)	BI	24"	Sow outside in fall or inside in spring		Culinary, cosmetics
Catmint	*Nepetamussinii*	P	18"	Root divisions		Lovely purple flowers, ant & insect repellent
Catnip	*Nepeta cataria*	P	18"	Root divisions or sow inside; SS	Sandy soil	Tea, cat tonic, insect repellent, cosmetics

continued

HERB	BOTANICAL NAME	LIFE CYCLE	AVERAGE HEIGHT	GROWING	SPECIFIC NEEDS (assume full sun unless otherwise noted)	BASIC USES
Chervil	*Anthriscus cerefolium*	HA	24"	Sow outside in fall	Shade	Culinary
Chives	*Allium schoenoprasum*	P	12"	Sow inside or outside early spring	Rich soil	Culinary, fresh or dried floral arrangements
Clary sage	*Salvia viridis*	BI	12"	Sow outside in late summer or inside in early spring	Sandy, dry soil	Arrangements, potpourri fixative, cosmetics
Comfrey	*Symphytum officinalis*	P	36"	Root division in early spring	Rich, moist soil; part shade OK	External healing, cosmetics
Coriander	*Coriandrum sativum* ("Chinese parsley")	HA	24"	Sow inside; SS		Culinary, potpourri
Costmary	*Chrysanthemum balsamita* ("Bible Leaf")	P	36"	Root division	Will grow in shade but not blossom	Culinary, potpourri, cosmetics
Dill	*Anethum graveolens*	A	30"	Sow outside	Rich soil	Culinary
Fennel	*Foeniculum vulgare*	A	30"	Sow outside by itself	Well-limed soil	Culinary, cosmetic
Fenugreek	*Trigonella foenumgraecum*	A	18"	Sow outside	Rich soil	Maple flavoring, sugar substitute, medicinal
Feverfew	*Chrysanthemum parthernium*	P	36"	Early spring sowing or root division	May not remain perennial if winter soil too wet or if allowed to go to seed	Arrangements, insect repellent, cosmetics, potpourri
Garlic	*Allium sativum*	P	24"	Plant bulbs in fall, bulb division	Moist, rich soil	Culinary, medicinal, cosmetic
Geraniums (Scented)	*Pelargonium*	TP	18"	Stem cuttings		Culinary, potpourri, cosmetics
Horehound	*Marrubium vulgare* (White)	P	18"	Sow indoors; SS; root division	Loves hot, dry soil	Garden edgings, bouquets, candy, coughdrops
Hyssop	*Hyssopus officinalis*	P	24"	Sow indoors	Well-limed soil; partial shade OK	Potpourri fixative, white fly deterrent, cosmetics

continued

HERB	BOTANICAL NAME	LIFE CYCLE	AVERAGE HEIGHT	GROWING	SPECIFIC NEEDS (assume full sun unless otherwise noted)	BASIC USES
Lady's Mantle	*Alchemilla vulgaris*	P	12"	Root division; SS		Sleep pillows, arrangements, medicinal, cosmetic
Lavender (English)	*Lavendula angustifolia*	P	24"	Sow indoors, stem cuttings, root division, layering	Well-drained soil	Potpourri, cosmetics, arrangements, medicinal
Lemon balm	*Melissa officinalis*	P	24"	Sow inside; SS; root division	Part shade OK	Culinary, potpourri, cosmetic
Lemon verbena	*Aloysia triphylla*	TP	36"	Stem cuttings	Rich soil	Culinary, potpourri, medicinal, cosmetic
Lovage	*Levisticum officinale*	P	6'	Sow inside or outside	Moist, rich soil; part shade OK	Celery flavor for cooking, salt substitute; cosmetics
Marjoram (Sweet)	*Origanum majorana*	TP	12"	Sow inside or outside	Rich soil	Culinary, potpourri, medicinal
Mints	*Mentha* family	P	18-30"	Root divisions, generally	Most like moist soil and part shade	Culinary, potpourri, bouquets, medicinal, cosmetic
Oregano	*Oreganum vulgare*	P	24"	Root division	Lime	Culinary
Parsley (Curly)	*Petroselinum crispum*	BI	12"	Sow outside	Rich soil; part shade OK, 2nd year harvest negligible	Very nutritious when fresh; cosmetics
Pennyroyal (English)	*Mentha pulegium*	P	12"+	Sow inside	Moist soil; part shade OK	Insect repellent, cosmetics potpourri (can be toxic if taken in large doses)
Pineapple sage	*Salvia elegans*	TP	36"	Stem cuttings		Culinary, potpourri, bouquets
Rosemary	*Rosmarinus officinalis*	TP	1-4'	Stem cuttings	Loves misting of foliage	Culinary, potpourri, cosmetics, incense
Rue	*Ruta graveolens*	P	24"	Sow inside; root division	Part shade OK	Insect deterrent, hedges, bouquets
Safflower	*Carthamus tinctorius*	A	30"	Sow inside midspring		Coloring and flavoring food, dye, cosmetics
Saffron	*Crocus sativus*	P	8"	Plant bulbs in fall	Rich soil, part shade	Coloring and flavoring food

continued

HERB	BOTANICAL NAME	LIFE CYCLE	AVERAGE HEIGHT	GROWING	SPECIFIC NEEDS (assume full sun unless otherwise noted)	BASIC USES
Sage	*Salvia officinalis*	P	24"	Sow inside; stem cuttings, root divisions	Well-limed soil	Culinary, cosmetic, medicinal
Salad burnet	*Poterium sanguisorba*	P	18"	Sow inside; root division		Cucumber flavor for salads
Santolina (Gray)	*Santolina chamaecyparissus*	P	24"	Stem cuttings		Hedges and knot gardens, potpourri
Shallot	*Allium ascalonicum*	P	15"	Plant bulbs in early spring; bulb division	Rich soil	Onion flavor and substitute
Sorrel (French)	*Rumex scutatus*	P	18"	Sow outside; SS	Re-sow every 3 yrs.	Culinary
Southernwood	*Artemisia abrotanum*	P	3'	Root divisions; layerings, cuttings		Insect deterrent, potpourri, cosmetics, arrangements, wreaths
Summer savory	*Satureja hortensus*	A	18"	Sow inside in peat pots, or outside		Culinary – the "Green Bean" herb
Sweet cicely	*Myrrhis odorata*	P	3'	Root division or seeds outside in fall	Rich soil; part shade OK	Anise-flavor sugar substitute, cosmetics, arrangements
Sweet woodruff	*Gallium odoratum*	P	10"	Root divisions; stem cuttings	All-shade leafy moist soil	Culinary, potpourri, ground cover
Sweet wormwood	*Artemisia annua*	HA	5'	Sow inside or out; SS	Needs plenty of room (3' wide)	Fragrant wreaths, arrangements, potpourri
Tansy	*Tanecetum vulgare*	P	3'	Root division	Toxic to cattle; do not plant where livestock graze	Ant and insect deterrent, fresh and dried arrangements, dye, cosmetics
Tarragon (French)	*A. dracunculus* variety *sativa*	P	30"	Root divisions or layering		Culinary, cosmetic, medicinal

continued

HERB	BOTANICAL NAME	LIFE CYCLE	AVERAGE HEIGHT	GROWING	SPECIFIC NEEDS (assume full sun unless otherwise noted)	BASIC USES
Thyme (Upright)	*T. vulgaris*	P	12"	Root division or layering		Culinary, cosmetic, medicinal
Winter savory	*Satureja montana*	P	12"	Sow inside; layering		Culinary
Wormwood	*Artemisia absinthium*	P	36"	Sow inside; root division	Part shade OK	Insect repellent, wreaths, arrangements, medicinal
Yarrow	*Achillea species*	P	24"	Root division		Wreaths, arrangements, cosmetics

Explanation of Terms:

A   =   annual, a plant having life for one growing season only; started by seed.

HA =   hardy annual, having a one-year life cycle, but self-sowing freely.

P   =   perennial, a plant with a life cycle of three or more seasons.

TP =   tender perennial, which will be killed by frost or severe cold weather. In cold climates these plants should be wintered over in the house, greenhouse, or coldframe. In warm climates these herbs should be given protection if a freeze is expected.

BI =   biennial, a plant which takes two years to mature, but quickly goes to seed the second year, necessitating annual plantings for consistent harvests.

SS =   self-sows, so allow some of the plants to go to seed and dry in the garden.

Source: *The Pleasure of Herbs,* Phyllis Shaudys

TIME CHART FOR PROPAGATING HERBS FROM SEED

SEED	COMMON NAME	FALL [1] OUTDOORS	FEBRUARY INDOORS	MARCH-APRIL INDOORS	MAY [3] IN PLACE	GERMINATION TIME (in days)	PLANT SPACING
Agastache	Anise hyssop			X		7-10	1½ '
Allium tuberosum	Garlic chives			X		14-21	Clumps
Anethum graveolens	Dill	X		X	X	21-25	4-8"
Angelica archangelica*	Angelica		X		X	21-25	3'
Anthriscus cerefolium*	Chervil		X		X	7-14	6-8"
Artemisia annua	Sweet Annie			X	X	7-10	2-4'
Borago officinalis	Borage			X	X	7-10	1'
Calendula officinalis	Calendula; pot marigold		X	X		10-14	12-15"
Carum carvi	Caraway	X		X		10-14	6-9"
Chrysanthemum parthenium	Feverfew; pyrethrum			X		7-14	9-12"
Coreopsis tinctoria	Calliopsis; dye plant			X		7-10	8-12"
Coriandrum satitum	Coriander	X		X		10-14	8-10"
Cuminum cyminum	Cumin			X	X	10-14	6"
Foeniculum vulgare	Fennel	X		X	X	10-14	8-12"
Isatis tinctoria*	Woad; dyer's weed			X		10-14	8"
Levisticum officinale	Lovage		X			10-14	12-15"
Lippia graveolens	Mexican oregano			X		7-10	Clumps
Marrubium vulgare	Horehound	X		X		10-14	8-10"
Matricaria recutita	German chamomile			X		7-10	8"

continued

SEED	COMMON NAME	FALL[1] OUTDOORS	FEBRUARY INDOORS	MARCH-APRIL INDOORS	MAY[3] IN PLACE	GERMINATION TIME (in days)	PLANT SPACING
*Myrrhis odorata**	Sweet cicely		X	X	X	30+	2'
Nepeta cataria	Catnip	X		X		7-10	1½ -2'
Nigella sativa	Bitter fitch; bible plant			X		10-14	1½ '
Ocimum	Basil			X		7-10	1'
Origanum majorana	Sweet marjoram			X		8-14	6-8"
Petroselinum crispum	Curly parsley	X	X			14-21	6-8"
Poterium sanguisorba	Burnet		X			8-10	15"
Rumex scutatus	French sorrel			X		14-21	6"
Salvia sclarea	Clary sage			X		14-21	1'
Satureja hortensis	Summer savory			X		10-15	4-6"
Tropaeolum majus [2]	Nasturtium			X		9-14	6-9"
Verbascum thapsus	Mullein			X		21-28	2'
Viola	Violet family			X	X	10-14	6-8"

KEY:
* Sow as soon as ripe or keep refrigerated
[1] Not always reliable
[2] Soak in warm water 24 hours
[3] These resent transplanting; use extreme care if alternate method is used

Source: *Herbal Treasures,* Phyllis V. Shaudys

Specific Herbs for Special Locations and Individual Interests

PARTIAL SHADE GARDENS			
Aconite	Coneflower	Lily-of-the-valley	Snakeroot
Angelica	Costmary	Lovage	Sweet cicely
Bee balm	English pennyroyal	Lungwort	Sweet flag
Borage	Fennel	Mints (not catnip)	Sweet woodruff
Carpet bugleweed	French tarragon	Mother-of-thyme	Valerian
Chervil	Good-King-Henry	Parsley	Wild ginger
Chives	Lady's-mantle	Roman chamomile	Wintergreen
Comfrey	Lemon balm	Running myrtle	Wormwood
Common (or sweet) violet	Liatris	St.-John's-wort	Yarrow
ROCK GARDENS			
Artemisia (Silver mound)	Costmary	Lady's-mantle	Santolina
Basils	Curry plant	Lavender	Southernwood
Bedstraw	Dittany	Lavender cotton	Scented geraniums
Burnet	Garlic chives	Mints	Sweet marjoram
Calendula	Germander	Pansy	Thymes
Catmint	Golden oregano	Parsley	Violet
Chamomiles	Golden, red, or silver sage	Pennyroyal	Wild ginger
Chives	Horehound	Rosemary	
Clove pink	Hyssop	Saffron	
HIGH EDGINGS			
Bay (in hot climates)	Germander	Lovage	Scented basils (holy, anise,
English lavender	Hyssop	Roman wormwood	licorice, cinnamon)
Fernleaf tansy	Lemon balm	Rosemary (in hot climates)	Southernwood
Feverfew	Lemon verbena	Rue	Sweet Annie

continued

GROUND COVERS			
Bedstraw (sun)	Coltsfoot (sun, in waste places)	Lady's-mantle (shade)	Running myrtle (shade)
Carpet bugleweed (sun or partial shade)	Common violet (part shade)	Lavender cotton (sun)	Sweet woodruff (part shade)
	Creeping thymes (sun)	Lily-of-the-valley (shade)	Wild ginger (part shade)
Catmint (part shade)	Dead nettle (sun)	Mints (sun or shade)	Wintergreen (shade)
Catnip (sun)	Ground ivy (sun or part shade, in waste areas)	Oregano (sun)	Woolly betony (sun)
Chamomile, Roman (sun)		Pennyroyal (part shade)	Wormwood (part shade)

SALAD GARDENS			
Anise (leaves)	Dill (leaves, umbrels)	Lime balm (leaves)	Rose (petals)
Basil (leaves)	Fennel (leaves, umbrels)	Lovage (leaves)	Savory (leaves)
Borage (leaves)	Garlic chives	Marjoram (leaves)	Shallot
Burnet (leaves)	Good-King-Henry (leaves)	Mints (leaves)	Sorrel (leaves)
Calendula (petals)	Lamb's quarters (leaves)	Mustard (white, young seedlings)	Sweet violet (petals)
Chervil (leaves)	Leek (leaves)	Nasturtium (leaves, petals)	Tarragon (leaves)
Chicory, or witloof (leaves)	Lemon balm (leaves)	Oregano (leaves)	Thyme (leaves)
Chive (leaves, blossoms)	Lemon catnip	Parsley (leaves)	Watercress

POTPOURRI GARDENS			
Ambrosia	Fennel	Orange bergamot mint	Spearmint
Anise hyssop	Florentine iris (orrisroot)(fixative)	Patchouli	Sweet flag (calamus)(fixative)
Bay	Lavender	Peppermint	Sweet marjoram
Bergamot	Lemon balm	Pineapple sage	Sweet violet
Chamomile	Lemongrass	Roses	Sweet woodruff
Clary sage (fixative)	Lemon thyme	Scented basils	Vetiver root (khus-khus)
Clevelandii sage (fixative)	Lemon verbena	Scented geraniums	
Clove pink	Lime balm	Southernwood	

continued

TEA GARDENS

Agrimony	Catmint	Lemon balm	Rosemary
Angelica	Catnip	Lemon-scented marigold	Saffron
Anise (seeds)	Chamomile	Lemon verbena	Scented geraniums (rose and lemon)
Anise hyssop	Costmary	Lime balm	Sweet marjoram
Basils	Dill (seeds)	Lovage	Thymes
Bergamot	Fennel (seeds)	Mints	Wintergreen
Calendula (petals)	Garden sage	Pennyroyal (do not use if you are pregnant)	Yarrow
Caraway (seeds)	Horehound	Rosehips	

LOW EDGINGS / BONSAI

LOW EDGINGS				BONSAI
Beach wormwood	Clove pink	Parsley	Winter savory	Dwarf lavender
Carpet bugleweed	Dead nettle	Pennyroyal		Hyssop
Catmint	Dwarf basils	Sweet woodruff		Rosemary
Chives	Germander	Upright thyme		Rue

CONTAINER GARDENS / SHAKESPEARE GARDENS

CONTAINER GARDENS				SHAKESPEARE GARDENS
Alliums	Dittany	Marjoram	Saffron	Bay
Artemisia (Silver mound)	Garlic	Marigold	Sage	Calendula
Basils	Garlic chives	Mignonette	Savory	Garlic
Bay	Hyssop	Mints	Scented geraniums	Lemon balm
Calendula	Lavender	Oregano	Thymes	Pansy
Chamomiles	Lavender cotton	Pansy	Violet	Poppy
Chives	Lemon balm	Parsley	Wormwood	Rosemary
Clove pink	Lemon catnip	Pennyroyal		
Curry plant	Lemon verbena	Rosemary		
Dill	Lime balm	Rue		

continued

SPECIFIC HERBS FOR SPECIAL LOCATIONS AND INDIVIDUAL INTERESTS (CONTINUED)

BEE GARDENS		EVERLASTINGS TO DRY	POND GARDENS
Anise hyssop	Lemon balm	Artemisia	Angelica
Bee balm	Mints	Feverfew	Chives
Borage	Oregano	Goldenrod	Japanese parsley
Comfrey	Pennyroyal	Lavender	Lemon balm
Creeping santolina	Sage	Rue	Lovage
Fenugreek	Sweet basil	Sweet marjoram	Sweet flag
German chamomile	Thymes	Tansy	Valerian
Horehound	Winter savory	Yarrow	Watercress
Hyssop	Woolly betony		

FRAGRANCE GARDENS			REPELLING INSECTS
Catmint	Lemon balm	Scented geraniums	Anise
Chamomile	Lemon verbena	Southernwood	Basil, sweet
Clove pink	Lime balm	Sweet cicely	Catnip
Coriander	Mignonette	Sweet flag	Garlic chives
Costmary	Mints	Sweet marjoram	Lavenders
Creeping santolina	Oregano	Sweet woodruff	Mints
Curry plant	Patchouli	Tansy	Parsley
Dill	Pennyroyal	Thymes	Rosemary
Fennel	Rosemary	Valerian	Sages
Hyssop	Sages	Violets	Thymes, garden
Lady's-mantle	Savory		
Lavender	Scented basils		

continued

HERBS & PLANTS FOR A DYER'S GARDEN		SILVER-GRAY HERBS	BIBLICAL HERBS
Agrimony	Marigold	Artemisia (Silver Beacon,	Aloe
Bay	Mullein	Silver Kings, Silver Queen	Anise
Bedstraw	Parsley	Catmint	Coriander
Bloodroot	Pearly everlasting	Clove pink	Costmary
Blue iris	Queen-Anne's-lace	Curry plant	Cumin
Blueberry	Red clover	Dittany	Garlic
Brown-eyed-Susan	Rhubarb	Everlasting	Hyssop
Butterfly weed	Rue	Fringed and Roman wormwood	Lady's bedstraw
Catnip	Safflower	Horehound	Mandrake
Chrysanthemum	St. John's-wort	Lamb's-ears	Mint
Clematis	Scotch broom	Lamium (Silver Beacon)	Mustard
Coreopsis	Sunflower	Lavender	Nigella
Cornflower	Tansy	Lavender cotton	Pasqueflower
Elderberry	Teasel	Sages	Rose
Golden marguerite	Weld	Sea holly	Rosemary
Goldenrod	Wild oregano (Pot marjoram)	Silver sage	Rue
Indian paintbrush	Woad	Silver thyme	Saffron
Lady's-mantle	Zinnia	Woolly betony	Sesame
Lily-of-the-valley		Woolly lavender	Wormwood

TO SCREEN AN UNSIGHTLY AREA		HERBS FOR BEES, BIRDS, AND BUTTERFLIES	
Bee balm	Valerian	Anise	Dill
Comfrey	White mugwort	Bee balm	Safe
Fennel	Yarrow	Borage	Thyme

continued

HERB FLOWERS FOR COLOR-COORDINATED GARDENS					
BLUE		**WHITE**		**RED**	
Sage	Borage	Garlic chives	Dropwort	Bergamot	
Clevelandii sage	Lungwort	Angelica	White flag	Cardinal flower	
Anise hyssop	Dwarf Russian comfrey	Chamomiles	Roses	Hollyhock	
Dwarf catnip	Hyssop	Camphor plant	Basils (sweet, lemon, bush)	Scarlet pimpernel	
Rosemary	Blue flag	Boneset	Florentine iris (orrisroot)	Roses	
Cornflower	False indigo	Feverfew	German statice	Pineapple sage	
Chicory	Larkspur	Lily-of-the-valley	Pineapple mint	Crimson thyme	
Love-in-a-mist	Pansy	White mugwort	Sweet cicely	Nasturtium	
YELLOW		White yarrow			
Nasturtium	Witch hazel	**PURPLE**		**PURPLE-ROSE**	
Goldenrod	Rue	Lavenders	Saffron	Germander	
Santolina	Bedstraw	Violets	Pansy	Annual clary sage	
Tansy	Yarrow	Ajuga	Spearmint	Annual statice	
Primrose	Lady's-mantle	Catmint	Peppermint	Joe-Pye weed	
Mignonette	Evening primrose	Oregano	Black peppermint	Pyrethrum	
St.-John's-wort	Calendula	Wild bergamot	Orange mint	Rosey yarrow	
Yellow flag	Curry plant	Oregano thyme		Valerian	
Silver germander	Dill	**PINK**		**ROSE-LAVENDER**	
ORANGE	**ROSE**	Fenugreek	Damask rose	Heliotrope	
Butterfly weed	Giant allium	Dittany-of-Crete	Foxglove	Chives	
Calendula	Cardoon	Hollyhock	English pennyroyal	Purple coneflower	
Coltsfoot	Betony	Hyssop	Dwarf monarda	Pasqueflower	
Nasturtium	Sesame	Clove pink	Basils (dark opal, thrysiflora,	Saffron	
Elecampane		Cat thyme	purple, holy, cinnamon		

Source: *The Harvest Gardener,* Susan McClure

VARIETIES OF MINT

COMMON NAME	BOTANICAL NAME	VARIETY	AVERAGE HEIGHT	DESCRIPTION
Apple mint	*Mentha suaveolens* formerly *M. rotundifolia*)		2½'	Often called "woolly mint." Delicate spearmint-apple flavor. Grayish-green hue, light purple flowers. Use for tea and to garnish applesauce.
Black peppermint	*Mentha piperita*	'Vulgaris'	15"	Superior fragrance and flavor! Forest-green leaves with deep purple veins and stems, purple flowers. Breathtaking freshness for tea, potpourri, tussie-mussies, bouquets. Used in Creme-de-Menthe.
Orange mint	*Mentha aquatica* formerly *M. piperita, 'Vulgaris'*)	'crispa'	18"	Also called "citrus mint" or "bergamot mint." Luscious lemon-orange scent. Grass-green leaves with reddish-purple stems and runners, lavender flowers. A bath mint, room deodorizer, tea or punch, and mice-repellent. "Eau-de-Cologne" mint is a superb fruity-sweet variation.
Pennyroyal	*Mentha pulegium*	(English)	12"	Creeping, matted growth style. Pungent medicinal aroma. Can be toxic, so not recommended for culinary use, especially by childbearing-age women. Small green leaves, violet-blue flowers. Superb flea and insect repellent. Aromatic ground cover. Easy to grow from seeds. Winter mulch necessary in cold climates.
Peppermint	*Mentha x piperita*	'officinalis'	2'	Sometimes called "white peppermint." Will ward off harmful insects from members of the cabbage family in the vegetable garden. Grass-green leaves with reddish-purple undertones, violet flowers. Fresh bouquet, a bathroom or kitchen freshener and insect repellent; makes tea, potpourri, and tussie-mussies.
Pineapple mint	*Mentha suaveolens* formerly *M. rotundifolia*)	'Variegata'	12"	Stunning pineapple scent. Taste does not equal fragrance. Garden accent plant. Creamy patches of color on apple-green leaves, off-white flowers. Garnish for fruit salads; lovely in tussie-mussies or bouquets of yellow roses. A conversation piece in garden!
Spearmint	*Mentha spicata*	'Viridis'	2'	Also known as "lamb mint," "pea mint," "garden mint." Sensational fragrance and flavor! Nice for picnic table centerpiece; will deter flies. Light green leaves, violet-gray flowers. For mint sauce or juleps, jelly, tea, fruit salads or punch, with carrots or peas.

Source: *Pleasure of Herbs,* Phyllis Shaudys

Harvesting and Preserving Herbs

HERB	WHAT & WHEN TO HARVEST	HOW TO PRESERVE
Ambrosia	Flowering stems when green or beige	Dry in bunches or wreath shape
Angelica	Side leaf stalks in fall of 1st year; more often in 2nd year	S/D leaves; freeze or crystallize
Anise	Flowers & leaves when seeds turn brown	S/D leaves & seeds
Artemisia (Silver)	Flowering stems when seedheads are whitest in late summer	Dry in bunches, vases, or wreath shape
Basil	Prune top half of plants whenever lush growth before flowering	S/D, then oven-crisp. Or oil, vinegar, freezer, or pesto
Bay, Sweet	Individual leaves sparingly until established; then top ¼ when lush or when transplanting to larger pots	S/D
Bergamot	Top half of plant when flowering	Dry in vases, bags or bunches
Borage	Prune tops for early leaf harvest; then top half when flowering	S/D leaves; candy flowers
Calendula	When flowering	S/D
Chamomile (annual)	Top half when flowers turn from gold to brown; leave some to self-sow	S/D, or bags
Chamomile (perennial)	Prune as desired if for ground cover	S/D
Caraway	Seedheads when brown	S/D
Catmint	Top ⅓ after flowering for second bloom	Bunches
Catnip	Top ½ early and late summer before blossoming	Bunches or bags
Chervil	Outer leaves in fall and 2nd spring; preserve central growth and some seed-heads	In butter, oil, or freezer
Chives	Snip outer leaves regularly all season; cut flowers in spring	Scissor-snip for freezer; vinegar
Clary sage	When flowering	S/D
Comfrey	Top ½, or more, 2 or 3 times during lush summer growth	S/D
Coriander	Foliage as needed, but allow some to go to seed; harvest when seeds turn brown.	Seedheads in bags; leaves in oil or freeze
Costmary	Leaves in mid-summer and early fall	S/D
Dill	Top ½ of plants when seedheads are beige; may trim foliage lightly earlier	Bunches or oil; vinegar or freeze

continued

HERB	WHAT & WHEN TO HARVEST	HOW TO PRESERVE
Fennel	Whole plant when flowering; may trim foliage earlier	S/D or vinegar, oil, or freezer
Fenugreek	Seed pods when ripe in fall	S/D or syrup
Feverfew	Flowers when blooming in mid-summer	Bunches
Garlic	Flowers in spring; bulbs late summer after leaves have died down	Braid, air-dry in nylon; oil, vinegar
Geraniums, scented	Prune whenever lush growth	S/D or candy or jelly
Horehound	Top ½ when flowering, but may prune leaves in spring & early fall	Bunch dry; candy
Hyssop	Top ⅓ in early and late summer	Bunch dry
Lady's-mantle	Prune foliage early in season, then when flowering	Screen or bunch
Lavender	Cut back top ⅓ of branches just before flowers open up	Screen, bunch, vase
Lemon balm	Top half early, mid, or late summer, before flowering	Bunch or bag; candy, vinegar, or jelly
Lemon verbena	Top half mid-summer and early fall before bringing inside	S/D, candy or jelly
Lovage	Half of top leaves in late spring and early fall	Bunch dry & oven crisp, or preserve in oil or freeze
Marjoram	Top third mid-summer & early fall before flowering	S/D then oven crisp
Mints	Top half, or more in late spring, mid-summer, and early fall	Bunch or Bag-dry. Candy, ice cubes, vinegar jelly
Oregano	Cut top half in summer before flowering, then again in early fall	Bunch or bag-dry, then oven-crisp; vinegar, oil
Parsley	Outer leaves when lush, leaving central growth	Bunch, oven, or freeze
Pennyroyal	Prune in early summer; top half when flowering in fall	S/D
Pineapple sage	Top third when lush foliage	S/D or bunches
Rosemary	Top fourth when established & lush in northern gardens or pots	S/D, bunches, oil or vinegar or jelly
Rue	Prune top half in spring and when flowering	Bunches or bags
Safflower	Petals when flowering	Paper bags
Saffron	Stigmas in the fall	On white paper towel in dark place
Sage	Prune top third in early spring and again in mid-summer	S/D or bunches; oil, vinegar, or freeze

continued

HERB	WHAT & WHEN TO HARVEST	HOW TO PRESERVE
Salad burnet	Prune young leaves often; cut off flowering stalks	S/D or vinegar or freeze
Santolina	Prune in early spring and as necessary for neatness	S/D or bunches
Shallot	Bulbs when foliage yellows	Sun-dry; store in mesh or nylon out of light; oil
Sorrel	Cut back flowering stems for later crop	Use fresh young leaves for cooking or freeze
Southernwood	Cut back by a third in early spring; half of plant in late summer	Bunches or in open paper bags
Summer savory	Top half in mid-summer and early fall before flowering	S/D
Sweet cicely	Leaves as needed in late spring and early fall before they darken	S/D, bunches, or freeze
Sweet woodruff	Cut back half of plant when flowering in spring; and repeat in early fall	S/D
Sweet wormwood	Harvest whole plants when flowering in green or brown; leave some to self-sow	Dry in vases or wreath shape
Tansy	Can prune in mid-spring and then cut top half or more when flowering in fall	Bunch or vase-dry
Tarragon (French)	Prune top half in mid-spring, summer, and fall	Vinegar, oil, or freezer, cubes, or S/D
Thyme	Top third in spring when lush and before flowering in summer	S/D or vinegar, oil, or jelly
Winter savory	Prune tops lightly when lush growth in spring & summer	S/D
Wormwood	Cut back top half in late spring, late summer, and mid-fall	Bunches or vases
Yarrow	Cut stems when flowering	Bunches or vases

S/D = screen dry

Source: *Pleasure of Herbs,* Phyllis Shaudys

ANNUAL AND PERENNIAL FLOWERS

COMMON NAME	BOTANICAL NAME	PLANTING DISTANCE	MAINTENANCE	PLANT HEIGHT	* LIGHT	** MOISTURE	*** TEMPERATURE	**** HARDINESS
African daisy	*Arctotis stoechadifolia*	8-10"	medium	10-12"	S	d	c	H
Ageratum	*Ageratum houstonianum*	5-7"	low	4-8"	S, PSh	a,m	m	HH
Amaranthus	*Amaranthus*	15-18"	medium	18-36"	S	d	m, h	HH
Anchusa	*Anchusa capensis*	4-6"	medium	9-18"	S	d, a	m, h	HH
Aster	*Compositae,* several genera	6-18"	high	6-30"	S, PSh	m	m	HH
Balsam	*Impatiens balsamina*	10-15"	low	12-36"	S, PSh	m	h	T
Begonia, tuberous	*Begonia* spp.	8-10"	low	8-10"	PSh, Sh	m	c, m	T
Begonia, wax	*Begonia* spp.	7-9"	low	6-8"	S, PSh, Sh	a	m	HH
Black-eyed Susan vine	*Thunbergia alata*	12-15"	medium	3-6"	S, PSh	m	m	HH
Browallia	*Browallia speciosa*	8-10"	low	10-15"	PSh, Sh	m	c	HH
Calendula	*Calendula officinalis*	8-10"	high	3-4"	S, LSh	m	c, m	H
Candytuft	*Iberis* spp.	7-9"	low	8-10"	S	d, a	any	HH
Celosia	*Celosia* spp.	6-8"	low	6-15"	S	d	m, h	HH
Clarkia	*Clarkia* spp.	8-10"	high	18-24"	S, LSh	d, a	c	H
Coleus	*Coleus* spp.	8-10"	low	10-24"	PSh, Sh	a, m	m, h	T
Cornflower	*Centaurea* spp.	6-12"	medium	12-36"	S	d, a	m	VH
Cosmos	*Cosmos* spp.	9-18"	medium	18-30"	S	d, a	m	HH
Creeping zinnia	*Sanuitalis procumbens*	5-7"	medium	5-16"	S	d, a	m, h	HH
Dahlberg daisy	*Chrysanthemum tenuiloba*	4-6"	low	4-8"	S	d, a	m, h	HH

continued

COMMON NAME	BOTANICAL NAME	PLANTING DISTANCE	MAINTENANCE	PLANT HEIGHT	* LIGHT	** MOISTURE	*** TEMPERATURE	**** HARDINESS
Dahlia	*Dahlia* spp.	8-10"	high	8-15"	S, LSh	a, m	m	T
Dianthus	*Dianthus* spp.	7-9"	low	6-10"	S, PSh	a	c, m	HH
Dusty miller	*Compositae,* several genera	6-8"	low	8-10"	S, PSh	d, a	m, h	HH
Flowering cabbage, kale	*Brassica oleracea*	15-18"	low	15-18"	S	m	c	VH
Forget-me-not	*Cynoglossum amabile*	8-12"	low	12-24"	PSh	m	c	H
Four o'clock	*Mirabilis jalapa*	12-18"	low	18-36"	PSh	d, a	any	T
Fuchsia	*Fuchsia* x *hybrida*	8-10"	high	12-24"	PSh, Sh	m	m	T
Gaillardia	*Gaillardia* spp.	8-15"	medium	10-18"	S, LSh	d, a	m, h	HH
Gazania	*Gazania* spp.	8-10"	high	6-10"	S	d, a	m, h	HH
Geranium	*Pelargonium* spp.	10-12"	high	10-15"	S	a, m	m	T
Gerbera	*Gerbera* spp.	12-15"	medium	12-18"	S	m	m	HH
Gloriosa daisy	*Rudbeckia* spp.	12-24"	low	18-36"	S, LSh	a	m, h	HH
Gomphrena	*Gomphrena globosa*	10-15"	medium	9-30"	S	d	m, h	HH
Hibiscus	*Hibiscus* spp.	24-30"	medium	48-60"	S, LSh	m	m	H
Impatiens	*Impatiens* spp.	8-10"	low	6-18"	PSh, Sh	m	m	T
Ivy geranium	*Pelargonium peltatum*	10-12"	medium	12-24"	S	a	m	T
Kochia	*Kochia scoparia*	18-24"	low	24-36"	S	d	m, h	HH
Lantana	*Lantana* spp.	8-10"	medium	10-12"	S	a	m	T
Lavatera	*Lavatera trimestris*	12-15"	medium	18-30"	S	d, a	m	H
Lobelia	*Lobelia erinus*	8-10"	low	3-5"	S, PSh	m	c, m	HH
Marigold, African	*Tagetes erecta*	12-15"	high	18-30"	S	a	m	HH

continued

COMMON NAME	BOTANICAL NAME	PLANTING DISTANCE	MAINTENANCE	PLANT HEIGHT	* LIGHT	** MOISTURE	*** TEMPERATURE	**** HARDINESS
Marigold, French	*Tagetes patula*	3-6"	high	5-10"	S	a	m	HH
Mexican sunflower	*Tithonia rotundifolia*	24-30"	medium	48-60"	S	d	m, h	T
Monkey flower	*Mimulus* spp.	5-7"	low	6-8"	PSh, Sh	m	c	HH
Nasturtium	*Tropaeolum majus*	8-12"	low	12-24"	S, LSh	d	c, m	T
New Guinea impatiens	*Impatiens hawkeri*	10-12"	low	10-12"	S, LSh	m	m	T
Nicotiana	*Nicotiana* spp.	8-10"	low	12-15"	S, PSh	m	m, h	HH
Ornamental pepper	*Capsicum annuum*	5-7"	low	4-8"	S, PSh	m	m, h	HH
Pansy	*Viola* spp.	6-8"	medium	4-8"	S, PSh	m	c	VH
Petunia	*Petunia* spp.	10-12"	medium	6-12"	S	d	m, h	HH
Phlox	*Phlox drummondii*	7-9"	low	6-10"	S	m	c, m	H
Portulaca	*Portulaca grandiflora*	6-8"	low	4-6"	S	d	h	T
Salpiglossis	*Salpiglossis sinuata*	10-12"	medium	18-24"	S	m	c	HH
Salvia	*Salvia* spp.	6-8"	low	12-48"	S, PSh	a, m	m, h	HH
Scabiosa	*Scabiosa* spp.	8-12"	high	12-24"	S	m	m	HH
Snapdragon	*Antirrhinum majus*	6-8"	medium	6-15"	S	a	c, m	VH
Spider flower	*Cleome hasslerana* or *c. spinosa*	12-15"	low	30-48"	S	d	m, h	HH
Statice	*Limonium* spp.	12-24"	medium	12-36"	5	d	m, h	HH
Stock	*Matthiola incana*	10-12"	high	12-24"	5	m	c	H
Strawflower	*Helichrysum* spp.	7-9"	medium	15-48"	5	d	m, h	HH
Sunflower (dwarf)	*Helianthus* spp.	12-24"	high	15-48"	S	d	h	T
Sweet alyssum	*Lobularia maritima*	10-12"	low	3-5"	S, PSh	a, m	m	H

continued

COMMON NAME	BOTANICAL NAME	PLANTING DISTANCE	MAINTENANCE	PLANT HEIGHT	* LIGHT	** MOISTURE	*** TEMPERATURE	**** HARDINESS
Sweet pea	*Lathyrus odoratus*	6-15"	medium	24-60"	S	m	c, m	H
Verbena	*Verbena* spp.	5-7"	medium	6-10"	S	d, a	h	T
Wishbone flower	*Torenia fournieri*	6-8"	low	8-12"	PSh, Sh	m	c	HH
Vinca	*Vinca* spp.	6-8"	low	4-12"	S, PSh	any	m, h	HH
Zinnia	*Zinnia* spp.	4-24"	high	4-36"	S	d, a	m, h	T

KEY:

* Light:
S   = Full sun
LSh = Light shade
PSh = Part shade
Sh   = Full shade

** Moisture:
d = dry
a = average
m = moist

*** Temperature:
c = cool (below 70°F)
m = moderate
h = hot (above 85°F)

**** Hardiness:
VH = very hardy, will withstand heavy frost
H = hardy, will withstand light frost
HH = half hardy, will withstand cool weather, but not frost
T = tender, will do poorly in cool weather, will not withstand frost

Source: *Landscaping With Annuals,* Ann Reilly

ANNUALS PLANTING GUIDE

BOTANICAL NAME	COMMON NAME	GERMINATION TIME (days)	INDOOR SOWING (# of weeks before transplanting outdoors)	OUTDOOR SOWING (# of weeks before last frost)	OUTDOOR TRANSPLANTING (# of weeks before last frost)	PLANTING DISTANCE (inches)
Ageratum houstonianum	Ageratum	5-10	6-8	last frost	last frost	9-12
Amaranthus species	Joseph's-coat, Love lies bleeding	10-15	3-4	last frost	last frost	12-24
Antirrhinum majus	Snapdragon	10-14	6-8	2	last frost	6-8
Arctotis stoechadifolia	African daisy	21-35	6-8	4	4	10-12
Begonia semperflorens	Wax begonia	15-20	10-12	—	last frost	6-8
Brassica oleracea	Ornamental kale and cabbage	10-18	6-8	—	first frost in fall	12-15
Browallia speciosa	Browallia	14-21	6-8	—	last frost	8-10
Calendula officinalis	Pot marigold	10-14	4-6	6	4	10-12
Callistephus chinensis	China aster	10-14	6-8	last frost	last frost	6-15
Capsicum annuum	Ornamental pepper	21-25	6-8	—	last frost	6-8
Catharanthus roseus	Vinca, periwinkle	15-20	10-12	—	last frost	8-10
Celosia cristata	Celosia, cockscomb	10-15	4-6	last frost	last frost	6-12
Centaurea cyanus	Bachelor's button	7-14	4-6	6	4	6-12
Chrysanthemum species	Annual chrysanthemum	10-18	8-10	last frost	last frost	12-15
Cleome hasslerana	Spider flower	10-14	4-6	last frost	last frost	24-30
Coleus x *hybridus*	Coleus	10-15	6-8	—	last frost	10-12

continued

BOTANICAL NAME	COMMON NAME	GERMINATION TIME (days)	INDOOR SOWING (# of weeks before transplanting outdoors)	OUTDOOR SOWING (# of weeks before last frost)	OUTDOOR TRANSPLANTING (# of weeks before last frost)	PLANTING DISTANCE (inches)
Consolida ambigua	Larkspur	8-15	6-8	4-6	4-6	12-24
Coreopsis tinctoria	Calliopsis	5-10	6-8	last frost	last frost	8-10
Cosmos bipinnatus	Cosmos	5-10	5-7	last frost	last frost	9-18
Dahlia hybrids	Dahlia	5-10	4-6	last frost	last frost	6-30
Dianthus species	Dianthus, pinks	5-10	8-10	last frost	last frost	6-12
Dimorphotheca sinuata	Cape marigold	10-15	4-5	last frost	last frost	6-8
Eschscholzia californica	California poppy	10-12	—	4-6	—	6-8
Euphorbia species	Annual poinsettia, snow-on-the-mountain	10-15	6-8	last frost	last frost	8-12
Gaillardia pulchella	Blanket flower	15-20	4-6	last frost	last frost	8-12
Gazania ringens	Treasure flower	8-14	4-6	last frost	last frost	8-12
Gerbera lamesonii	Transvaal daisy	15-25	8-10	—	last frost	10-12
Helianthus species	Sunflower	10-14	—	last frost	—	24-36
Helichrysum bracteatum	Strawflower	7-10	4-6	last frost	last frost	9-12
Iberis species	Candytuft	10-15	6-8	last frost	last frost	6-8
Impatiens balsamina	Balsam	8-14	6-8	last frost	last frost	10-12
Impatiens wallerana	Impatiens	15-20	10-12	—	last frost	8-12
Ipomoea species	Morning-glory	5-7	4-6	last frost	last frost	12-15
Kochia scoparia	Burning bush	10-15	4-6	last frost	last frost	15-18

continued

BOTANICAL NAME	COMMON NAME	GERMINATION TIME (days)	INDOOR SOWING (# of weeks before transplanting outdoors)	OUTDOOR SOWING (# of weeks before last frost)	OUTDOOR TRANSPLANTING (# of weeks before last frost)	PLANTING DISTANCE (inches)
Lathyrus odoratus	Sweet pea	20-30	—	6-8	—	12-15
Lavatera hybrids	Tree mallow	15-20	—	4-6	—	18-24
Lobelia erinus	Lobelia	15-20	10-12	—	last frost	4-6
Lobularia maritima	Sweet alyssum	8-15	4-6	4	2	5-8
Machaeranthera tanacetifolia	Tahoka daisy	25-30	6-8	4-6	4-6	6-8
Matthiola incana	Stock	7-10	6-8	last frost	last frost	12-15
Mimulus species	Monkey flower	8-12	10-12	—	2	6-8
Mirabilis jalapa	Four-o'clock	7-10	4-6	last frost	last frost	12-18
Moluccella laevis	Bells-of-Ireland	25-35	—	6-8	—	12-15
Nemesia strumosa	Nemesia	7-14	4-6	last frost	last frost	6-8
Nemophila menziesii	Baby-blue-eyes	7-12	—	6-8	—	6-9
Nicotiana alata	Flowering tobacco	10-20	6-8	last frost	last frost	10-12
Nierembergia species	Cupflower	15-20	10-12	—	last frost	4-6
Pelargonium x *hortorum*	Geranium	5-15	12-15	—	last frost	10-12
Petunia x *hybrida*	Petunia	10-12	10-12	—	last frost	10-12
Phlox drummondii	Annual phlox	10-15	—	6-8	—	6-8
Portulaca grandiflora	Rose moss	10-15	4-6	last frost	last frost	12-15
Reseda odorata	Mignonette	5-10	—	4-6	—	10-12
Salpiglossis sinuata	Painted-tongue	15-20	6-8	—	last frost	8-12

continued

BOTANICAL NAME	COMMON NAME	GERMINATION TIME (days)	INDOOR SOWING (# of weeks before transplanting outdoors)	OUTDOOR SOWING (# of weeks before last frost)	OUTDOOR TRANSPLANTING (# of weeks before last frost)	PLANTING DISTANCE (inches)
Sanvitalia procumbens	Creeping zinnia	10-15	—	last frost	—	5-7
Schizanthus x *wisetonensis*	Poor-man's orchid	20-25	10-12	—	last frost	12-15
Tagetes erecta	African marigold	5-7	4-6	—	last frost	12-18
Tagetes patula	French marigold	5-7	4-6	last frost	last frost	6-8
Thunbergia alata	Black-eyed Susan vine	10-15	6-8	last frost	last frost	10-12
Tithonia rotundifolia	Mexican sunflower	5-10	6-8	last frost	last frost	24-30
Torenia fournieri	Wishbone flower	15-20	10-12	—	last frost	6-8
Tropaeolum majus	Nasturtium	7-12	—	last frost	—	8-12
Verbena x *hybrida*	Verbena	20-25	12-14	—	last frost	6-8
Viola x *wittrockiana*	Pansy	10-20	6-8	—	4-6	4-6
Zinnia elegans	Zinnia	5-7	4-6	last frost	last frost	6-18

Source: *Starting Seeds Indoors,* Ann Reilly

PERENNIALS PLANNING GUIDE

| COMMON NAME | BOTANICAL NAME | ZONE | PLANT HEIGHT | | | CUT FLOWERS |
			UNDER 2'	2-3'	OVER 3'	
Astilbe	Astilbe x arendsii	4		x		
Avens	Geum species	6	x			
Baby's-breath	Gypsophila paniculata	3		x		x
Balloon flower	Platycodon grandiflorus	3	x			x
Basket-of-gold	Aurinia saxatilis	3	x			
Bear's-breech	Acanthus mollis	8			x	
Beard-tongue						
Common	Penstemon barbatus	3	x	x		x
Bedding	P. x gloxinioides	7	x			x
Bee balm	Monarda didyma	4			x	x
Bellflower						
Carpathian bellflower	Campanula carpatica	3	x			
Dane's-blood	C. glomerata	3		x		x
Canterbury-bells	C. medium	3		x		
Peachleaf bells	C. persicifolia	3	x	x		x
Scotch harebell	C. rotundifolia	2	x			
Betony	Stachys grandiflora	3	x			x
Lamb's ears	S. byzantina	4	x			
Bishop's hat	Epimedium species	4	x			
Blackberry lily	Belamcanda chinensis	5		x		
Blanket flower	Gaillardia x grandiflora	3	x	x		x

FLOWER COLOR	FLOWER SEASON			LIGHT			SOIL		
	SPRING	SUMMER	FALL	SUN	PARTIAL SHADE	SHADE	DRY	MOIST, WELL DRAINED	WET
white, pink, red		x			x			x	
orange, yellow	x	x		x	x			x	
white		x		x				x	
white, blue, pink		x		x	x			x	
yellow	x			x			x	x	
white, lilac, rose		x		x				x	
red, pink, purple		x		x			x	x	
red		x		x			x	x	
red, pink, white		x		x	x			x	
white, blue		x	x	x	x			x	
violet		x		x	x			x	
blue, white, rose		x		x	x			x	
white, blue		x		x	x			x	
blue		x		x	x			x	
pink		x		x				x	
pink		x		x			x	x	
red, yellow, white	x				x			x	
orange		x		x				x	
red, yellow		x	x	x			x	x	

continued

| COMMON NAME | BOTANICAL NAME | ZONE | PLANT HEIGHT | | | CUT FLOWERS |
			UNDER 2'	2-3'	OVER 3'	
Bleeding-heart	*Dicentra eximia*	3	x			x
	D. formosa	3	x			x
	D. spectabilis	2		x		x
Blue plumbago	*Ceratostigma plumbaginoides*	5-6	x			
Blue stars	*Amsonia tabernaemontana*	3		x		x
Bugbane						
Cohosh bugbane	*Cimicifuga racemosa*	3			x	x
Kamchatka bugbane	*C. simplex*	3			x	x
Bugleweed	*Ajuga reptans*	3	x			
Bugloss	*Anchusa azurea* var.	3	x	x	x	x
Butterfly flower	*Asclepias tuberosa*	3		x		x
Campion						
Maltese cross	*Lychnis chalcedonica*	3		x		x
Rose campion	*L. coronaria*	3		x		
Catchfly	*L. viscaria*	3	x			
Candytuft	*Iberis sempervirens*	3	x			
Carnation						
Allwood pinks	*Dianthus* x *allwoodii*	4	x			x
Sweet william	*D. barbatus*	5	x			x
Maiden pinks	*D. deltoides*	4	x			x
Cottage pinks	*D. plumarius*	3	x			x

FLOWER COLOR	FLOWER SEASON			LIGHT			SOIL		
	SPRING	SUMMER	FALL	SUN	PARTIAL SHADE	SHADE	DRY	MOIST, WELL DRAINED	WET
pink		x	x	x	x			x	
pink		x	x	x	x			x	
pink, white	x			x	x			x	
blue		x	x	x	x			x	
blue	x			x	x			x	x
white		x			x	x		x	
white			x		x	x		x	
white, blue		x			x			x	
blue		x	x	x	x			x	
orange		x		x				x	
red		x		x	x			x	
magenta		x		x				x	
white, red		x		x				x	
white	x	x		x				x	
salmon	x	x		x				x	
white, pink, red	x	x		x				x	
pink	x	x		x				x	
white, pink, red	x	x		x				x	

continued

| COMMON NAME | BOTANICAL NAME | ZONE | PLANT HEIGHT | | | CUT FLOWERS |
			UNDER 2'	2-3'	OVER 3'	
Carolina lupine	*Thermopsis caroliniana*	3			x	x
Catmint	*Nepeta* x *Faassenii*	3	x			
Chinese forget-me-not	*Cynoglossum nervosum*	5	x			
Chinese-lantern plant	*Physalis franchetii*	3		x		x
Christmas rose						
Stinking hellebore	*Helleborus foetidus*	6	x			
Corsican rose	*H. lividus corsicus*	8	x			
Christmas rose	*H. niger*	3	x			
Lenten rose	*H. orientalis*	4	x			
Chrysanthemum	*Chrysanthemum* x *morifolium*	4-5	x	x	x	x
Painted daisy	*C. coccineum*	3		x		x
Shasta daisy	*C.* x *superbum*	4		x		x
Cinquefoil	*Potentilla* species	4	x			
Columbine	*Aquilegia* hybrids	4		x		x
Coneflower	*Rudbeckia* species	3		x		x
Coralbells	*Heuchera* varieties	3	x			x
Cranesbill						
Spotted	*Geranium maculatum*	4	x			
Bloodred	*G. sanguineum*	3	x			
Cupid's-dart	*Catananche caerulea*	4	x			x
Dame's-rocket	*Hesperis matronalis*	3			x	x
Daylily	*Hemerocallis* species	3	x	x	x	

FLOWER COLOR	FLOWER SEASON			LIGHT			SOIL		
	SPRING	SUMMER	FALL	SUN	PARTIAL SHADE	SHADE	DRY	MOIST, WELL DRAINED	WET
yellow		x		x			x	x	
lavender		x		x				x	
blue		x		x				x	
orange			x	x	x			x	
	x				x	x		x	
	x				x	x		x	
	x				x	x		x	
	x				x	x		x	
all but blue			x	x				x	
white, pink, red	x	x		x				x	
white		x		x				x	
pink, yellow, red		x	x	x	x			x	
red, blue, yellow, white, pink	x	x		x	x			x	
yellow		x	x	x				x	
red, pink				x	x			x	
pink		x		x				x	
pink		x		x				x	
blue		x		x			x		
purple, white		x		x	x			x	
yellow, orange, red		x	x	x	x			x	

continued

| COMMON NAME | BOTANICAL NAME | ZONE | PLANT HEIGHT | | | CUT FLOWERS |
			UNDER 2'	2-3'	OVER 3'	
Delphinium	*Delphinium* x *belladonna*	3		x	x	x
	D. elatum	2		x	x	x
	D. grandiflorum	3		x		x
Desert-candle	*Eremurus* species	4&6			x	x
False dragonhead	*Physostegia virginiana*	4		x		x
False indigo	*Baptisia australis*	3			x	x
False starwort	*Boltonia asteroides*	3			x	x
Ferns						
Maidenhair	*Adiantum pedatum*	3	x			
Lady	*Athyrium filix-femina*	3		x		
Japanese painted	*A. goeringianum Pictum*	3	x			
Hay-scented	*Dennstaedtia punctilobula*	3		x		
Wood	*Dryopteris* species	3		x		
Ostrich	*Matteuccia pensylvanica*	3			x	
Sensitive	*Onoclea sensibilis*	3		x		
Cinnamon	*Osmunda cinnamomea*	3			x	
Royal	*O. regalis* var. *spectabilis*	3			x	
Common	*Polypodium virginianum*	3	x			
Christmas	*Polystichum acrostichoides*	3	x			
Flax						
Golden	*Linum flavum*	5	x			
Blue	*L. perenne*	5	x			

FLOWER COLOR	FLOWER SEASON			LIGHT			SOIL		
	SPRING	SUMMER	FALL	SUN	PARTIAL SHADE	SHADE	DRY	MOIST, WELL DRAINED	WET
blue		x		x	x				
blue, purple, pink, white		x		x	x				
white, blue		x		x	x				
white, pink, yellow		x		x				x	
white, pink		x	x	x	x			x	
blue		x		x			x	x	
white			x	x				x	
					x	x		x	
				x	x			x	
					x	x		x	
					x	x		x	
					x	x		x	
					x	x		x	
				x	x			x	
					x	x		x	x
					x	x		x	x
					x	x		x	x
					x	x		x	
yellow		x		x				x	
blue		x		x				x	

continued

COMMON NAME	BOTANICAL NAME	ZONE	PLANT HEIGHT			CUT FLOWERS
			UNDER 2'	2-3'	OVER 3'	
Fleabane	*Erigeron* hybrids	5-6		x		x
Foxglove						
Yellow	*Digitalis grandiflora*	3			x	x
Merton's	*D.* x *mertonensis*	5			x	x
Common	*D. purpurea*	5			x	x
Gas plant	*Dictamus albus*	3		x		x
Gay-feather	*Liatris* species	3		x	x	x
Gentian	*Gentiana* species	3	x			
Globeflower	*Trollius* species	3		x		x
Globe thistle	*Echinops ritro*	3			x	x
Goatsbeard	*Aruncus sylvester*	3			x	
Golden marguerite	*Anthemis tinctoria*	3		x		x
Goldenrod	*Solidago* hybrids	4		x		x
Greek valerian	*Polemonium caeruleum*	3		x		
Hardy aster	*Aster* varieties	4-5		x	x	x
Hardy begonia	*Begonia grandis*	6	x			
Hardy fuchsia	*Fuchsia magellanica*	7		x		
Hardy orchid	*Bletilla*	3	x			x
Hen-and-chickens	*Sempervivum tectorum*	4	x			
Hollyhock	*Alcea rosea*	3			x	
Iris	*Iris* species	3-4	x	x	x	x
Jupiter's-beard	*Centranthus ruber*	4		x		x
Lady's-mantle	*Alchemilla mollis*	3	x			x

FLOWER COLOR	FLOWER SEASON			LIGHT			SOIL		
	SPRING	SUMMER	FALL	SUN	PARTIAL SHADE	SHADE	DRY	MOIST, WELL DRAINED	WET
blue, pink		x		x			x	x	
yellow		x			x			x	
pink		x			x			x	
purple, pink		x			x			x	
pink, white		x		x				x	
white, pink		x	x	x				x	
blue		x			x			x	
yellow		x		x	x			x	x
blue		x	x	x			x	x	
white		x			x				x
yellow		x		x	x		x		
yellow			x	x			x	x	
white, blue	x	x		x	x			x	
white, pink, purple, blue, red		x	x				x		
pink		x	x		x			x	
purple, red		x			x			x	
pink		x			x			x	
pink		x		x			x	x	
pink, red, yellow, white		x		x	x			x	
all colors	x	x		x	x			x	
white, red		x		x	x			x	
yellow-green		x			x		x	x	

continued

| COMMON NAME | BOTANICAL NAME | ZONE | PLANT HEIGHT | | | CUT FLOWERS |
			UNDER 2'	2-3'	OVER 3'	
Lavender cotton	*Santolina chamaecyparissus*	5	x			
Leopard's-bane	*Doronicum caucasicum*	3	x			x
Lily-of-the-valley	*Convallaria majalis*	2	x			x
Lily-turf	*Liriope muscari*	6	x			
Lobelia						
Cardinal flower	*Lobelia cardinalis*	3			x	
Great blue lobelia	*L. siphilitica*	4		x		
Loosestrife gooseneck	*Lysimachia clethroides*	3		x		
Yellow	*L. punctata*	5		x		
Lungwort	*Pulmonaria* species	4	x			
Lupine	*Lupinus polyphyllus*	4			x	x
Mallow						
Hollyhock mallow	*Malva alcea* var. *fastigiata*	4			x	
Musk mallow	*M. moschata*	3			x	
Marsh marigold	*Caltha palustris*	3	x			
Meadow rue	*Thalictrum aquilegifolium*	5		x		x
Yunnan	*T. delavayi*	4			x	x
Lavender mist	*T. rochebrunianum*	5			x	x
Meadowsweet	*F. vulgaris* 'Flore'	3	x			
Queen-of-the-prairie	*Filipendula rubra* 'Venusta'	2			x	
Queen-of-the-meadow	*F. ulmaria* 'Flore Pleno'	3			x	
Mist flower	*Eupatorium coelestinum*	6	x			x
Joe-Pye weed	*E. purpureum*				x	

FLOWER COLOR	FLOWER SEASON			LIGHT			SOIL		
	SPRING	SUMMER	FALL	SUN	PARTIAL SHADE	SHADE	DRY	MOIST, WELL DRAINED	WET
yellow		X	X	X			X	X	
yellow	X			X	X			X	
pink, white	X				X	X		X	
lavender		X	X		X			X	
red		X	X	X	X			X	X
blue		X	X	X	X			X	
white		X		X	X			X	
yellow		X		X	X			X	
pink, white, blue, red	X				X	X		X	
blue, pink, red, white, yellow		X		X				X	
pink, white		X		X				X	
pink, white		X		X				X	
yellow	X				X	X			X
pink, white	X	X		X	X			X	
mauve		X	X	X	X			X	
mauve		X	X	X	X			X	
white		X		X	X				
white, pink		X		X	X			X	
white		X		X	X				
lavender			X	X	X			X	
purple			X		X	X			X

continued

COMMON NAME	BOTANICAL NAME	ZONE	PLANT HEIGHT			CUT FLOWERS
			UNDER 2'	2-3'	OVER 3'	
Monkshood						
Azure	*Aconitum fisheri*	3		x		
Common	*A. napellus*	3		x		x
Orange sunflower	*Heliopsis scabra*	4			x	
Oriental poppy	*Papaver orientale*	3		x	x	x
Ornamental grasses						
Giant reed	*Arundo donax*	7			x	
Feather Reed	*Calamagrostis acutiflora* 'Stricta'	5			x	x
Japanese sedge	*Carex morrowii* var. *expallida*	5	x			
Pampas	*Cortaderia selloana*	7			x	x
Ravenna	*Erianthus revennae*	6			x	x
Blue fescue	*Festuca ovina* var. *glauca*	4	x			
Eulalia	*Miscanthus sinensis*	4			x	x
Variegated purple moor	*Molinia caerulea*	4		x		x
Fountain	*Pennisetum alopecuroides*	5			x	x
Giant feather	*Stipa gigantea*	5			x	x
Ribbon	*Phalaris arundinacea* var. *picta*	3	x			
Ornamental onion	*Allium senescens*	3	x			x
Chives	*A. schoenoprasum*	4	x			x
Garlic chives	*A. tuberosum*	4	x			x
Pearly everlasting	*Anaphalis margaritacea*	3	x			x
Peony	*Paenoia* species	3		x		x

FLOWER COLOR	FLOWER SEASON			LIGHT			SOIL		
	SPRING	SUMMER	FALL	SUN	PARTIAL SHADE	SHADE	DRY	MOIST, WELL DRAINED	WET
blue			X	X	X			X	
blue, white	X	X		X	X			X	
orange, yellow		X	X	X			X	X	
orange, red, pink, white		X		X				X	
red		X		X				X	
beige		X	X	X				X	
white		X		X				X	
white		X	X	X				X	
silver, purple		X		X				X	
white		X		X				X	
beige		X	X	X				X	
beige		X	X	X				X	
silver-rose		X	X	X				X	
yellow		X	X	X				X	
white		X	X	X				X	
mauve		X		X				X	
pink		X		X				X	
white		X		X				X	
white		X	X		X		X		
white, red, pink	X	X		X				X	

continued

COMMON NAME	BOTANICAL NAME	ZONE	PLANT HEIGHT			CUT FLOWERS
			UNDER 2'	2-3'	OVER 3'	
Perennial cornflower						
John Coutts	*Centaurea hypoleuca*	3		x		x
Knapweed	*C. macrocephala*	2-3			x	x
Mountain bluet	*C. montana*	2-3		x		x
Perennial forget-me-not	*Myosotis scorpioides*	3	x			
Perennial sunflower	*Helianthus x multiflorus*	4			x	x
Swamp sunflower	*H. angustifolius*	6			x	x
Perennial sweet pea	*Lathyrus latifolius*	4			x	x
Phlox						
Early	*Phlox carolina*	3		x		x
Wild blue	*P. divaricata*	3	x			x
Garden	*P. paniculata*	3		x	x	x
Creeping	*P. stolonifera*	3	x			
Moss pink	*P. subulata*	3	x			
Pincushion flower	*Scabiosa caucasica*	3		x		x
Plantain lily	*Hosta* species	3	x			
Plume poppy	*Macleaya cordata*	3			x	
Prickly pear	*Opuntia humifusa*	6	x			
Primrose	*Primula* species	5	x			
Purple coneflower	*Echinacea purpurea*	3			x	x
Purple loosestrife	*Lythrum salicaria*	3			x	
Purple rockcress	*Aubrieta deltoidea*	4	x			
Ragwort	*Ligularia* species	4		x		

FLOWER COLOR	FLOWER SEASON			LIGHT			SOIL		
	SPRING	SUMMER	FALL	SUN	PARTIAL SHADE	SHADE	DRY	MOIST, WELL DRAINED	WET
mauve		x		x			x	x	
yellow		x		x			x	x	
blue		x		x			x	x	
blue, pink		x			x				x
yellow			x	x	x			x	
yellow			x	x	x			x	
pink		x	x	x				x	
white, pink, red		x		x	x			x	
blue	x	x		x	x			x	
pink, red, white		x	x	x	x			x	
pink, white, red, blue	x	x			x			x	
pink, white, red, blue	x	x		x				x	
blue, white, purple		x	x	x				x	
lavender, white		x			x	x		x	
white		x		x	x			x	
yellow		x		x			x		
white, red, blue, pink, yellow	x				x	x		x	
pink		x	x	x				x	
purple		x		x	x			x	
red, purple	x			x	x			x	
yellow		x		x	x			x	

continued

COMMON NAME	BOTANICAL NAME	ZONE	PLANT HEIGHT			CUT FLOWERS
			UNDER 2'	2-3'	OVER 3'	
Rock cress	*Arabis procurrens*	4	x			
Double rock cress	*A. caucasica* 'Flore Pleno'	3	x			x
Rose mallow	*Hibiscus moscheutos*	5			x	
Rue	*Ruta graveolens*	4	x			
Russian sage	*Perovskia atriplicifolia*	5		x		x
Saxifrage	*Bergenia cordifolia*	2	x			
	B. crassifolia	2	x			
Sea holly	*Eryngium* hybrids	5		x		x
Sea lavender	*Limonium latifolium*	3	x			x
Self-heal	*Prunella webbiana*	4	x			
Siberian bugloss	*Brunnera macrophylla*	3	x			
Snake grass	*Tradescantia* x *andersoniana*	4	x			
Sneezeweed	*Helenium autumnale*	3			x	x
Snow-in-summer	*Cerastium tomentosum*	4	x			
Snow-on-the-mountain	*Aegopodium podagraria variegatum*	3	x			
Solomon's-seal	*Polygonatum* species	4		x	x	
Speedwell	*Veronica* species	3	x			x
Spotted dead nettle	*Lamium maculatum*	3	x			
Spurge	*Euphorbia characias* 'Wulfenii'	8			x	
Baby's breath	*E. corollata*	3		x		
Cushion	*E. epithymoides*	4	x			
Stokes' aster	*Stokesia laevis*	5	x			x

FLOWER COLOR	FLOWER SEASON			LIGHT			SOIL		
	SPRING	SUMMER	FALL	SUN	PARTIAL SHADE	SHADE	DRY	MOIST, WELL DRAINED	WET
white	X			X			X	X	
white	X			X			X	X	
pink, white, red		X	X	X	X			X	
yellow		X		X				X	
violet-blue		X		X			X	X	
pink	X			X	X			X	
pink	X			X	X			X	X
gray-blue		X	X	X			X	X	
lavender		X	X	X			X	X	
pink, white			X			X		X	
blue	X				X	X	X	X	
blue, white, pink, purple	X				X	X		X	
yellow, red			X	X				X	
white		X		X			X	X	
white		X			X			X	
white	X	X			X	X		X	
blue, pink, white, purple		X		X				X	
pink	X	X		X	X			X	
yellow	X			X				X	
white		X		X				X	
yellow	X			X				X	
blue, white		X	X	X			X	X	

continued

COMMON NAME	BOTANICAL NAME	ZONE	PLANT HEIGHT			CUT FLOWERS
			UNDER 2'	2-3'	OVER 3'	
Stonecrop						
Aizoon	*Sedum aizoon*	5	x			
Autum joy	*Sedum* species	3		x		x
Kamtschat	*S. kamtschaticum*	3	x			
Ruby glow	*Sedum* species	3	x			
Siebold	*S. sieboldii*	3	x			
Showy	*S. spectabile*	3		x		x
Creeping	*S. spurium*	3	x			
Sundrops						
Ozark	*Oenothera missourensis*	4	x			
Evening primrose	*O. speciosa*	5	x			
Common	*O. tetragona*	4	x			
Sunrose	*Helianthemum nummularium*	5	x			
Sweet woodruff	*Asperula odorata*	3	x			
Thrift	*Armeria pseudarmeria*	6	x			
Sea pink	*A. maritima*	3	x			
Tickseed	*Coreopsis grandiflora/lanceolata*	5	x	x	x	x
Threadleaf	*C. verticillata*	3	x	x	x	x
Toadflax	*Linaria genistifolia*	3		x		x
Turtlehead	*Chelone lyonii*	3			x	
Violet	*Viola* species	4	x			x
Virginia bluebells	*Mertensia virginica*	3	x			

FLOWER COLOR	FLOWER SEASON			LIGHT			SOIL		
	SPRING	SUMMER	FALL	SUN	PARTIAL SHADE	SHADE	DRY	MOIST, WELL DRAINED	WET
yellow	x	x		x			x	x	
red			x	x			x	x	
yellow		x	x	x			x	x	
red			x	x			x	x	
pink			x	x			x	x	
pink, red, white		x	x	x			x	x	
red, pink		x		x			x	x	
yellow		x		x				x	
pink		x						x	
yellow		x		x				x	
pink, yellow, red		x		x				x	
white	x				x	x		x	
pink, white	x	x		x			x		
pink, white, red	x			x			x		
yellow		x		x			x	x	
yellow		x		x			x	x	
yellow		x		x				x	
pink		x	x	x	x			x	x
white, purple, pink, yellow	x				x			x	
blue	x				x			x	

continued

PERENNIALS PLANNING GUIDE (CONTINUED)

| COMMON NAME | BOTANICAL NAME | ZONE | PLANT HEIGHT | | | CUT FLOWERS |
			UNDER 2'	2-3'	OVER 3'	
Wild ginger	*Asarum europaeum*	5	x			
Windflower						
Japanese anemone	*Anemone* x *hybrida* var.	5		x	x	x
Pasque flower	*A. pulsatilla*	5	x			x
Japanese anemone	*A. vitifolia* 'Robustissima'	4		x		x
Wormwood	*Artemisia absinthium*	3		x		
Southernwood	*A. abrotanum*	5			x	
Silver King	*A. ludoviciana*	4		x		
Silver Mound	*A. schmidtiana*	3	x			
Yarrow	*Achillea*					
Fernleaf	*A. filipendulina*	3		x		x
Rosy	*A. millefolium*	2	x			x
Sneezewort	*A. ptarmica*	3		x		x
Woolly	*A. tomentosa*	3	x			
Yucca	*Yucca* species	3,5			x	

Source: *Perennials: 1001 Gardening Questions Answered,* Editors of Garden Way Publishing

FLOWER COLOR	FLOWER SEASON			LIGHT			SOIL		
	SPRING	SUMMER	FALL	SUN	PARTIAL SHADE	SHADE	DRY	MOIST, WELL DRAINED	WET
maroon	x					x		x	
white, pink			x		x			x	
lilac	x				x			x	
pink			x		x			x	
yellow		x		x			x	x	
yellow		x		x			x	x	
yellow		x		x			x	x	
yellow		x		x			x	x	
		x		x			x	x	
yellow	x	x		x			x	x	
white, rose		x		x			x	x	
white	x	x		x				x	
yellow		x		x			x	x	
white	x	x		x			x		

PLANTING INFORMATION FOR SELECTED PERENNIALS

BOTANICAL NAME	COMMON NAME	GERMINATION TIME (days)	INDOOR SOWING (# of weeks before transplanting outdoors)	OUTDOOR SOWING (# of weeks before last frost)	OUTDOOR TRANSPLANTING (# of weeks before last frost)	PLANTING DISTANCE (inches)
Achillea species	Yarrow	10-12	6-8	A	B	12-18
Alcea rosea	Hollyhock	10-14	6-8	A	B	18-36
Alyssum montanum	Basket-of-gold	7-14	6-8	C	B	6-8
Anchusa azurea	Summer forget-me-not	14-21	6-8	A	B	18-30
Chrysanthemum coccineum	Pyrethrum, painted daisy	20-25	6-8	A	B	10-12
Chrysanthemum x *morifolium*	Garden chrysanthemum	7-10	6-8	C	F	8-18
Chrysanthemum parthenium	Feverfew	10-15	4-6	C	B	6-12
Chrysanthemum x *superbum*	Shasta daisy	10-14	4-6	A	B	12-18
Coreopsis grandiflora	Tickseed	20-25	6-8	F	B	12-15
Delphinium species	Delphinium	8-15	6-8	A	B	12-24
Dicentra spectabilis	Bleeding heart	30+	8-10	H	B	24-30
Dictamnus albus	Gas plant	30-40	6-8	H	B	30-36
Digitalis species	Foxglove	15-20	6-8	A	B	15-24
Doronicum cordatum	Leopard's-bane	15-20	6-8	A	B	12-15
Echinacea purpurea	Purple coneflower	10-20	6-8	A	B	18-24
Erigeron species	Midsummer aster	15-20	6-8	D	B	10-12
Gaillardia x *grandiflora*	Blanket flower	15-20	4-6	C	B	8-15
Geranium sanguineum	Cranesbill	20-40	8-10	C	B	10-12

continued

BOTANICAL NAME	COMMON NAME	GERMINATION TIME (days)	INDOOR SOWING (# of weeks before transplanting outdoors)	OUTDOOR SOWING (# of weeks before last frost)	OUTDOOR TRANSPLANTING (# of weeks before last frost)	PLANTING DISTANCE (inches)
Geum species	Avens	21-28	6-8	A	B	12-18
Gypsophila species	Baby's-breath	10-15	6-8	A	B	18-24
Helleborus niger	Christmas rose	14-20	6-8	G	B	12-15
Hemerocallis hybrids	Daylily	21-50	9-15	D	B	18-36
Heuchera sanguinea	Coralbells	10-15	6-8	D	B	9-15
Hibiscus moscheutos	Mallow	15-30	6-8	A	B	24-36
Hosta species	Plaintain lily	15-20	6-8	A	B	10-12
Iberis sempervirens	Candytuft	16-20	8-10	C	B	6-9
Kniphofia uvaria	Red-hot-poker, tritoma	10-20	6-8	C	B	18-24
Lathyrus latifolius	Perennial pea	20-30	4-6	C	B	10-12
Liatris species	Gay-feather	20-25	6-8	A	B	12-15
Linum species	Flax	20-25	—	A	—	10-12
Liriope muscari	Lilyturf	25-30	8-10	I	B	6-12
Lunaria annua	Money plant	10-14	6-8	C	F	12-15
Lupinus species	Lupine	20-25	6-8	C	B	18-24
Lychnis chalcedonica	Maltese-cross	21-25	6-8	A	B	12-15
Lythrum salicaria	Loosestrife	15-20	6-8	C	B	18-24
Monarda didyma	Beebalm	15-20	4-6	A	B	12-15
Myosotis scorpioides	Forget-me-not	8-14	6-8	H	B	8-12
Oenothera species	Evening primrose	15-20	6-8	I	B	6-12
Papaver species	Poppy	10-15	—	D	—	12-18
Penstemon species	Beard-tongue	20-30	8-10	D	B	12-18

continued

BOTANICAL NAME	COMMON NAME	GERMINATION TIME (days)	INDOOR SOWING (# of weeks before transplanting outdoors)	OUTDOOR SOWING (# of weeks before last frost)	OUTDOOR TRANSPLANTING (# of weeks before last frost)	PLANTING DISTANCE (inches)
Phlox paniculata	Phlox	25-30	8-10	I	B	24-36
Physostegia virginiana	False dragonhead	20-25	6-8	A	B	15-18
Platycodon grandiflorus	Balloon flower	10-15	6-8	A	B	12-18
Polemonium caeruleum	Jacob's-ladder	20-25	6-8	D	B	15-18
Primula species	Primrose	21-40	8-10	D	B	6-8
Rudbeckia hirta	Gloriosa daisy	5-10	4-6	A	B	12-18
Santolina chamaecyparissus	Lavender cotton	15-20	6-8	A	B	18-20
Scabiosa species	Pincushion flower	10-15	6-8	A	B	10-15
Sedum species	Stonecrop	15-30	6-8	—	B	6-8
Sempervivum species	Live-forever	15-30	6-8	—	B	4-8
Senecio species	Dusty Miller	10-15	8-10	A	B	8-10
Stokesia laevis	Stokes' aster	25-30	8-10	A	B	12-15
Thalictrum aquilegifolium	Meadow rue	15-30	8-10	H	B	12-18
Tradescantia species	Spiderwort	25-30	8-10	A	B	12-15
Trillium ovatum	Wake-robin	180+	—	H	—	10-12
Trollius europaeus	Globeflower	50-60+	—	H	—	8-10
Veronica species	Veronica, speedwell	15-20	6-8	A	B	12-15
Viola species	Viola, violet	10-20	8-10	F	B	6-8

Key:
A = Sow outdoors from early spring through summer up until 2 months before first fall frost.
B = Plant outdoors from early spring through summer up until 2 months before first fall frost.
C = Sow outdoors in early spring.
D = Sow outdoors in fall or early spring.
E = Plant outdoors in early to mid spring.

F = Sow outdoors in fall or from early spring through summer up until 2 months before first fall frost.
G = Sow outdoors in spring after danger of frost has passed.
H = Sow outdoors in fall.
I = Sow outdoors in fall, spring or early summer.

Source: *Starting Seeds Indoors,* Ann Reilly

Everlastings and Flower Preservation

EVERLASTINGS FOR EVERY GARDEN

COMMON NAME	BOTANICAL NAME	COLOR	ZONES*/ PLANT TYPE	COMMON NAME	BOTANICAL NAME	COLOR	ZONES*/ PLANT TYPE
THE EASIEST				**PLANTS FOR DRY, SHADY PLACES**			
Baby's-breath	*Gypsophila paniculata*	Pink, white	2	Bergenia	*Bergenia*	Pink, white	2
Bachelor's-button	*Centaurea cyanus*	Blue, pink	HA	Honesty	*Lunaria annua*	Silvery seed head	HB
Chives	*Allium schoenoprasum*	Pink, purple	2	Pearly everlasting	*Anaphalis margaritacea*	White	3
Delphinium	*Delphinium* spp.	Blue, pink, white	4-7	St.-John's-wort	*Hypericum* spp.	Yellow	3-7
Globe amaranth	*Gomphrena globosa*	Pink, purple, whte	HHA	Yarrow	*Achillea filipendulina*	Pink, yellow, white	2
Larkspur	*Consolida regalis*	Blue, pink, white	HHA	**PLANTS FOR WET, SUNNY PLACES**			
Love-in-a-mist	*Nigella damascena*	Blue, pink	HA	Beebalm	*Monarda didyma*	Pink, red	4
Pink poker	*Limonium suworowii*	Pink	HHA	False goat's-beard	*Astilbe biternata*	Pink, red	5
Starflower	*Scabiosa stellata*	Blue	HA	Forget-me-not	*Myosotis sylvatica*	Blue	HA
Statice	*Limonium sinuatum*	Blue, purple, white, yellow	HA	Foxglove	*Digitalis purpurea*	Pink, purple, white	4
Strawflower	*Helichrysum bracteatum*	All except blue	HHA	Loosestrife	*Lythrum alatum*	Rose	3
PLANTS FOR DRY, SUNNY PLACES							
Acroclinium, sunray	*Helipterum* spp.	Pink, yellow, white	HHA	Dusty miller	*Artemisia stellerana*	Yellow flowers, white stems	2
Baby's-breath	*Gypsophila paniculata*	Pink, white	2	Lavender	*Lavandula angustifolia*	Purple	5
Clary sage	*Salvia sclarea*	Pink, red, white	HA	Sea holly	*Eryngium maritima*	Blue	5
Cockscomb	*Celosia cristata*	Pink, purple, yellow	HHA	Yarrow	*Achillea filipendulina*	Pink, yellow, white	HP/2

continued

COMMON NAME	BOTANICAL NAME	COLOR	ZONES*/ PLANT TYPE
PLANTS FOR MOIST, SHADY PLACES			
Foxglove	*Digitalis purpurea*	Pink, white	4
Goldenrod	*Solidago*	Yellow	4
Meadowrue	*Thalictrum*	Gray-green leaves, pink flowers	2-5
HERBS THAT DRY WELL			
Bay leaves	*Lauris nobilis*	Leaves	7
Chives	*Allium schoenoprasum*	Flower, seed heads	2
Feverfew	*Chrysanthemum parthenium*	Flowers	5
Lamb's ears	*Stachys byzantina*	Leaves	5
Lavender	*Lavandula angustifolia*	Flowers	5
Rosemary	*Rosmarinus officinalis*	Leaves, flowers	8
Rue	*Ruta graveolens*	Seed heads	4
Sage	*Salvia officinalis*	Leaves, flowers	4
Sweet marjoram	*Origanum majorana*	Flowers	9
Tansy	*Tanacetum vulgare*	Flower heads	4
Thyme	*Thymus vulgaris*	Leaves	4
Wormwood	*Artemisia absinthium*	Leaves	4
Yarrow	*Achillea* spp.	Flower heads	HP

Plant type:
HA = Hardy Annual
HHA = Half-hardy Annual
HP = Hardy Perennial
HB = Biennial

* Chart shows coldest hardiness zone tolerated by a species. Where a specific species is not named on the chart, look for a species appropriate to the hardiness range indicated.

Source: *The Able Gardener,* Kathleen Yeomans, R.N.

FLOWERS THAT PRESS WELL

COMMON NAME	BOTANICAL NAME	COMMENTS	COMMON NAME	BOTANICAL NAME	COMMENTS
Auricula	*Primula auricula*	Petals have many different colors	Geranium	*Pelargonium zonale*	Retains red shades well
Basket-of-gold	*Aunnia saxatilis*	Retains yellow color well	Golden marguerite	*Anthemis tinctona*	Press individual petals
Bear's-breech	*Acanthus* spp.	Retains purple color well	Goldenrod	*Solidago* spp.	Press small pieces
Blackberry; dewberry	*Rubus macropetalus*	Flowers are a delicate mauve-white	Heath	*Erica* spp.	Tiny flowers press well
Bleeding-heart	*Dicentra spectabilis*	Interesting shapes	Heather; Scotch heather	*Calluna vulgans*	Tiny flowers press well
Bracken	*Pteridium aquilinum*	Very useful foliage	Hydrangea	*Hydrangea paniculata*	Keeps color well
Buttercup, common	*Ranunculus acris*	Beautiful texture and gold color	Larkspur	*Consolida regalis*	Petals have interesting shapes
California poppy	*Eschscholzia californica*	Press individual petals	Lobelia	*Lobelia* spp. & var.	Use blue varieties
Calliopsis	*Coreopsis tinctoria*	Retains yellow color well	Mallowwort	*Malope* spp.	Deep pink petals; press individually
Christmas rose	*Helleborus niger*	Retains its interesting texture when pressed	Marigold, pot	*Calendula officinalis*	Pot and medicinal herb
Chrysanthemum	*Chrysanthemum* spp.	Press any petals of unusual shape	Montebretia	*Crocosmia crocosmiiflora*	Retains orange color well
Clematis	*Clematis* spp. & var.	Press wild and garden varieties	Pansy; violet	*Viola* spp. & var.	Small dark ones retain color well
Columbine	*Aquilegia* spp.	Press unusual shapes	Primrose, English	*Primula vulgaris*	Dainty pale yellow flowers
Coneflower	*Rudbeckia* spp.	Press petals separately	Purple coneflower	*Echinacea purpurea*	Press individual petals
Crocus, autumn	*Colchicum autumnale*	Press petals separately	Sage, blue	*Salvia azurea*	A half-hardy blue salvia
Dahlia	*Dahlia* spp. & var.	Press petals with interesting shapes	Tulips	*Tulipa* spp.	Retains texture and lasts a long time
Delphinium	*Delphinium* spp. & var.	Petals have interesting shapes	Wallflower	*Cheiranthus cheiri*	Yellow and bronze flowers press well
Dusty Miller	*Senecio cinerana*	Florists often sell this plant in pots	Windflower	*Anemone* spp.	Press petals separately
Freesia	*Freesia* x *hybrida*	Press flat or open	Yellow oxeye	*Telekia speciosa*	Press yellow petals separately
Gentian	*Gentiana acaulis*	Beautiful blue color			

Source: *Flowers That Last Forever,* Betty E.M. Jacobs

PLANTS THAT HAVE INTERESTING SEED HEADS OR SEEDPODS

COMMON NAME	BOTANICAL NAME	PLANT TYPE	COMMON NAME	BOTANICAL NAME	PLANT TYPE
Aconite, winter	*Eranthis hyemalis*	Hardy bulbs	Cress, field penny	*Thlaspi arvense*	Wild, common, annual weed
African lily	*Agapanthus africanus*	Rhizomatous; propagated by division	Crown-imperial	*Fritillaria imperialis*	Hardy bulb
Alyssum, sweet	*Lobularia maritima*	Annual; grown from seed	Cupid's-dart	*Catanache caerulea*	Hardy perennial
Anemone; windflower	*Anemone coronaria*	Hardy bulb	Delphinium	*Delphinium* spp.& var.	Hardy perennials
Angelica	*Angelica archangelica*	Biennial herb; propagate by seed	Dill	*Anethum graveolens*	Annual herb
Bear's-breech	*Acanthus* spp.	Hardy perennial	Dock; sorrel	*Rumex* spp.	Hardy perennials; wild
Bluebell, English	*Endymion non-scriptus*	Wild, hardy bulb	Fennel	*Foeniculum vulgare*	Hardy perennial herb
Blue false indigo	*Baptisia ausfralis*	Hardy perennial	Foxglove(s)	*Digitalis* spp.	Hardy biennial
Blue lace flower	*Trachymene coerulea*	Annual; grown from seed	Gas plant; burning bush	*Dictamnus albus*	See Burning bush
Bouncing bet	*Saponaria officinalis*	Hardy perennial	Gladiolus	*Gladiolus* spp.& var.	Half-hardy biennial bulbs
Burning bush; gas plant	*Dictamnus albus*	Hardy perennial	Globe thistle, small	*Echinops ritro*	Hardy perennial
Canterbury-bells	*Campanula medium*	Hardy perennial	Goat's-beard; Jack-go-to-bed-at-noon	*Tragopogon pratensis*	Biennial; wild
Cattail, common	*Typha latifolia*	Wild; found in ditches	Grape hyacinth	*Muscari* spp.& var.	Hardy bulbs
Chervil	*Anthriscus cerefolium*	Annual herb	Hellebore	*Helleborus* spp.	Hardy perennials
Chinese-lantern plant	*Physalis alkekengi*	Hardy perennial	Hollyhock	*Alcea rosea*	Hardy perennial
Chive	*Allium schoenoprasum*	Hardy perennial herb	Honesty	*Lunaria annua*	Hardy biennial
Clarkia	*Clarkia* spp.	Annuals; grown from seed	Iris	*Iris* spp.	Hardy perennial rhizome; also propagated by seed
Clematis	*Clematis* spp.	Hardy perennials; climbers	Iris, scarlet-seeded; iris, stinking	*Iris foetidissima*	Very interesting pods
Columbine	*Aquilegia* spp.	Hardy perennials	Jerusalem sage	*Phlomis fruticosa*	Hardy shrub
Cress, American; cress, early winter	*Barbarea verna*	Edible hardy perennial	Joe-Pye-weed	*Eupatorium purpureum*	Hardy perennial weed

continued

COMMON NAME	BOTANICAL NAME	PLANT TYPE	COMMON NAME	BOTANICAL NAME	PLANT TYPE
Knapweed	*Centaurea* spp.	Perennial and annual weeds	Red-hot-poker	*Kniphofia uvaria*	Hardy perennial
Knotweed	*Polygonum* spp.	Hardy annual weeds	Rhododendron	*Rhododendron* spp. & var.	Hardy shrubs
Larkspur	*Consolida regalis*	Hardy annual	Rose-of-Sharon	*Hibiscus syriacus*	Hardy shrub
Leek, garden	*Allium ampeloprasum* (Porrum Group)	Biennial vegetable	Rose-of-Sharon	*Hypericum calycinum*	Hardy perennial shrub
Love-in-a-mist; wild fennel	*Nigella damascena*	Hardy annual	Rue, common	*Rutagraveolens*	Hardy perennial shrub
Lily	*Lilium* spp.	Hardy and half-hardy bulbs	Rush	*Juncus* spp.	Hardy perennials
Lupine	*Lupinus* spp. & var.	Hardy perennials and annuals	Sage, mealy-cup	*Salvia farinacea*	Half-hardy annual
Mallow	*Malva* spp.	Hardy perennials	Sedge	*Carex* spp.	Hardy perennials
Milkweed	*Asclepias* spp.	Hardy and half-hardy perennials	Shepherd's-purse	*Capsella bursa-pastoris*	Hardy annual, common weed
Okra	*Abelmoschus esculentus*	Half-hardy perennial	Squill	*Scilla* spp.	Hardy bulbs
Onion	*Allium cepa*	Hardy perennial; grown as an annual	Snapdragon, common	*Antirrhinum majus*	Half-hardy annual
Onion, edible	*Allium* spp.	Onions, leeks, chives, etc.	Sorrel; dock	*Rumex* spp.	Hardy perennials; wild, edible
Onion, ornamental	*Allium* spp.	Hardy perennials	St.-John's-wort	*Hypericum* spp.	Hardy perennial
Onion, wild	*Allium* spp.	Hardy perennials	Sweet Cicely; myrrh	*Myrrhis odorata*	Hardy perennial herb
Orach	*Atriplex hortensis*	Hardy annual	Tansy, common	*Tanacetum vulgare*	Hardy perennial herb
Peony, common garden	*Paeonia lactiflora* var.	Hardy perennial	Teasel	*Dipsacus sativus*	Hardy biennial
Pincushions	*Scabiosa atropurpurea* var.	Hardy annual	Thistle	*Cirsium* spp.	Mostly biennials
Poppy	*Papaver* spp. & var.	Hardy annuals, biennials, and perennials	Tulip	*Tulipa* spp. & var.	Hardy bulbs
Queen-Anne's-lace	*Daucus carota*	Hardy biennial	Witch hazel	*Hamamelis* spp.	Hardy trees
Queen-of-the-meadow	*Filipendula ulmaria*	Hardy perennial	Yucca	*Yucca* spp.	Hardy and half-hardy perennials

Source: *Flowers That Last Forever,* Betty E.M. Jacobs

PLANTS THAT AIR DRY WELL

COMMON NAME	BOTANICAL NAME	DRYING TIPS	COMMON NAME	BOTANICAL NAME	DRYING TIPS
Ageratum	*Ageratum*	Blue & white flowers dry well	Dusty Miller	*Artemisia stellerana*	Foliage dries well
Bear's-breech	*Acanthus*	Dry flowers and foliage	False dragonhead; obedience	*Physostegia virginiana*	Dry calyx-covered runners
Bird-of-paradise	*Strelitzia reginae*	Dry flowers	False goat's-beard	*Astilbe biternata*	Dry when blooms open at base
Blanket flower	*Gaillardia aristata*	Dry flowers	Goldenrod	*Solidago*	Dry before flowers fully mature
Blazing-star	*Liatris spicata*	Dry when flowers at top of spike are open	Heath	*Erica*	Dry before flowers fully mature
Blue lace flower	*Trachymene coerulea*	Dry when flowers are fully open	Heather	*Calluna*	Dry before flowers fully mature
Box, common	*Buxus sempervirens*	Dry foliage	Hop, common	*Humulus lupulus*	Dry foliage & flowers
Broom	*Cytisus*	Tie stems in curves while drying	Hydrangea	*Hydrangea paniculata*	Cut before frost when green or pinkish
Broom	*Genista*	Tie stems in curves while drying	Hydrangea, florist's; hydrangea, French	*Hydrangea macrophylla*	Cut in fall after color changes
Broom, Scotch	*Cytisus scopanus*	Best broom for holding curves	Lady's-mantle	*Alchemilla*	Cut flowers when mature
Candle larkspur	*Delphinium elatum*	Dry before lowest flower is open	Lamb's-ears	*Stachys byzantina*	Dry the wooly foliage
Chrysanthemum	*Chrysanthemum*	For pom-poms	Larkspur	*Consolida regalis*	Cut stems when flowers open
Clary sage	*Salvia sclarea*	Dry flowers and foliage	Lavender	*Lavandula*	Dry when all flowers on spike open
Coneflower	*Rudbeckia*	Remove petals, dry centers	Lavender cotton	*Santolina chamaecyparissus*	Silver foliage dries well
Cornflower; bachelor's-button	*Centaurea cyanus*	Wire, then dry buds & immature flowers	Mimosa	*Acacia dealbata*	Flowers dry well; remove foliage

continued

PLANTS THAT AIR DRY WELL (CONTINUED)

COMMON NAME	BOTANICAL NAME	DRYING TIPS	COMMON NAME	BOTANICAL NAME	DRYING TIPS
Montebretia	*Crocosmia crocosmiiflora*	Flowers dry well	Rue, common	*Ruta graveolens*	Gray-green foliage retains scent
Oats	*Avena sativa*	Turns beige when dry	Rush	*Juncus* spp.	Cut sparingly in the wild
Onions; leeks; garlic; chives; etc.	*Allium* spp.	Leeks especially	Sage, blue; mealy-cup sage	*Salvia farinacea*	Flowers and foliage dry well
Peony	*Paeonia* spp.	Double white, pink, and red dry best	Sedge	*Carex* spp.	Cut sparingly in the wild
Pincushions	*Scabiosa atropurpurea*	Cut when petals have fallen	Silver-dollar gum	*Eucalyptus polyanthemos*	One of the many florist's varieties
Plantain lily	*Hosta* spp.	Dry foliage	Silver king artemisia	*Artemisia ludoviciana albula*	Dry foliage
Protea; king protea	*Protea cynaroides*	Dry white, red, bicolored	Silver-leaved mountain gum	*Eucalyptus pulverulenta*	One of the many florist 's varieties
Pussy willow	*Salix caprea, S. discolor*	Cut before catkins are open	Sweet corn; Indian corn	*Zea mays*	Dry leaves and tassels at all stages
Queen-Anne's-lace	*Daucus carota*	Cut just before white flowers mature	Sweet-sultan	*Centaurea moschata*	Flowers are thistlelike and fragrant
Ravenna grass	*Erianthus ravennae*	Cut before seeds mature	Tansy, common	*Tanacetum vulgare*	Dry compact yellow flower heads
Rocket larkspur	*Consolida ambigua*	Dry foliage and flower buds	Wheat, common	*Triticum aestivum*	Cut at different stages of development
Rosemary	*Rosmarinus officinalis*	Retains its fragrance when dried	Zinnia	*Zinnia* spp.	Dry mature yellow, green, and white flowers

Source: *Flowers That Last Forever,* Betty E.M. Jacobs

Plants That Can Be Preserved in Glycerine

COMMON NAME	BOTANICAL NAME	COMMENTS	COMMON NAME	BOTANICAL NAME	COMMENTS
Barberry	*Berberis* spp.	Wild and cultivated species	Ivy	*Hedera* spp. & var.	Immerse strands to preserve
Bay	*Lauris nobilis*	Kitchen herb	Laurel, Japanese	*Aucuba japonica*	Not to be confused with Bay
Beech	*Fagus* spp.		Laurel, mountain	*Kalmia latifolia*	Not to be confused with Bay
Bells-of-Ireland	*Moluccella laevis*	Total immersion is best	Laurel, Portugal	*Prunus lusitanica*	Not to be confused with Bay
Blackberry; dewberry	*Rubus macropetalus*	Wild and cultivated plants	Lime tree; linden	*Tilia* spp.	Flowers and bracts preserve well
Box; boxwood	*Buxus* spp.	Turns golden-yellow	Lily-of-the-valley	*Convallaria majalis*	Immerse leaves only in solution
Bracken	*Pteridium aquilinum*	A fern; rewarding to preserve	Magnolia	*Magnolia* spp.	
Broom, Scotch	*Cytisus scoparius*		Maple	*Acer* spp.	Many species, Japanese maple esp.
Camellia, common	*Camellia japonica*		Montebretia	*Crocosmia crocosmiiflora*	Preserve the seed heads
Clematis	*Clematis* spp.	Garden and wild species	Oak	*Quercus* spp.	
Cotoneaster	*Cotoneaster* spp.	Hardy deciduous shrubs	Old-man's-beard	*Clematis vitalba*	This is the wild clematis
Dogwood	*Cornus* spp.	Illegal to pick in the wild	Oregon grape	*Mahonia aquifolium*	
Dock	*Rumex* spp.	Common weeds	Peony	*Paeonia officinalis*	Mature foliage and seed heads
Elaeagnus	*Elaeagnus* spp.	Use evergreen species	Prunus	*Prunus* spp.	Especially the dark-leaved varieties
Eucalyptus	*Eucalyptus* spp.	Especially the "florist's variety"	Rhododendron; azalea	*Rhododendron* spp. & var.	Submerge individual leaves
Forsythia; golden-bells	*Forsythia* spp.		Rosemary	*Rosmarinus officinalis*	Retains its perfume
Hawthorn	*Crataegus* spp.		Rowan	*Sorbus aucuparia*	Leaves and berries can be preserved
Heath	*Erica* spp.		Rue, common	*Ruta graveolens*	One of the bitter herbs
Heather	*Calluna* spp.		Salal	*Gaultheria shallon*	Found in northwestern coastal forests
Holly	*Ilex* spp.	Most species & cultivars will preserve	Viburnum; arrowwood	*Viburnum* spp.	Ornamental shrubs
Hop, common	*Humulus lupulus*		Willow	*Salix* spp.	*S. tortuosa* has an interesting form
Hydrangea	*Hydrangea paniculata*				

continued

Plants That Can Be Preserved in Glycerine (continued)

PLANT MATERIAL PRESERVED IN GLYCERINE — SOME DOs AND DON'Ts

DO store it in an upright position, whenever possible, in an area that is neither damp nor too warm.

DO store leaves, which have been preserved individually, between sheets of tissue paper.

DO wipe off any condensation that forms on the foliage, then wash it in warm water and dry it with a soft cloth. **DO** this and you will prevent mildew from forming on it.

DO store glycerine-preserved material by itself. If stored with dried-plant material, that dry material could absorb moisture from it.

DON'T put silica gel in any container containing glycerine-preserved material.

DON'T store it in airtight containers. If it is stored in cardboard boxes, **DO** make air holes in them.

Source: *Flowers That Last Forever,* Betty E.M. Jacobs

Wildflowers That Air Dry Well

Bergamot
Black-eyed Susan
Butterfly weed
Cattail
Dock
Goldenrod
Joe-Pye weed
Milkweed
Mullein
Pearly everlasting
Pussy willow
Tansy
Teasel

Plants with Attractive Seed Pods for Dried Arrangements

Bittersweet
Chinese lantern
Columbine
Delphinium
Globe thistle
Honesty
Iris
Lily
Poppy
Conifers

Source: *The Flower Arranger's Garden,* Patricia R. Barrett

FLOWERS THAT DRY WELL IN SILICA GEL

Aster	Clematis	Forget-me-not, garden	Lavender cotton	Poppy
Azalea	Columbine	Forsythia; golden-bells	Lily	Primrose, English
Bells-of-Ireland	Coneflower	Foxglove	Lily, African	Queen-Anne's-lace
Bird-of-paradise	Cornflower; bachelor's button	Freesia	Lily-of-the-valley	Rhododendron
Bleeding-heart	Crocus	Fuchsia	Love-in-a-mist	Rose
Blue lace flower	Cup-and-saucer vine; Mexican ivy	Gentian	Marigold	Snow-on-the-mountain
Blue sage	Daffodil	Gentian sage	Marigold, pot	Stock, evening
Buttercup, common	Dahlia, annual and perennial	Geranium	Marguerite; daisy, Paris	Sunflower, common
Buttercup, double	Daisy, African	Gladiolus	Marsh mallow	Tickseed
Butterfly bush	Daisy, English	Globe thistle, small	Mimosa	Tulip
Camellia, common	Daisy, gloriosa	Grape hyacinth	Mock orange	Verbena, garden
Candytuft	Daisy, Paris; Marguerite	Heath	Mexican sunflower	Veronica; speedwell
Canterbury-bells	Daisy, shasta	Heather	Pansy; violet	Violet, sweet
Carnation	Daisy, Transvaal	Hollyhock	Pasque flower	Water lily, European white
Chamomile	Delphinium	Hyacinth, common	Peony	Windflower
Christmas rose	Dogwood	Hydrangea	Phlox	Yarrow
Chrysanthemum	Edelweiss	Larkspur	Pincushions	Zinnia
Clary sage	Feverfew	Lavender	Pinks	

Source: *Flowers That Last Forever,* Betty E.M. Jacobs

Bulbs

Types of Fleshy-Rooted Plants

BULBS		CORMS	TUBERS AND TUBEROUS ROOTS AND STEMS		RHIZOMES
Amaryllis	Iris (bulbous)	Crocus	Anemone	Cyclamen	Bird-of-paradise
Daffodil	Lily	Colchicum	Begonia (tuberous)	Dahlia	Canna
Glory-of-the-snow *(Chionodoxa)*	Scilla	Freesia	Black callus	Desert candle	Calla lily
	Snowdrop	Gladiolus	Bleeding heart	Gloxinia	Iris
Grape hyacinth *(Muscari)*	Trout lily	Tritoma	Caladium		Lily-of-the-valley
	Tuberose				Mint
Hyacinth	Tulip				Rhubarb

Source: *Secrets of Plant Propagation,* Lewis Hill

Bulbs for Greenhouses and Sunspaces

NAME	PLANTING TIME	PLANTING DEPTH	GROWING CONDITIONS	PROPAGATION	COMMENTS
Achimenes, see Gloxinia					
Amaryllis *Amaryllidaceae Hippeastrum*	September-October for February-March (treated bulbs for January)	Half bulb depth	60-70°F (min 55°F). Full sun. Feed after flowering.	Detach 1½ " offsets as growth begins. Grow on, will flower when 3-3½ ". Sow seed in March (60-65°F), takes 2-8 years to bloom.	Keep fairly dry after leaves yellow, very dry if below 55°F. Water sparingly when new growth appears, usually early winter. Water more after bud appears.
Anemone *Ranunculaceae Anemone*	September-October for January-March	2"	50°F (60°F when in flower). Full sun.	Sow seed in late summer, takes several years to bloom.	Needs good drainage. Water sparingly until growing well. Reduce water in winter.
Crocus *Iridaceae Crocus*	September-October for December-February (8-10 weeks in dark plus 2-4 in light)	Just cover corm.	35-45°F in darkness until well rooted. Then 50°F in full sun.	Offsets will bloom the following year. Sow seed in summer, takes 2-4 years to bloom.	Winter-flowering varieties will be ready first. Species crocus have smaller but more plentiful flowers than hybrids. Do not try to mix colors as they are likely to bloom at different times. Chionodoxa, snowdrops, and scillas can be grown like crocuses.

continued

NAME	PLANTING TIME	PLANTING DEPTH	GROWING CONDITIONS	PROPAGATION	COMMENTS
Cyclamen *Primulaceae* *Cyclamen*	August for winter	Leave half of corm showing.	Day, 55-65°F, night, 50-55°F. Good, indirect light or partial sun. Use ordinary potting mix. Maintain humidity, especially if over 65°F.	Sow seed in August or September (60°F). Takes up to 2 months to sprout, 15-18 months to bloom. Can take leaf cuttings with a bit of corm attached.	Keep moist but provide good drainage and avoid wetting corm. Keep fairly dry and allow to rest after blooming in August, as new leaves appear, repot if necessary and begin watering to restart growth. Do not feed if repotted. Twist off faded leaves and flowers to remove all of stalk.
Daffodil, see Narcissus					
Freesia *Iridaceae* *Freesia*	August-November for December-April	1"	Day, 65°F, night 50°F (min 45°F). Full sun.	Sow seed in spring (60°F). Do not transplant. Takes 9-12 months to bloom.	Water sparingly until buds appear. Best discarded after blooming. Support leaves and flowers with canes or grow in hanging baskets.
Gloxinia and Achimenes *Gesneriaceae* *Sinningia speciosa* *Achimenes*	January-April for summer	Gloxinia crown level with surface. Achimines 3-4 rhizomes per 4" pot. Lay horizontally ½" below surface.	Day 65-75°F, night 65°F. (min 60°F, max 70°F). Partial shade or good indirect light. Water well. Maintain humidity. Give high potash feed after flowering. Use ½ peat, ½ vermiculite mix with extra lime. 5" pot.	Divide tubers of rhizomes in March. Root 2-4" stem cuttings in June with sliver of tuber attached. Or take leaf cuttings of gloxinias nicking the main veins and laying flat on peat-sand mix. Sow gloxinia seed in fall or winter (70°F) in light. Takes 6-9 months.	Needs humid warm atmosphere, but avoid wetting leaves. Gradually dry off when leaves yellow, then store at 50-60°F, in darkness. Repot and begin watering sparingly in early spring.
Hyacinth *Liliaceae* *Hyacinthus*	Prepared bulbs: September-November for December-February. Unprepared bulbs: October for March-April (both bloom 3-5 weeks after being brought into light).	Leave tip of bulb showing	35-45°F in darkness until well rooted and buds showing, usually 10-14 weeks. Then 50°F for 10 days in semishade. Then 55-60°F in full sun till blooms; then 60°F.		Specially prepared bulbs should be used for very early flowers. Can be grown in sand, sand and peat, bulb fiber, pebbles, or just water. Large flowers will need staking. Bulbs grown in soil can be planted outdoors (6" deep) after flowering. Grape hyacinths are more difficult to grow.

NAME	PLANTING TIME	PLANTING DEPTH	GROWING CONDITIONS	PROPAGATION	COMMENTS
Iris *Iridaceae* *Iris reticulata* and others	November-January for February-April	Leave tip of bulb showing	40-50°F until buds color, then 60-65°F.	Divide tubers after leaves die back. Offsets will bloom in 1-3 years.	Buy specially treated bulbs for forcing. Not as easy to grow as hyacinths and narcissi.
Lily-of-the-Valley *Liliaceae* *Convallaria* *majalis*	October-November for February-March	Leave tip of bulb showing.	40-50°F until January then 60-70°F. Partial shade.		Buy specially prepared pips for forcing. Keep moist.
Narcissus *Amaryllidaceae* *Narcissus*	September-November for December-March (Tazettas 5-8 weeks after planting; others 8-10 weeks in dark, plus 3-4 weeks in light).	Leave tip of bulb showing.	35-45°F in darkness (except Tazettas, which can be placed in cold, sunny place immediately) until well rooted, then 50-55°F in full sun till bloom, then 60°F.	Offsets will bloom in 1-2 years. Sow seed in summer when ripe; takes 3-7 years to bloom; usually poor quality.	Buy specially prepared bulbs for very early flowers. Tazetta narcissi (with several flowers on one stalk, e.g., Paper white or Soleil d'Or) will bloom sooner than others. Plant in sand, gravel, bulb fiber, or soil. Keep some in dark longer for succession of blooms. Flowers may need staking if too hot, last longer if cool. After blooming hardy varieties potted in soil can be grown on, gradually drying off as leaves yellow, then planted outside (6" deep).
Tuberose *Agavaceae* *Polianthes* *tuberosa*	Plant late autumn or winter. Keep frost free. Tubers will wait till 60-65°F to sprout.	1" deep, 3 in a 7" pot.	65-80°F after leaves appear. Full sun.	Offsets, but unlikely to bloom.	3' tall, extremely fragrant and beautiful flowers. Buy tubers and discard after flowering. Plant in moist soil, but don't water unless bone dry until leaves appear.
Tulip *Liliaceae* *Tulipa*	September-October for January-February (8-12 weeks in dark, plus 3-5 weeks in light).	Leave tip of bulb showing. Put flat side of bulb toward outside of pot.	35-45°F in darkness until well rooted, usually 6-10 weeks, then 50-60°F in full sun.	Some produce offsets that will bloom 2-3 years. Sow seed in summer to bloom in 5-7 years; usually poor quality.	Single and double earlies will bloom soonest and are easiest to force.

Source: *Sunspaces,* Peter Clegg & Derry Watkins

Spring-Flowering Bulbs

FLOWER	HEIGHT	BLOOMING TIME	PLANTING DEPTH
Snowdrop	4-6"	Early spring	4"
Crocus	3-5"	Early spring	3-4"
Anemone blanda (Wildflower)	5"	Early spring	2"
Grape hyacinth (Muscari)	6-10"	Early spring	3"
Early tulips	10-13"	Early spring	6"
Hyacinth	12"	Early spring	6"
Daffodil	12"	Midspring	6"
Darwin hybrid tulips	28"	Midspring	6"
Crown imperial *(Fritillaria imperialis)*	30-48"	Midspring	5"
Late tulips	36"	Late spring	6"
Dutch iris	24"	Late spring	4"
Allium giganteum	48"	Late spring	10"

Source: *Landscaping with Bulbs,* Ann Reilly

Summer-Flowering Bulbs

FLOWER	HEIGHT	PLANTING TIME	PLANTING DEPTH	SPACING
Acidanthera	20"	Early spring	2"	5"
Anemones de Caen, St. Brigid	18"	South, Sept.-Jan. North, Early spring	2"	3"
Dahlia large varieties	48"	After last frost	4"	24"
dwarf varieties	12"		4"	6"
Galtonia	40"	April-May	5"	10"
Gladiolus large flowering	60"	April-mid June	3-4"	6"
small flowering	30"		3-4"	6"
Lily	3-7'	Fall or early spring	8"	8"
Montbretia	24"	April-end of May	4"	4"
Ranunculus	12"	South, Sept.-Jan.	2"	8"
Tigridia	16"	Early spring	3"	6"

Ground Covers and Ornamental Grasses

Ground Covers

| GROUND COVER | CONDITIONS | | | | CHARACTERISTICS | | | | | |
	SUN OR SHADE	WATER REQRMNTS	SOIL TYPE	SPACING	HEIGHT	FOLIAGE TYPE	GROWTH RATE	FLOWER COLOR	FRUIT COLOR	EROSION CONTROL
Aegopodium podagraria 'Variegatum'	S-PS	All	All	6-15"	8-12"	H	F	W	–	*
Ajuga, all	All	D-M	All	12-18"	6"	H	F	Bu-Pr	–	–
Campsis radicans	All	M	All	3'	18-24"	H	F	O-R	–	–
Celastrus scandens (vine)	All	D-M	L	3'	4-6'	D	R	Y-W	O	–
Ceratostigma plumbaginoides	S-PS	D-M	SL	12-18"	1'	H	F	Bu	–	–
Cornus sericea 'Kelseyi'	S-PS	M-W	L	18-24"	2'	D	M	W	W	–
Cotoneaster, low types	S-PS	M	L	18-36"	1-3'	D	F	W-Pk	R-O	*
Euonymus fortunei and cvs	All	D-M	All	6-24"	1-3'	E	F	W	R-O	*
Forsythia suspensa and cvs	S-PS	M	L	18-30"	4-6'	D	F	Y	–	*
Genista x 'Lydia'	S	D-M	S-L	18-24"	1'	D	M	Y	–	–
Grasses, ornamental	S-PS	All	All	1-6'	V	V	M-F	V	V	*
Hedera helix and cvs	All	M	All	8-12"	6-8"	E	S-M	–	–	*
Hemerocallis, all	S-PS	D-M	All	18-24"	1-4"	H	M	V	–	*
Hosta, all	All	M-W	All	18-24"	1-3'	H	M	V	–	*
Houttuynia cordata 'Chameleon'	All	M-W	All	12-18"	6"	H	R	W	–	*

Key:

CONDITIONS
SUN OR SHADE: S = Sun, PS = Partial Shade, Sh = Shade,
    All = Sun through Shade
WATER REQUIREMENTS: D = Dry, M = Moist, but well drained,
    W = Wet, All = Dry through Wet
SOIL TYPE: S = Sand, L = Loam, All = Sand through Clay
SPACING IS DETERMINED BY THE SIZE OF THE PLANT USED:
Examples: Rooted Cutting = 6-12", Peat Pot = 12-18", Container = 18-36"

CHARACTERISTICS
FOLIAGE TYPE: H = Herbaceous, D = Deciduous, S = Semi-Evergreen,
    E = Evergreen, C = Coniferous
GROWTH RATE: S = Slow, M = Medium, F = Fast, R = Rampant
FLOWER, FRUIT, AUTUMN & WINTER COLORS IF SHOWY: W = White, Pk = Pink,
    R = Red, O = Orange, Y = Yellow, Br = Brown, Bu = Blue, Bk = Black, Bz = Bronze,
    Gn = Green, Gy = Gray, Pr = Purple, L = Lavender, V = Varies, according to variety,
    F = Fragrant

continued

GROUND COVERS (CONTINUED)

GROUND COVER	CONDITIONS				CHARACTERISTICS						
	SUN OR SHADE	WATER REQRMNTS	SOIL TYPE	SPACING	HEIGHT	FOLIAGE TYPE	GROWTH RATE	FLOWER COLOR	FRUIT COLOR	EROSION CONTROL
Hydrangea petiolaris (vine)	S-PS	M	All	3'	1'	D	F	W	–	*
Hypericum, most	S	D-M	S-L	6-24"	1-3'	D	F	Y	–	–
Itea spp.	S-PS	M	S-L	3'	2-3'	D	F	W	–	*
Juniperus, low types	S	D-M	All	2-4'	4"-3'	E	M-F	–	Bu	*
Lavandula, all	S	D-M	S-L	12-18"	1'	H-D	M	L	–	*
Leucothoe, most	S-PS	M	S-L	2-4'	2-4'	E	F	W	–	–
Ligustrum obtusifolium regelianum	All	M	All	2-5'	5-6'	D	F	W	Bu-Bk	–
Liriope, all	S-PS	D-M	S-L	12-18"	2'	H	S-M	L-Bu	–	*
Lonicera x *brownii* 'Dropmore Scarlet' (vine)	S-PS	M	L	3'	30"	D	M-F	R	–	*
japonica 'Halliana' (vine)	S-PS	M	All	18"-3'	2'	D	R	Y-W	–	*
pileata	S-PS	M	S-L	1-2'	1'	D	M	Y-W	Pr	*
xylosteum 'Emerald Mound'	S-PS	M	All	2'	2-3'	D	M	Y-W	R	–
Mahonia aquifolium	All	D-M	S-L	2-3'	3-6'	S	M	Y	Bu	*
Microbiota decussata	All	D-M	S-L	2-4'	1'	E	M	–	–	*
Ophiopogon p. cv. 'Ebknizam'-Ebony Knight®	S	D-M	S-L	6-12"	6"	H	S	–	Bk	*

Key:

<u>CONDITIONS</u>

SUN OR SHADE: S = Sun, PS = Partial Shade, Sh = Shade,
  All = Sun through Shade
WATER REQUIREMENTS: D = Dry, M = Moist, but well drained,
  W = Wet, All = Dry through Wet
SOIL TYPE: S = Sand, L = Loam, All = Sand through Clay
SPACING IS DETERMINED BY THE SIZE OF THE PLANT USED:
Examples: Rooted Cutting = 6-12", Peat Pot = 12-18", Container = 18-36"

<u>CHARACTERISTICS</u>

FOLIAGE TYPE: H = Herbaceous, D = Deciduous, S = Semi-Evergreen,
  E = Evergreen, C = Coniferous
GROWTH RATE: S = Slow, M = Medium, F = Fast, R = Rampant
FLOWER, FRUIT, AUTUMN & WINTER COLORS IF SHOWY: W = White, Pk = Pink,
  R = Red, O = Orange, Y = Yellow, Br = Brown, Bu = Blue, Bk = Black, Bz = Bronze,
  Gn = Green, Gy = Gray, Pr = Purple, L = Lavender, V = Varies, according to variety,
  F = Fragrant

continued

Ground Covers (continued)

GROUND COVER	CONDITIONS				CHARACTERISTICS					
	SUN OR SHADE	WATER REQRMNTS	SOIL TYPE	SPACING	HEIGHT	FOLIAGE TYPE	GROWTH RATE	FLOWER COLOR	FRUIT COLOR	EROSION CONTROL
Pachysandra terminalis and cvs	All	M	All	6-12"	6"	E	S	W	–	*
Parthenocissus tricuspidata (vine)	S-PS	M	All	2-4'	18"	D	F	Gn-W	–	*
Polygonum spp.	S-PS	M	S-L	1-3'	V	D	R	V	–	–
Potentilla, most	S	D-M	S-L	18-24"	2-3'	D	M	V	–	–
Prunux x cv. 'Snofozam'-Snow Fountains	S	M	All	4-6'	2-3'	D	F	W	–	–
Rhus aromatic a and cvs	S-PS	D	All	2-3'	2-3'	D	F	Gn-Y	R	*
Rosa wichuraiana and cvs	S	M	S-L	18"-3'	10"	D	F	W	–	*
Salix x *cottetii* 'Bankers'	S-PS	M-W	All	18"-4'	3-6'	D	F-R	–	–	*
purpurea 'Streamco'	S-PS	M-W	All	18"-6'	12-15"	D	F-R	–	–	*
Spiraea japonica and cvs	S	M	All	6-12"	12-15"	D	M	Pk	–	–
nipponica and cvs	S-PS	M	All	2-3'	3-5'	D	M	W	–	–
Stephanandra incisa 'Crispa'	S-PS	M	All	18-24"	2-3'	D	F	Y-W	–	*
Symphoricarpos x *chenaultii* 'Hancock'	All	M	All	18-24"	2'	D	F	Pk	Pk	*
Taxus baccata repandens	All	M	All	3'	2-4'	E	S-M	–	R	–
Vinca minor and cvs	All	M	All	6-12"	6"	E	F	L-Bu	–	*

Key:

CONDITIONS
SUN OR SHADE: S = Sun, PS = Partial Shade, Sh = Shade,
  All = Sun through Shade
WATER REQUIREMENTS: D = Dry, M = Moist, but well drained,
  W = Wet, All = Dry through Wet
SOIL TYPE: S = Sand, L = Loam, All = Sand through Clay
SPACING IS DETERMINED BY THE SIZE OF THE PLANT USED:
Examples: Rooted Cutting = 6-12", Peat Pot = 12-18", Container = 18-36"

CHARACTERISTICS
FOLIAGE TYPE: H = Herbaceous, D = Deciduous, S = Semi-Evergreen,
  E = Evergreen, C = Coniferous
GROWTH RATE: S = Slow, M = Medium, F = Fast, R = Rampant
FLOWER, FRUIT, AUTUMN & WINTER COLORS IF SHOWY: W = White, Pk = Pink,
  R = Red, O = Orange, Y = Yellow, Br = Brown, Bu = Blue, Bk = Black, Bz = Bronze,
  Gn = Green, Gy = Gray, Pr = Purple, L = Lavender, V = Varies, according to variety,
  F = Fragrant

Source: Reprinted with permission of James W. Zampini of Lake County Nursery, Inc. Copyright 1986-1992.

GROUND COVERS FOR SMALL GARDENS

COMMON NAME	BOTANICAL NAME	LIGHT REQUIREMENTS	HARDINESS ZONES*
Baby's tears	*Soleirolia soleirolii*	Shade	9
Bearberry	*Arctostaphylos* spp.	Sun	7-10
Bugleweed	*Ajuga* spp.	Partial or full shade	2
Campanula	*Campanula* spp.	Partial or full shade	3-6
Corsican mint	*Mentha requienni*		7
Creeping thyme	*Thymus* spp.	Sun	4-5
Honeysuckle	*Lonicera* spp.	Sun	3-7
Ice plant	*Mesembryanthemum* spp.	Sun	10
Spike moss	*Selaginella* spp.	Sun/Partial shade	10
Pachysandra	*Pachysandra* spp.	Partial to full shade	4-5
Periwinkle	*Vinca* spp.	Partial to full shade	4-7
St.-John's-wort	*Hypericum* spp.	Sun/Partial shade	3-7
Sedum	*Sedum* spp.	Sun	2-10
Star jasmine	*Trachelospermum jasminoides*	Sun	8

* Chart shows coldest hardiness zone tolerated by a species. Where a specific species is not named on the chart, look for a species appropriate to the hardiness range indicated.

Source: *The Able Gardener,* Kathleen Yeomans, R.N.

ORNAMENTAL GRASSES

| ORNAMENTAL GRASS | CONDITIONS | | | | CHARACTERISTICS | | | | | | |
	SUN OR SHADE	WATER REQRMNTS	SOIL TYPE	SPACING	HEIGHT	TEXTURE	GROWTH HABIT	FOLIAGE COLOR	FLOWER COLOR	WINTER EFFECT	EROSION CONTROL
Calamagrostis x *acutifolia* 'Karl Foerster'	S-PS	D-M	S-L	2-3'	5-6'	M	N-U	Gn	R-Bz	*	–
Carex buchananii	S	M	L	1-2'	2'	F	U-N	Bz	B	*	–
morrowii 'Aurea-variegata'	S	M	L	<1'	F	A-C	Y-Gn	–	–	–	
Chasmanthium latifolium	S-PS	D-M	L	18-30"	2-3'	M	UA-N	Gn	Gn-Bz	*	–
Deschampsia caespitosa 'Goldgehaenge'	All	D-M	L	2-3'	1-3'	F-M	UA-O	Gn	W-Gn	–	–
Deschampsia 'Viviparia'	All	D-M	L	2-3'	18-24"	F-M	UA-O	Gn	W-Gn	–	–
Elymus arenaria	S	M-W	S-L	1-2'	2'	C	O-C	Bu	B-Gn	–	*
Erianthus ravennae	S	D-M	L	3-5'	<12'	C	U-O	Gn	W	*	*
Festuca cinerea 'Blaufuchs'	S-PS	D-M	S-L	9-15"	<1'	F	T-C	Bu-Gy	–	*	–
Festuca ovina glauca 'Elijah Blue'	S-PS	D-M	L	12-15"	8-10'	F	M	Bu	–	*	–
Glyceria maxima 'Variegata'	S-PS	D-M	S-L	18-30"	2-3'	F-M	M	Gn-Y	W	*	–
Helictotrichon sempervirens	S-PS	D-M	S-L	18-30"	2-3'	F-M	T-M	Bu-Gy	B-Br	*	–
Imperata cylindrica 'Red Baron'	S-PS	M	L	1-2'	12-18"	M	U-C	R	B	–	

Key:

CONDITIONS

SUN OR SHADE: S = Sun, PS = Partial Shade, Sh = Shade,
  All = Sun through Shade
WATER REQUIREMENTS: D = Dry, M = Moist, but well drained,
  W = Wet, All = Dry through Wet
SOIL TYPE: S = Sand, L = Loam, All = Sand through Clay
SPACING IS DETERMINED BY THE SIZE OF THE PLANT USED:
  Examples: Rooted Cutting = 6-12", Peat Pot = 12-18",
  Container = 18-36"

CHARACTERISTICS

FOLIAGE TYPE: H = Herbaceous, D = Deciduous, S = Semi-Evergreen, E = Evergreen,
  C = Coniferous
TEXTURE: C = Coarse, M = Medium, F = Fine
GROWTH HABIT: A = Arching, C = Clump, M = Mound, N = Narrow, O = Open, T = Tufted,
  U = Upright
FLOWER, FRUIT, AUTUMN & WINTER COLORS IF SHOWY: W = White, Pk = Pink, R = Red,
  O = Orange, Y = Yellow, Br = Brown, Bu = Blue, Bk = Black, Bz = Bronze, Gn = Green, Gy = Gray,
  Pr = Purple, L = Lavender, V = Varies, according to variety, F = Fragrant, B = Beige

continued

| ORNAMENTAL GRASS | CONDITIONS | | | | CHARACTERISTICS | | | | | | |
	SUN OR SHADE	WATER REQRMNTS	SOIL TYPE	SPACING	HEIGHT	TEXTURE	GROWTH HABIT	FOLIAGE COLOR	FLOWER COLOR	WINTER EFFECT	EROSION CONTROL
Miscanthus sinensis 'Giganteus'	S-PS	D-M	S-L	3-5'	8-10'	M	U-A	Gn	W	*	*
s. 'Gracillimus'	S-PS	D-M	L	3-5'	3-6'	F	U-A	Gn-W	R-Pk	*	*
s. 'Morning Light'	S-PS	D-M	L	2-3'	4'	M	N-U	Gy-Gn-W	R-Pk	*	*
s. purpurascens	S	D-M	L	3-4'	3-4'	M	U-C	Bz	W	*	*
s. strictus	S-PS	D-M	L	2-3'	6'	M	N-U	G-Y	Y	*	*
s. 'Variegatus'	S	D-M	L	3-5'	3-6'	M	U-O	Gn-W	Pk	*	*
s. 'Zebrinus'	S	D-M	L	3-5'	4-7'	M	UN-O	Go-Y	Y-R	–	*
Ophiopogon planiscapus 'Ebknizam'-Ebony Knight®	S	D-M	S-L	6-9"	6"	M	O-M	Bk	Bk	–	–
Panicum virgatum	S	D-M	S-L	3-5'	3-6'	M	U-N	Gn	R-Pr	*	*
Panicum virgatum 'Haense Herms'	S	D-M	S-L	2-3'	4'	M-F	M	Gn	W-Pk	–	*
Pennisetum alopecuroids	S	D-M	S-L	3-5'	4'	M-F	M	Gn	Br-B	–	*
a. 'Hameln'	S-PS	D-M	S-L	18-24"	1-2'	M-F	M	Gn	Bz-B	–	*
a. 'Moudry'	S-PS	D-M	S-L	2-3'	3-4'	M-F	M	Gn	B	–	*
Phalaris arundinacea 'Picta'	S-PS	All	L	1-2'	1-2'	M	U-O	Gn-W	W-P	–	*

Key:

CONDITIONS
SUN OR SHADE: S = Sun, PS = Partial Shade, Sh = Shade,
  All = Sun through Shade
WATER REQUIREMENTS: D = Dry, M = Moist, but well drained,
  W = Wet, All = Dry through Wet
SOIL TYPE: S = Sand, L = Loam, All = Sand through Clay
SPACING IS DETERMINED BY THE SIZE OF THE PLANT USED:
  Examples: Rooted Cutting = 6-12", Peat Pot = 12-18",
  Container = 18-36"

CHARACTERISTICS
FOLIAGE TYPE: H = Herbaceous, D = Deciduous, S = Semi-Evergreen, E = Evergreen,
  C = Coniferous
TEXTURE: C = Coarse, M = Medium, F = Fine
GROWTH HABIT: A = Arching, C = Clump, M = Mound, N = Narrow, O = Open, T = Tufted,
  U = Upright
FLOWER, FRUIT, AUTUMN & WINTER COLORS IF SHOWY: W = White, Pk = Pink, R = Red,
  O = Orange, Y = Yellow, Br = Brown, Bu = Blue, Bk = Black, Bz = Bronze, Gn = Green, Gy = Gray,
  Pr = Purple, L = Lavender, V = Varies, according to variety, F = Fragrant, B = Beige

Wildflower and Grass Region Map

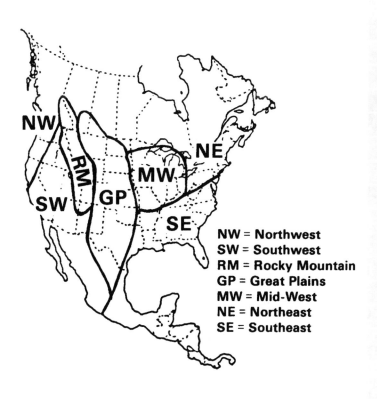

NW = Northwest
SW = Southwest
RM = Rocky Mountain
GP = Great Plains
MW = Mid-West
NE = Northeast
SE = Southeast

Some wildflowers are "hardy" and tolerate freezing temperatures, while others are "tender" and are killed by frosts. Take your local climate into consideration when selecting wildflowers, remembering that sunny southern slopes are usually warmer, and shady northern slopes may be substantially cooler, than the average climate of a region. For example, if you live in a northern region you may be able to grow more southerly wildflowers on south-facing, protected slopes.

Source: *Creating a Wildflower Meadow*, Henry W. Art

Varieties of Bunch Grass and Where They Grow Best

COMMON NAME	BOTANICAL NAME	NE	MW	SE	GP	RM	SW	NW
Big bluestem	*Andropogon gerardii*	X	X	X		X		
Blue grama	*Bouteloua gracilis*		X	X	X	X	X	
Broomsedge	*Andropogon virginicus*	X	X	X	X			
Buffalo grass	*Buchloe dactyloides*		X	X	X	X	X	
California oat grass	*Danthonia californica*					X	X	X
Tufted hair grass	*Deschampsia caespnosa*	X	X	X	X	X	X	X
Indian grass	*Sorghastrum nutans*	X	X	X	X		X	
Indian ricegrass	*Oryzopsis hymenoides*				X	X	X	X
June grass	*Koeleria cristata*		X	X	X	X	X	X
Little bluestem	*Andropogon scoparius*	X	X	X	X	X		
Needlegrass	*Stipa spartea*	X	X	X	X	X	X	X
Northern dropseed	*Sporobolus heterolepsis*	X	X	X	X	X		
Poverty three-awn	*Aristida divaricata*		X	X	X	X		
Sheep fescue	*Festuca ovina*	X	X	X	X	X	X	X
Side oats grama	*Bouteloua curtipendula*	X	X	X	X	X	X	
Silver bluestem	*Bothriochloa saccharoides*				X	X		X
Switch-grass	*Panicum virgatum*	X	X	X	X		X	
Western wheatgrass	*Agropyron smithii*	X	X	X	X	X	X	X

WILDFLOWERS

Hardiness Zones of Selected Wildflowers

COMMON NAME	1	2	3	4	5	6	7	8	9	10	COMMON NAME	1	2	3	4	5	6	7	8	9	10
Blue flax											Black-eyed Susan HA										
Bunchberry											Purple coneflower										
Pasqueflower											Mayapple										
Elephantheads											Purple prairie clover										
Canada anemone											Bloodroot										
Shinleaf											Culver's root										
Pink lady's slipper											Compass plant										
Larger blue flag											Wintergreen										
Purple trillium											Jack-in-the-pulpit										
False Solomon's seal											Eastern columbine										
Blanketflower											Turtlehead										
False dragonhead											Silky aster										
Cardinal flower											White trillium										
Platte River penstemon											Gayfeather										
Old-man-of-the-mountain											Wild bergamot										
Yellow fawn lily											Groundnut										
Closed gentian											Virginia bluebells										
Showy tick trefoil											Butterfly weed										
Leadplant											Eastern trout lily										
Yellow clintonia											Wood lily										
Colorado columbine											Wild leek										
Wild ginger											Rocky Mountain penstemon										
New England aster											Bear grass										
Dutchman's breeches											Giant evening primrose										
White baneberry											Bitterroot										
Sharp-lobed hepatica											Mule's ears										

continued

Hardiness Zones of Selected Wildflowers (continued)

COMMON NAME	1	2	3	4	5	6	7	8	9	10
Spring beauty				■	■	■	■	■		
Nodding wild onion				■	■	■	■	■		
Eastern shooting star				■	■	■	■	■		
Bluets				■	■	■	■	■		
Missouri evening primrose				■	■	■	■	■		
Desert mallow				■	■	■	■	■		
Goatsbeard				■	■	■	■	■		
Coralbells				■	■	■	■	■		
Pasture rose				■	■	■	■	■		
Lance-leaved coreopsis				■	■	■	■	■		
Partridgeberry				■	■	■	■	■		
Rattlesnake master				■	■	■	■	■		
Spiderwort					■	■	■	■		
Solomon's seal					■	■	■	■		
Meadow beauty					■	■	■	■		
Standing cypress						■	■	■		
Mexican hat				■	■	■	■	■		
Douglas's wallflower						■	■	■		
California poppy							■	■		
Desert marigold							■	■		
Southwestern verbena							■	■		
Indian pink							■	■		
Golden yarrow							■	■		
Western shooting star							■	■		
Showy penstemon							■	■		

COMMON NAME	1	2	3	4	5	6	7	8	9	10
Douglas's iris									■	■
Blue dicks									■	■
Chocolate lily									■	■
Blue-eyed grass									■	■
Golden stars									■	■
Scarlet sage (WA)									■	■
Our Lord's candle									■	■
American bellflower (HA)										
Annual phlox (WA)										
Baby blue-eyes (HA)										
Blazing star (HA)										
Chinese houses (HA)										
Cosmos (TA)										
Farewell-to-spring (HA)										
Goldfields (SA)										
Linanthus (TA)										
Owl's clover (HA)										
Prickly poppy (TA)										
Purple annual lupine (HA)										
Purple heliotrope (TA)										
Sky lupine (HA)										
Snow-on-the-mountain (HA)										
Tidy tips (SA)										
Wind poppy (TA)										

WA (Winter Annual): Planted in fall, flowers next spring or summer.

HA (Hardy Annual): Planted in fall or spring, grows early spring to early fall.

SA (Semi-Hardy Annual): Planted in early spring, grows spring to summer.

TA (Tender Annual): Planted in mid- or late spring, grows summer.

Source: *A Garden of Wildflowers,* Henry W. Art

pH Preferences of Selected Wildflowers

COMMON NAME	3	4	5	6	7	8	9	10
Pink lady's slipper		▮						
Meadow beauty		▮—▮						
Yellow clintonia		▮———▮					
Bunchberry		▮———▮					
Wood lily		▮—————▮				
Partridgeberry		▮—————▮				
Shinleaf			▮—▮					
Wintergreen			▮————▮				
Pasture rose			▮————▮				
Mayapple		▮—————————▮				
Solomon's seal		▮—————————▮				
Purple trillium			▮——————▮			
Butterfly weed			▮——————▮			
Culver's root			▮————————▮		
Jack-in-the-pulpit				▮———▮			
False Solomon's seal				▮———▮			
Yellow fawn lily				▮———▮			
Silky aster				▮———▮			
Eastern shooting star			▮—————————▮		
Groundnut				▮———▮			
Spring beauty				▮———▮			
Eastern trout lily				▮———▮			
Bloodroot				▮———▮			
Larger blue flag				▮———▮			
False dragonhead				▮———▮			
Bluets				▮———▮			

COMMON NAME	3	4	5	6	7	8	9	10
Turtlehead			▮——————▮			
Purple prairie clover				▮—▮			
Goatsbeard			▮—————————▮		
Wild ginger			▮—————————▮		
Closed gentian			▮————————▮		
Wild bergamot			▮————————▮		
Blue flax			▮————————▮		
New England aster			▮————————▮		
Gayfeather			▮————————▮		
Spiderwort			▮————————▮		
Cardinal flower			▮————————▮		
White baneberry				▮—————————▮	
Eastern columbine				▮—————————▮	
Bear grass				▮———▮			
Wild leek				▮———▮			
Canada anemone				▮———▮			
Coralbells				▮———▮			
American bellflower				▮———▮			
White trillium				▮———▮			
Virginia bluebells			▮—————————▮		
Western shooting star				▮———▮			
Sharp-lobed hepatica				▮———▮			
Pasqueflower				▮———▮			
Colorado columbine				▮———▮			
Dutchman's breeches				▮———▮			
Mexican hat				▮———▮			

continued

COMMON NAME	3	4	5	6	7	8	9	10
Golden yarrow								
Prickly poppy								
Farewell-to-spring								
Lance-leaved coreopsis								
Chocolate lily								
Bitterroot								
Douglas's iris								
Douglas's wallflower								
Sky lupine								
Purple annual lupine								
California poppy								
Snow-on-the-mountain								
Standing cypress								
Leadplant								
Baby blue-eyes								
Giant evening primrose								
Tidy tips								
Owl's clover								
Elephantheads								
Linanthus								
Showy penstemon								
Rocky Mountain penstemon								
Blanketflower								
Purple heliotrope								
Annual phlox								

COMMON NAME	3	4	5	6	7	8	9	10
Blazing star								
Chinese houses								
Old-man-of-the-mountain								
Desert marigold								
Golden stars								
Blue dicks								
Missouri evening primrose								
Black-eyed Susan								
Scarlet sage								
Platte River penstemon								
Indian pink								
Compass plant								
Blue-eyed grass								
Cosmos								
Desert mallow								
Wind poppy								
Showy tick trefoil								
Goldfields								
Nodding wild onion								
Southwestern verbena								
Purple coneflower								
Mule's ears								
Rattlesnake master								
Our Lord's candle								

Note: The optimum pH is the mid-range of the shaded area.

Source: *A Garden of Wildflowers*, Henry W. Art

Plant Height of Selected Wildflowers

COMMON NAME	6"	1'	2'	3'	4'	5'	10'
Partridgeberry							
Wintergreen							
Sharp-lobed hepatica							
Old-man-of-the-mountain							
Pasqueflower							
Bitterroot							
Eastern trout lily							
Bluets							
Bunchberry							
Tidy tips							
Spiderwort							
Goldfields							
Blue-eyed grass							
Spring beauty							
Yellow clintonia							
Shinleaf							
Wild leek							
Chocolate lily							
Wild ginger							
Missouri evening primrose							
Owl's clover							
Linanthus							
Sky lupine							
White trillium							
Purple trillium							
Southwestern verbena							

COMMON NAME	6"	1'	2'	3'	4'	5'	10'
Annual phlox							
Bloodroot							
Dutchman's breeches							
Meadow beauty							
Indian pink							
Eastern shooting star							
Elephantheads							
Eastern columbine							
Baby blue-eyes							
Jack-in-the-pulpit							
Purple annual lupine							
Virginia bluebells							
Western shooting star							
Mayapple							
Desert marigold							
Larger blue flag							
Golden stars							
Douglas's iris							
Mule's ears							
Closed gentian							
Pink lady's slipper							
Canada anemone							
Chinese houses							
Platte River penstemon							
Golden yarrow							
Lance-leaved coreopsis							

continued

PLANT HEIGHT OF SELECTED WILDFLOWERS (CONTINUED)

COMMON NAME	6"	1'	2'	3'	4'	5'	10'	15'
Silky aster								
Nodding wild onion								
Wind poppy								
Scarlet sage								
Coralbells								
White baneberry								
Yellow fawn lily								
California poppy								
Groundnut								
Colorado columbine								
Rocky Mountain penstemon								
Blue flax								
Butterfly weed								
Turtlehead								
Pasture rose								
Solomon's seal								
Wood lily								
Douglas's wallflower								
Snow-on-the-mountain								
Farewell-to-spring								
False Solomon's seal								
Purple prairie clover								
Black-eyed Susan								
Purple heliotrope								
Prickly poppy								

COMMON NAME	6"	1'	2'	3'	4'	5'	10'	15'
Blazing star								
Cardinal flower								
Gayfeather								
Rattlesnake master								
Desert mallow								
Mexican hat								
Leadplant								
Blue dicks								
Wild bergamot								
False dragonhead								
Blanketflower								
Showy penstemon								
New England aster								
Purple coneflower								
Standing cypress								
Bear grass								
American bellflower								
Culver's root								
Showy tick trefoil								
Giant evening primrose								
Cosmos								
Compass plant								
Goatsbeard								
Our Lord's candle								

Note: The optimum pH is the mid-range of the shaded area.

Source: *A Garden of Wildflowers,* Henry W. Art

Soil Moisture Conditions Required for Selected Wildflowers

COMMON NAME	WET	DAMP	MODERATELY OR MOIST	SEASONALLY DRY	ARID
Elephantheads	■	■			
Bunchberry		■	■		
Larger blue flag		■	■		
Turtlehead	■	■	■		
Meadow beauty	■	■	■		
Jack-in-the-pulpit	■	■	■		
Groundnut	■	■	■		
Cardinal flower	■	■	■		
Bluets		■	■	■	
False dragonhead	■	■			
Wintergreen	■	■	■	■	
Pink lady's slipper	■	■	■	■	
Blue-eyed grass	■	■	■	■	
Yellow clintonia			■		
Baby blue-eyes			■		
Culver's root			■		
New England aster			■		
Eastern trout lily			■		
Nodding wild onion			■		
Goatsbeard			■		
False Solomon's seal			■		
Yellow fawn lily			■		
Sharp-lobed hepatica			■		
Wild ginger			■		
Wild leek			■		
Eastern shooting star			■	■	

COMMON NAME	WET	DAMP	MODERATELY OR MOIST	SEASONALLY DRY	ARID
Mayapple			■	■	
Douglas's iris			■	■	
Dutchman's breeches			■	■	
Bloodroot			■	■	
Virginia bluebells			■	■	
Standing cypress		■	■	■	■
Canada anemone			■	■	
Giant evening primrose			■	■	
Showy tick trefoil			■	■	
Eastern columbine			■	■	
Goldfields			■	■	
Shinleaf			■	■	
Snow-on-the-mountain			■	■	
Partridgeberry			■	■	
Purple coneflower			■	■	
Spiderwort			■	■	
Annual phlox			■	■	
Gayfeather			■	■	
Solomon's seal			■	■	
Colorado columbine			■	■	
Wind poppy			■	■	
White baneberry			■	■	
Closed gentian			■	■	
Pasture rose		■	■	■	
White trillium		■	■	■	
Purple trillium		■	■	■	

continued

COMMON NAME	WET	DAMP	MOIST	MODERATELY OR SEASONALLY DRY	ARID
Spring beauty			▓		
Chinese houses			▓		
American bellflower			▓		
Western shooting star			▓		
Black-eyed Susan		▓	▓	▓	
Compass plant		▓	▓	▓	
Wood lily			▓	▓	
Wild bergamot			▓	▓	
California poppy			▓	▓	
Old-man-of-the-mountain			▓	▓	
Tidy tips			▓	▓	
Rattlesnake master			▓	▓	
Coralbells			▓	▓	
Mule's ears				▓	
Cosmos				▓	
Farewell-to-spring				▓	
Rocky Mountain penstemon				▓	
Owl's clover				▓	
Platte River penstemon				▓	
Blazing star				▓	
Showy penstemon				▓	
Silky aster				▓	▓
Purple heliotrope				▓	▓
Lance-leaved coreopsis				▓	▓
Blanketflower				▓	▓

COMMON NAME	WET	DAMP	MOIST	MODERATELY OR SEASONALLY DRY	ARID
Douglas's wallflower			▓	▓	
Linanthus			▓	▓	
Mexican hat			▓	▓	
Bear grass			▓	▓	
Blue flax			▓	▓	
Southwestern verbena				▓	
Leadplant				▓	
Pasque flower				▓	
Golden stars				▓	
Butterfly weed				▓	
Our Lord's candle				▓	
Scarlet sage				▓	
Chocolate lily				▓	
Sky lupine				▓	
Golden yarrow				▓	
Purple annual lupine				▓	
Prickly poppy				▓	
Indian pink				▓	
Purple prairie clover				▓	
Blue dicks				▓	
Missouri evening primrose				▓	▓
Desert mallow				▓	▓
Desert marigold					▓
Bitterroot					▓

Note: The optimum pH is the mid-range of the shaded area.

Source: *A Garden of Wildflowers*, Henry W. Art

COMMON NAME	OPEN, FULL SUN	FILTERED SUN, PARTIAL SHADE	LIGHT SHADE	HEAVY SHADE	COMMON NAME	OPEN, FULL SUN	FILTERED SUN, PARTIAL SHADE	LIGHT SHADE	HEAVY SHADE
Blazing star	X				Lance-leaved coreopsis	X			
Nodding wild onion	X				Blue flax	X			
Southwestern verbena	X				Cosmos	X			
Leadplant	X				Sky lupine	X			
Giant evening primrose	X				Douglas's wallflower	X			
Missouri evening primrose	X				Mule's ears	X			
Owl's clover	X				Tidy tips	X			
Elephantheads	X				California poppy	X			
Platte River penstemon	X				Old-man-of-the-mountain	X			
Prickly poppy	X				Mexican hat	X			
Rocky Mountain penstemon	X				Blanketflower	X			
Purple prairie clover	X				Blue-eyed grass	X			
Purple heliotrope	X				Snow-on-the-mountain	X			
Butterfly weed	X				Linanthus	X			
Annual phlox	X				Showy penstemon	X			
Purple annual lupine	X				Pasqueflower	X	X		
Bitterroot	X				Purple coneflower	X	X		
Desert marigold	X				Closed gentian		X	X	
Golden stars	X				Coralbells		X	X	
Blue dicks	X				Indian pink		X	X	
Golden yarrow	X				Wild bergamot	X	X	X	
Rattlesnake master	X				Bluets	X	X	X	
Scarlet sage	X				Yellow fawn lily		X	X	
Desert mallow	X				Black-eyed Susan	X	X		
Our Lord's candle	X				Cardinal flower	X	X		
Compass plant	X				Showy tick trefoil	X	X	X	

continued

Light Conditions Required for Selected Wildflowers (continued)

COMMON NAME	OPEN, FULL SUN	FILTERED SUN, PARTIAL SHADE	LIGHT SHADE	HEAVY SHADE	COMMON NAME	OPEN, FULL SUN	FILTERED SUN, PARTIAL SHADE	LIGHT SHADE	HEAVY SHADE
New England aster		▓			Wood lily		▓		
Spring beauty		▓			Wild leek		▓		
Gayfeather		▓			Wintergreen		▓	▓	
Farewell-to-spring		▓			Spiderwort		▓	▓	▓
Meadow beauty		▓			Yellow clintonia	▓	▓	▓	
Baby blue-eyes		▓			Bloodroot	▓	▓	▓	▓
Standing cypress		▓			Eastern trout lily	▓	▓	▓	▓
Silky aster		▓			Mayapple	▓	▓	▓	▓
Larger blue flag		▓			Solomon's seal	▓	▓	▓	▓
Groundnut		▓			Goatsbeard	▓	▓	▓	▓
Bear grass		▓			Wind poppy	▓	▓	▓	▓
Canada anemone		▓			Pink lady's slipper	▓	▓	▓	▓
Goldfields	▓	▓			Chinese houses		▓	▓	
Pasture rose		▓	▓		Sharp-lobed hepatica		▓	▓	
Virginia bluebells		▓	▓		False Solomon's seal	▓	▓	▓	
Bunchberry		▓	▓		Western shooting star	▓	▓	▓	
Eastern columbine		▓	▓		Jack-in-the-pulpit		▓	▓	
Douglas's iris		▓	▓		Partridgeberry		▓	▓	
Eastern shooting star		▓	▓		Wild ginger		▓	▓	
False dragonhead		▓	▓		Dutchman's breeches		▓	▓	
Colorado columbine		▓	▓		Purple trillium		▓	▓	
Turtlehead		▓	▓		White trillium		▓	▓	
American bellflower		▓	▓		White baneberry		▓	▓	
Culver's root		▓	▓		Shinleaf		▓	▓	▓
Chocolate lily		▓							

Note: The optimum pH is the mid-range of the shaded area.

Source: *A Garden of Wildflowers*, Henry W. Art

FLOWERING PROGRESSION OF SELECTED WILDFLOWERS

COMMON NAME	LATE WINTER	EARLY SPRING	MID-SPRING	LATE SPRING	EARLY SUMMER	SUMMER	LATE SUMMER	EARLY FALL	FALL
Pasqueflower		■	■						
Sharp-lobed hepatica		■	■						
Baby blue-eyes	■	■							
Blue-eyed grass		■	■						
Spring beauty			■						
Bloodroot			■						
Western shooting star			■						
Bitterroot			■						
Wild ginger			■						
Dutchman's breeches			■						
Eastern trout lily			■						
Owl's clover			■	■					
Blue dicks			■	■					
Purple trillium			■	■					
Desert mallow			■	■					
Virginia bluebells			■	■					
Goldfields			■	■					
Blazing star			■	■					
Mayapple			■	■					
Chocolate lily			■	■					
Douglas's iris			■	■					
Our Lord's candle			■	■					
Purple annual lupine			■	■					
Wind poppy			■	■					
White baneberry				■					
Goatsbeard				■					
Pink lady's slipper			■						
Canada anemone			■						
White trillium			■						
Eastern shooting star			■						
Golden stars			■						
Jack-in-the-pulpit			■	■					
Yellow fawn lily		■	■						
Bluets			■	■					
Chinese houses			■	■					
Tidy tips			■	■					
Douglas's wallflower			■	■					
Sky lupine			■	■					
Yellow clintonia			■	■					
Solomon's seal				■					
False Solomon's seal				■					
Wild leek				■					
Eastern columbine			■	■	■				
Purple heliotrope			■	■	■				
Linanthus			■	■	■				
Golden yarrow			■	■	■				
Mule's ears			■	■	■				
Indian pink			■	■	■				
Spiderwort			■	■	■				
Larger blue flag					■				
Bunchberry					■				
Pasture rose					■				

continued

FLOWERING PROGRESSION OF SELECTED WILDFLOWERS (CONTINUED)

COMMON NAME	LATE WINTER	EARLY SPRING	MID-SPRING	LATE SPRING	EARLY SUMMER	SUMMER	LATE SUMMER	EARLY FALL	FALL
Rocky Mountain penstemon				▓					
Showy penstemon				▓					
Farewell-to-spring				▓					
Platte River penstemon				▓					
Annual phlox			▓	▓	▓	▓	▓		
Bear grass				▓	▓				
American bellflower				▓	▓				
Prickly poppy				▓	▓				
Leadplant				▓	▓				
Lance-leaved coreopsis				▓	▓				
Missouri evening primrose				▓	▓				
Colorado columbine				▓	▓				
Partridgeberry			▓	▓	▓				
Southwestern verbena			▓	▓	▓	▓			
Coralbells				▓	▓	▓			
Butterfly weed			▓	▓	▓	▓			
Wood lily				▓	▓				
Wild bergamot				▓	▓				
Elephantheads				▓	▓				
Old-man-of-the-mountain				▓	▓				
Shinleaf				▓	▓				
Standing cypress				▓	▓				
Nodding wild onion				▓	▓				
Groundnut				▓	▓				
Meadow beauty				▓	▓				

COMMON NAME	LATE WINTER	EARLY SPRING	MID-SPRING	LATE SPRING	EARLY SUMMER	SUMMER	LATE SUMMER	EARLY FALL	FALL
Blue flax						▓	▓		
California poppy			▓	▓	▓	▓	▓		
Desert marigold			▓	▓	▓	▓	▓		
Cosmos					▓	▓			
Mexican hat					▓	▓			
Purple coneflower					▓	▓			
Black-eyed Susan					▓	▓			
Compass plant					▓	▓			
Culver's root					▓	▓			
False dragonhead					▓	▓			
Rattlesnake master					▓	▓			
Purple prairie clover					▓	▓			
Blazing star					▓	▓			
Wintergreen				▓	▓	▓	▓		
Snow-on-the-mountain				▓	▓	▓	▓		
Scarlet sage				▓	▓	▓	▓		
Showy tick trefoil						▓	▓		
Cardinal flower						▓	▓		
Turtlehead						▓	▓		
Blanketflower						▓	▓		
Giant evening primrose						▓	▓		
Closed gentian						▓	▓		
Silky aster								▓	▓
New England aster							▓	▓	▓

Source: *A Garden of Wildflowers,* Henry W. Art

FLOWER COLOR OF SELECTED WILDFLOWERS

COMMON NAME	BROWN	WHITE	PINK	RED	ORANGE	YELLOW	GREEN	BLUE	PURPLE	LAVENDER
Chocolate lily	■								■	
Purple trillium				■						
Jack-in-the-pulpit							■			
Wild ginger	■								■	
Groundnut	■									
Douglas's iris		■								
Partridgeberry		■								
Bloodroot		■								
Our Lord's candle		■								
Canada anemone		■								
Wintergreen		■								
False Solomon's seal		■								
Mayapple		■								
White baneberry		■								
Shinleaf		■								
Culver's root		■								
Linanthus		■								
Bear grass		■								
Goatsbeard		■								
Dutchman's breeches		■								
Prickly poppy		■								
Bunchberry		■								
White trillium		■	■							
Turtlehead		■	■							
Bitterroot		■	■							
Cosmos			■	■						

COMMON NAME	BROWN	WHITE	PINK	RED	ORANGE	YELLOW	GREEN	BLUE	PURPLE	LAVENDER
Sharp-lobed hepatica		■	■				■		■	■
Rattlesnake master		■					■			
Wild leek		■								
Snow-on-the-mountain		■					■			
Sky lupine		■						■		
Colorado columbine		■						■		
Pasqueflower		■								■
Pink lady's slipper			■							
Pasture rose			■							
Spring beauty			■							
Coralbells			■	■						
Elephantheads			■	■						
Farewell-to-spring			■	■						
Eastern columbine			■			■				
Annual phlox			■						■	
Showy penstemon								■	■	
Showy tick trefoil								■		■
Nodding wild onion			■							
Western shooting star			■							
False dragonhead			■							
Eastern shooting star			■						■	
Scarlet sage				■						
Meadow beauty			■							
Cardinal flower				■						
Standing cypress				■						
Indian pink				■						

continued

FLOWER COLOR OF SELECTED WILDFLOWERS (CONTINUED)

COMMON NAME	BROWN	WHITE	PINK	RED	ORANGE	YELLOW	GREEN	BLUE	PURPLE	LAVENDER
Wood lily				X	X					
Wind poppy				X						
Blanketflower				X	X	X				
Douglas's wallflower					X	X				
Mexican hat				X		X				
Owl's clover									X	
Purple prairie clover									X	X
Purple coneflower				X						
Desert mallow					X					
Black-eyed Susan						X				
Butterfly weed					X					
California poppy					X					
Old-man-of-the-mountain						X				
Lance-leaved coreopsis						X				
Giant evening primrose						X				
Tidy tips						X				
Compass plant						X				
Eastern trout lily						X				
Golden yarrow						X				
Golden stars						X				
Goldfields						X				
Blazing star						X				
Yellow clintonia						X				
Yellow lawn lily						X				
Missouri evening primrose						X				

COMMON NAME	BROWN	WHITE	PINK	RED	ORANGE	YELLOW	GREEN	BLUE	PURPLE	LAVENDER
Mule's ears						X				
Desert marigold						X				
Solomon's seal						X	X			
Blue flax								X		
Blue dicks								X	X	
Baby blue-eyes								X		
American bellflower								X		
Purple annual lupine									X	X
Platte River penstemon									X	
Closed gentian								X	X	
Blue-eyed grass								X		
Larger blue flag								X		
Rocky Mountain penstemon								X		
Purple heliotrope										X
Spiderwort									X	X
Chinese houses										X
Virginia bluebells									X	X
Bluets										X
New England aster										X
Leadplant									X	
Silky aster										X
Southwestern verbena										X
Wild bergamot										X
Gayfeather										X

Source: *A Garden of Wildflowers*, Henry W. Art

POISONOUS PLANTS

Selected Poisonous Plants/158

SELECTED POISONOUS PLANTS

BOTANICAL NAME	COMMON NAME	POISONOUS PART OF PLANT	BOTANICAL NAME	COMMON NAME	POISONOUS PART OF PLANT
Abrus precatorius	rosary pea	A single rosary pea seed causes death.	*Buxus sempervirens*	common box	Leaves; may cause rash
Acokanthera spp.	bushman's poison	All parts very poisonous	*Calonyction* spp.	moonflower	Seeds
Aconitum spp.	monkshood	All parts, especially roots and seeds, very poisonous. Characterized by digestive upset and nervous excitement.	*Cephalanthus occidentalis*	buttonbush	Leaves
Adonis aestivalis	summer adonis	Leaves and stem	*Cestrum* spp.	cestrum, night-blooming jessamine	Leafy shoots
Aesculus spp.	horsechestnut, buckeye	Leaves and fruit	*Cicuta*	water hemlock	All parts fatal, cause violent and painful convulsions
Ailanthus altissima	tree of heaven	Leaves, flowers; may cause rash	*Clematis vitalba*	traveller's joy	Leaves
Amaryllis belladonna	belladonna lily	Bulbs	*Colchicum autumnale*	autumn crocus, meadow saffron	Leaves are very poisonous
Anemone patens	pasque flower	Young plants and flowers	*Conium maculatus*	poison hemlock	All parts
Arisaema triphyllum	jack-in-the-pulpit	All parts, especially roots, (like dumb cane) contain small needle-like crystals of calcium oxalate that cause intense irritation and burning of the mouth and tongue.	*Convallaria majalis*	lily-of-the-valley	Leaves and flowers very poisonous
Asclepias spp.	milkweeds	Leaves and stems	*Corynocarpus laevigata*	karaka nut	Seeds
Asparagus officinalis	asparagus	Spears contain mercaptan, a substance which may cause kidney irritation if eaten in large amounts; young stems; may cause rash	*Crinum asiaticum*	crinum lily	Bulbs
Baileya multiradiata	desert marigold	Whole plant	*Crotalaria* spp.	canary bird bush	Seeds
Brunsvigia rosea	garden amaryllis, naked lady	Bulbs	*Cypripedium* spp.	ladyslipper orchid	Hairy stems and leaves; may cause rash

continued

BOTANICAL NAME	COMMON NAME	POISONOUS PART OF PLANT	BOTANICAL NAME	COMMON NAME	POISONOUS PART OF PLANT
Cytisus laburnum (see Laburnum)			*Fragaria* spp.	strawberry	Fruit; may cause rash.
Daphne spp.	daphne	Bark, leaves and fruit fatal. A few berries can kill a child.	*Gelsemium sempervirens*	yellow jessamine	Flowers and leaves; roots; may cause rash.
Datura spp.	angel's trumpet, thorn apple, jimsonweed	All parts cause abnormal thirst, distorted sight, delirium, incoherence and coma. Has proved fatal.	*Ginkgo biloba*	ginkgo, maidenhair tree	Fruit juice; may cause rash.
Delphinium spp.	larkspur, delphinium	Young plants and seeds cause digestive upset; may be fatal.	*Gloriosa* spp.	climbing lily	All parts
Dicentra spp.	Dutchman's breeches, bleeding-heart	Leaves and tubers may be poisonous in large amounts; fatal to cattle.	*Hedera helix*	English ivy	Leaves and berries
Dieffenbachia seguine	dumb cane	Stems and leaves cause intense burning and irritation of mouth and tongue. Death can occur if base of tongue swells enough to block the throat.	*Helenium* spp.	sneezeweed	Whole plant
Digitalis purpurea	foxglove	Leaves cause digestive upset and mental confusion; may be fatal in large amounts.	*Helleborus niger*	Christmas rose	Rootstocks and leaves; may cause rash.
Duranta repens	golden dewdrop	Fruits and leaves	*Heracleum lanatum*	cow parsnip	Leaves and root slightly poisonous; dangerous to cattle
Echium vulgare	blue weed	Leaves and stems; may cause rash.	*Heteromeles arbutifolia*	toyon, Christmas berry	Leaves
Euonymus europa	European burning bush	Leaves and fruit	*Hyacinthus*	hyacinth	Bulb causes nausea, vomiting; may be fatal.
Eupatorium rugosum	white snakeroot	Leaves and stems	*Hydrangea macrophylla*	hydrangea	Leaves
Euphorbia spp.	Euphorbias, snow-on-the-mountain, poinsettia	Milky sap; may cause rash. Leaves of poinsettia can kill a child.	*Hymenocallis americana*	spider-lily	Bulbs
Ficus spp.	figs	Milky sap; may cause rash.	*Hypericum perforatum*	St. John's Wort	All parts when eaten; may cause rash.

continued

BOTANICAL NAME	COMMON NAME	POISONOUS PART OF PLANT	BOTANICAL NAME	COMMON NAME	POISONOUS PART OF PLANT
Ilex aquifolium	English holly	Berries	*Malus*	apple	Seeds contain cyanic acid
Impatiens spp.	impatiens	Young stems and leaves	*Melia azedarach*	chinaberry	Fruit, flowers and bark
Iris spp.	iris	Rhizomes; may cause rash. If eaten causes digestive upset but not usually serious.	*Menispermum*	moonseed	Berries (resemble small wild grapes) may be fatal if eaten.
Jasminum	jessamine	Berries fatal.	*Myoporum laetum*	ngaio	Leaves very poisonous
Juglans spp.	walnut	Green hull juice; may cause rash.	*Narcissus* spp.	narcissus, daffodil	Bulbs cause nausea, vomiting, may be fatal.
Kalmia latifolia	mountain laurel	Leaves	*Nepeta hederacea*	ground ivy	Leaves and stems
Laburnum vulgare	golden chain	Leaves and seeds cause severe poisoning.	*Nerium oleander*	oleander	All parts extremely poisonous, affect the heart.
Lantana spp.	lantana	Foliage and green berries may be fatal.	*Nicotiana* spp.	tobaccos	Foliage
Laurus	laurels	All parts fatal	*Ornithogalum umbellatum*	star-of-Bethlehem	All parts cause vomiting and nervous excitement.
Ligustrum spp.	privet	Leaves and berries	*Oxalis cernua*	Bermuda buttercup	Leaves
Linum usitatissimum	flax	Whole plant, especially immature seed pods	*Papaver somniferum*	opium poppy	Unripe seed pod very poisonous
Lobelia spp.	lobelia	Leaves, stems, and fruit; may cause rash.	*Pastinaca sativa*	parsnip	Hairs on leaves and stems; may cause rash.
Lupinus spp.	lupines	Leaves, pods and especially seeds	*Philodendron* spp.	philodendron	Stems and leaves
Lycium halimifolium	matrimony vine	Leaves and young shoots	*Phoradendron* spp.	common mistletoe	Berries fatal.
Macadamia ternifolia	queensland nut	Young leaves	*Pittosporum* spp.	pittosporum	Leaves, stem and fruit very poisonous.
Maclura pomifera	osage orange	Milky sap; may cause rash.	*Podophyllum*	May apple	Apple, foliage and roots contains at least 16 active toxic principles, primarily in the roots. Children often eat the apple with no ill effects but several may cause diarrhea.

continued

BOTANICAL NAME	COMMON NAME	POISONOUS PART OF PLANT	BOTANICAL NAME	COMMON NAME	POISONOUS PART OF PLANT
Primula spp.	primrose	Leaves and stems; may cause rash.	*Senecio mikanioides*	German-ivy	Leaves and stems
Prunus spp.	cherries, peaches, plums	Seeds and leaves; seeds contain cyanic acid.	*Solanum dulcamara*	European bittersweet	Leaves and berries
Quercus	oak	Foliage and acorns. Takes a large amount to poison.	*Solanum nudiflorum*	black nightshade	Green berries poisonous but apparently harmless when full ripe.
Ranunculus spp.	buttercup	Leaves; may cause rash. If eaten, irritant juices may severely injure the digestive system.	*Solanum nigrum*	garden huckleberry nightshade	Unripe berries and leaves
Rhamnus spp.	coffee berry, buckthorn	Sap and fruit; may cause rash.	*Solanum pseudo-capsicum*	Jerusalem cherry	Fruit
Rheum rhaponticum	rhubarb	Leaves; may cause rash. Large amounts of raw or cooked leaves (contain oxalic acid) can cause convulsions, coma, followed by death.	*Solanum tuberosum*	Irish potato	Green skin on tubers
Rhododendron	rhododendron, azalea	Leaves and all parts may be fatal.	*Tanacetum vulgare*	common tansy	Leaves
Rhus diversiloba	poison oak	Leaves	*Taxus baccata*	yew	Foliage, bark and seeds fatal; foliage more toxic than berries
Ricinus communis	castor bean	Seeds fatal	*Thevetia peruviana*	yellow oleander	All parts
Robina pseudo-acacia	black locust	Young shoots, bark and seeds.	*Urtica* spp.	nettles	Leaves; may cause rash.
Rumex acetosa	sour dock	Leaves	*Veronica virginica*	culvers root	Roots
Sambucus canadensis	elderberry	Shoots, leaves and bark. Children have been poisoned by using the pithy stems for blowguns.	*Wisteria*	wisteria	Mild to severe digestive upset. Children sometimes poisoned by this plant.
Saponaria vaccaria	cow cockle	Seeds	*Zephyranthes* spp.	zephyr-lily	Leaves and bulbs
Sativus	autumn crocus	Vomiting and nervous excitement			

Source: *Carrots Love Tomatoes,* Louise Riotte

LAWNS

GRASS SEED MIXTURES BY PERCENTAGE

SITUATION	KENTUCKY BLUEGRASS	CREEPING RED FESCUE	WINTER-HARDY RYEGRASS
General use in a diversity of situations and soils	20	40	40
Full sun, good fertility and management	50	20	30
Quick cover, but persistent	20	20	60
Clay soil, full sun, densely growing sod	100	–	–
Putting-green turf, to be mowed short	100	–	–
Slope, never to be mowed	20	60	20
Temporary cover for summer	–	–	100 (annual)
Dry, sandy soils, open shade, or under trees	20	80	–
Moist shade much of day, under trees, or north side of house	30	40	30

Source: *Lawns and Landscaping: 1001 Gardening Questions Answered,* Editors of Garden Way Publishing

CHOOSING THE RIGHT LAWN FERTILIZER

GRADE	WHEN TO USE
5-20-10	For lawns testing low in phosphorus
5-10-10	For lawns not regularly fertilized, or for preparation of a seedbed for a new lawn
10-10-10	For lawns in need of extra phosphorus and potassium, but not generally impoverished
15-10-10	For lawns fertilized regularly but in need of more phosphorus
15-8-12	For lawns fertilized regularly but high in phosphorus
20-10-5	May be used for a lawn pep-up; contains too little potassium for regular use and, because of the high percentage of nitrogen, may result in greater disease susceptibility

COMMON LAWN PROBLEMS AND THEIR SOLUTIONS

PROBLEMS	SYMPTOM	SOLUTION
Anthills	Small mounds of sand or dirt on the lawn that can spread over and kill the grass.	Pour liquid pyrethrum or insecticidal soap down anthills. Make orange peel insecticide by mixing peels and orange juice in a food processor, then pour it down the anthills.
Armyworms	Patches of ragged grass.	Apply sabadilla dust.
Billbugs	Brown patches in June and July.	Plant resistant grasses. Aerate lawn, water deeply, and remove thatch. Apply rotenone or diatomaceous earth.
Broad-leaved weeds	Non-grassy lawn weeds. Not all have broad leaves.	Deep, infrequent watering. Mow grass high to shade weeds.
Chinch bugs	Yellow and brown patches in late spring and early fall.	Plant resistant grasses. Reduce nitrogen fertilizer and water well. Apply sabadilla dust.
Crabgrass	Short, light-green, hairy leaves on short stems.	To prevent crabgrass, use preemergent or postemergent herbicides. Mow high, fertilize heavily, water deeply and infrequently.
Drought damage	Many grasses, such as fescues, Bahia, Bermuda, and zoysia, turn brown, but live through all but the worst of droughts.	To protect plants during droughts, don't cut the grass closely and don't spread inorganic fertilizers such as 5-10-10. When you water, do so until water has reached to the deepest roots.
Fairy ring	As fungus in the soil breaks down organic matter, it releases nutrients and turns a circle of grass dark green.	Fairy grass doesn't harm a lawn, but you may wish to disguise its appearance by fertilizing well so that all the grass is the same color.
Fusarium blight	Patches of grass turn light green, then straw color, often with a patch of green in the center.	Avoid late spring/early summer fertilization. Mow high and remove clippings. Remove thatch.
Fusarium patch (pink snow mold)	Pale yellow areas, with pink along the edge, appearing in late winter and early spring.	Don't apply heavy nitrogen fertilizers or limestone in fall. Remove thatch.
Grubs	In late spring or late summer, grass turns brown in irregular patches, and sod lifts up easily.	Grubs are the larvae of many beetles, such as Japanese beetles, which feed on grass roots. Apply diatomaceous earth, Margosan-O (contains an extract of the neem tree), or beneficial nematodes. Use milky spore powder (*Bacillus popillae*) for Japanese beetle grubs.
Mites	Brown, thin patches.	Apply insecticidal soap frequently.
Mole tunnels	Uneven, heaved up ridges in the lawn.	Moles feed on grubs. If you get rid of the grubs, you will no longer have moles. You can also try traps in active tunnels (those that reappear a day or so after being tamped down). Avoid using poison; it's too dangerous to have around children and pets.

continued

COMMON LAWN PROBLEMS AND THEIR SOLUTIONS (CONTINUED)

PROBLEMS	SYMPTOM	SOLUTION
Scalped spots	Caused by cutting grass too closely, shaving the tops of bumps in your lawn, or cutting the grass too closely after not mowing for an extended period.	Level high spots, set the mower higher, and mow more frequently.
Sod webworms	Brown spots	Plant resistant grasses. Dethatch lawn. Apply *Bacillus thuringiensis (Bt)*.
Shade damage	Blades of grass are thin and dark green. Moss may be seen.	Prune overhanging trees and shrubs. Select shade-tolerant grass, such as fescues and some bluegrass varieties (Glade or Nugget) in the North, and St. Augustine grass in the South. Seed in fall and rake grass frequently to keep it free of leaves. If necessary, plant a ground cover, such as English ivy, pachysandra, or periwinkle instead of grass.
White or gray cast to lawn	Caused by dull lawn mower blades, which chew into grass, tearing it instead of clipping it.	Sharpen rotary mowers after every two or three mowings.

Source: *Lawns and Landscaping: 1001 Gardening Questions Answered,* Editors of Garden Way Publishing

APPROXIMATE CUTTING HEIGHTS FOR LAWNS

GRASS NAME	TYPE	HEIGHT IN INCHES*	GRASS NAME	TYPE	HEIGHT IN INCHES*	GRASS NAME	TYPE	HEIGHT IN INCHES*
NORTHERN GRASSES			**SOUTHERN GRASSES**			**TURF-TYPE GRASSES**		
Bentgrass	Creeping	¼–1	Bahiagrass		2½–4	Ryegrass	Perennial	1½–3½
	Colonial	½–1¼	Bermudagrass	Common	½–1½		Annual	1½–3½
Fescue	Red	2–4		Improved	¼–1	Zoysiagrass - (limited use in North)		½–2
	Chewing	1½–3	Carpetgrass		1½–2½	**NATIVE GRASSES–**		
	Tall	3–5	Centipedegrass		1½–2½	**MORE COMMON IN HARSHER & DRYER CLIMATES**		
Kentucky Bluegrass	Common	2–4	St. Augustinegrass		2–4	Buffalograss		1–2½
	Improved	1½–4	Zoysiagrass		½–2	Wheatgrass (Agropyron)		2–4

*Set your mower for about ½ inch lower than the cutting height indicated for your type of grass and mow where your grass reaches the cutting height. Let your grass grow to the higher cutting heights during hot weather and if your lawn is shaded.

Source: *Building a Healthy Lawn,* Stuart Franklin

TREES AND SHRUBS

CHARACTERISTICS AND GROWING INFORMATION FOR SELECTED SHRUBS AND CONIFERS

SHRUBS AND CONIFERS	CONDITIONS			CHARACTERISTICS										
	SUN OR SHADE	WATER REQMNTS	SOIL TYPE	FOLIAGE TYPE	HEIGHT	GROWTH HABIT	GROWTH RATE	FLOWER COLOR	FRUIT COLOR	AUTUMN COLOR	WINTER EFFECT	THORNS	HEDGING	HEDGE SPACING
Abelia x *grandiflora* and cvs	S-PS	M	L	S	D	M	M	W-Pk	–	–	–	–	I	2'
Acanthopanax sieboldiana	All	D-M	All	D	M	O	M-F	–	–	–	–	*	I	3'
Amelanchier canadensis and cvs	S-PS	D-M	S-L	D	L	O-U	M	W	R-Pr	Y-O-R	–	–	–	–
Andromeda polifolia	S-PS	M	All	E	D	M	S-M	W-Pk	–	–	*	–	–	–
Aralia spinosa	S-PS	M	All	D	L	U	F	W	Bk	Y	–	*	–	–
Arctostaphylos uva-ursi	S-PS	M	All	E	D	Pr	S-M	W-Pk	R	–	*	–	–	–
Aronia spp.	S-PS	All	All	D	S-M	V	M	W	R-Bk	R	–	–	F-I	24-30"
Azalea, Evergreen Hybrids	S-PS	M	L	E-S	D-S	V	M	V	–	V	*	–	I	15-24"
Deciduous Hybrids	S-PS	M	L	D	S-M	R	S	V	–	Y-O-R	–	–	I	15-36"
Berberis, most	S-PS	D-M	All	D	D-M	R	M	Y	R-O	V	V	*	F-I	15-24"
Berberis thunbergii 'Bogozam' Bonanza Gold™	S-PS	D-M	S-L	D	S	M-R	M	Y	R	Y	–	*	F-I	2-3'
Buddleia, most	S	D-M	S-L	D	M	U	F	V	–	–	–	–	I	30-36"
Buxus sempervirens 'Vardar Valley'	S-PS	M	All	E	D	R	S-M	–	–	–	*	–	F	2-3'
Callicarpa dichotoma	S-PS	M	All	D	S	U	S-M	Pk-L	Pr	–	–	–	I	4'

Key:

CONDITIONS
SUN OR SHADE: S = Sun, PS = Partial Shade, Sh = Shade, All = Sun through Shade
WATER REQUIREMENTS: D = Dry, M = Moist, but well drained, W = Wet, All = Dry through Wet
SOIL TYPE: S = Sand, L = Loam, All = Sand through Clay
CHARACTERISTICS
FOLIAGE TYPE: H = Herbaceous, D = Deciduous,

S = Semi-Evergreen, E = Evergreen, C = Coniferous
SHRUB HEIGHT: D = Dwarf (up to 3'), S = Small (3' to 6'), M = Medium (6' to 10'), L = Large (over 10')
GROWTH HABIT: I = Irregular, M = Mounding, O = Oval, Pr = Prostrate, Py = Pyramid, R = Round, U = Upright, W = Weeping, V = Varies, according to variety
GROWTH RATE: S = Slow, M = Medium, F = Fast

FLOWER, FRUIT, AUTUMN & WINTER COLORS IF SHOWY:
W = White, Pk = Pink, R = Red, O = Orange, Y = Yellow, Br = Brown, Bu = Blue, Bk = Black, Bz = Bronze, Gn = Green, Gy = Gray, Pr = Purple, L = Lavender, V = Varies, according to variety, F = Fragrant
HEDGING: F = Formal, I = Informal, V = Varies, depending on variety

continued

CHARACTERISTICS AND GROWING INFORMATION FOR SELECTED SHRUBS AND CONIFERS (CONTINUED)

SHRUBS AND CONIFERS	CONDITIONS			CHARACTERISTICS											
	SUN OR SHADE	WATER REQMNTS	SOIL TYPE	FOLIAGE TYPE	HEIGHT	GROWTH HABIT	GROWTH RATE	FLOWER COLOR	FRUIT COLOR	AUTUMN COLOR	WINTER EFFECT	THORNS	HEDGING	HEDGE SPACING
Calluna vulgaris and cvs	S-PS	M-D	All	E	D	M	S-M	V	–	–	*	–	–	–
Calycanthus florida	All	M	L	D	M	R	M	F/R-Br	Br	Y	–	–	I	3-5'
Caragana arborescens	S-PS	D-M	All	D	L	O-Py	M-R	Y	–	–	–	–	–	–
Caryopteris spp.	S	M	All	D	S	M	F	Y	–	–	–	–	I	15-24"
Chaenomeles japonica and cvs	S	D-M	All	D	D-S	M-R	M	V	Y-Gn	–	–	*	I	15-24"
speciosa and cvs	S	D-M	All	D	S-M	R	M	V	Y-Gn	–	–	*	I	2-3'
Chamaecyparis obtusa and cvs	S	M	L	E	D-L	V	S-M	–	–	V	*	–	F-I	–
pisifera and cvs	S	M	L	E	D-M	V	M	–	–	V	*	–	–	–
Clethra alnifolia and cvs	All	M-W	L	D	S-M	O-U	M	F/W-Pk	Br	Y	–	–	I	2-3'
Cornus, shrubby types	S-PS	M	L	D	D-M	V	F	W	V	V	V	–	I	30-36"
Coryluus avellana 'Contorta'	S-PS	M	L	D	M	R	M	W	Br	–	*	–	–	–
Cotinus coggygria and cvs	S	D-M	L	D	L	R	M	V	–	V	–	–	I	4'
Cotoneaster divaricata	S-PS	D-M	L	D	S	R	M-F	Pk	R	Y-R-Pr	–	–	I	30-36"
Cotoneaster, low types	S-PS	M	L	D	D	V	F	W-Pk	R-O	V	V	–	I	15-24"
Daphne cneorum 'Ruby Glow'	S-PS	M	S-L	E	D	M	S-M	Pk	–	–	*	–	–	–

Key:
CONDITIONS
SUN OR SHADE: S = Sun, PS = Partial Shade, Sh = Shade,
    All = Sun through Shade
WATER REQUIREMENTS: D = Dry, M = Moist, but well
    drained, W = Wet, All = Dry through Wet
SOIL TYPE: S = Sand, L = Loam, All = Sand through Clay
CHARACTERISTICS
FOLIAGE TYPE: H = Herbaceous, D = Deciduous,

S = Semi-Evergreen, E = Evergreen, C = Coniferous
SHRUB HEIGHT: D = Dwarf (up to 3'), S = Small (3' to 6'),
    M = Medium (6' to 10'), L = Large (over 10')
GROWTH HABIT: I = Irregular, M = Mounding, O = Oval,
    Pr = Prostrate, Py = Pyramid, R = Round, U = Upright,
    W = Weeping, V = Varies, according to variety
GROWTH RATE: S = Slow, M = Medium, F = Fast

FLOWER, FRUIT, AUTUMN & WINTER COLORS IF SHOWY:
    W = White, Pk = Pink, R = Red, O = Orange, Y = Yellow,
    Br = Brown, Bu = Blue, Bk = Black, Bz = Bronze,
    Gn = Green, Gy = Gray, Pr = Purple, L = Lavender,
    V = Varies, according to variety, F = Fragrant
HEDGING: F = Formal, I = Informal, V = Varies,
    depending on variety

continued

SHRUBS AND CONIFERS	CONDITIONS			CHARACTERISTICS											
	SUN OR SHADE	WATER REQMNTS	SOIL TYPE	FOLIAGE TYPE	HEIGHT	GROWTH HABIT	GROWTH RATE	FLOWER COLOR	FRUIT COLOR	AUTUMN COLOR	WINTER EFFECT	THORNS	HEDGING	HEDGE SPACING
Deutzia gracilis and cvs	S	M	All	D	S-M	O-U	S-M	V	–	–	–	–	F-I	30-36"
scabra and cvs	S	M	All	D	S-M	O-U	S-M	V	–	–	–	–	F-I	30-36"
Diervilla lonicera	S-PS	D-M	All	D	S	M	M	Y	–	–	–	–	–	–
Elaeagnus angustifolia	S	D-M	All	D	L	I-R	F	F/W-Y	Y	–	–	*	I	6'
'Tizam' P.P. 7750-Titan ®	S	D-M	All	D	L	R	F	F/W	R	–	–	*	I	3-5'
Erica, most	S	D-M	S-L	E-S	D	M	S	Y-Gn	–	V	*	–	–	–
Euonymus alata and cvs	S-PS	D-M	All	D	M-L	R	M	V	O-R	R	*	–	F-I	2-3'
fortunei and cvs	S-PS	D-M	All	E	D	V	V	–	–	V	*	–	–	–
f.cv. 'Spargozam'-Sparkle 'n Gold ®	S-PS	D-M	All	E	D	M	M-F	–	–	–	*	–	–	–
Forsythia x *intermedia* and cvs	S-PS	M	All	D	M-L	R	M	Y	–	–	–	–	I	2-5'
suspensa sieboldi	S-PS	M	L	D	M	W	F	Y	–	–	–	–	–	–
viridissima 'Bronxensis'	S-PS	M	All	D	D	M	M	Y	–	–	–	–	I	15-18"
Genista spp.	S	D-M	S-L	D	D	M	M	Y	–	–	*	–	–	–
Hamamelis spp.	S-PS	M	All	D	M-L	R	M	Y-R	Br	Y-O	–	–	I	4-6'
Hibiscus syriacus and cvs	S-PS	M	S-L	D	M-L	U	M	V	–	–	–	–	I	2-5'
Hippophae rhamnoides	S-PS	M	All	D	M-L	R	M-F	Y-W	O	–	–	–	–	–

Key:

CONDITIONS
SUN OR SHADE: S = Sun, PS = Partial Shade, Sh = Shade, All = Sun through Shade
WATER REQUIREMENTS: D = Dry, M = Moist, but well drained, W = Wet, All = Dry through Wet
SOIL TYPE: S = Sand, L = Loam, All = Sand through Clay
CHARACTERISTICS
FOLIAGE TYPE: H = Herbaceous, D = Deciduous,

S = Semi-Evergreen, E = Evergreen, C = Coniferous
SHRUB HEIGHT: D = Dwarf (up to 3'), S = Small (3' to 6'), M = Medium (6' to 10'), L = Large (over 10')
GROWTH HABIT: I = Irregular, M = Mounding, O = Oval, Pr = Prostrate, Py = Pyramid, R = Round, U = Upright, W = Weeping, V = Varies, according to variety
GROWTH RATE: S = Slow, M = Medium, F = Fast

FLOWER, FRUIT, AUTUMN & WINTER COLORS IF SHOWY:
W = White, Pk = Pink, R = Red, O = Orange, Y = Yellow, Br = Brown, Bu = Blue, Bk = Black, Bz = Bronze, Gn = Green, Gy = Gray, Pr = Purple, L = Lavender, V = Varies, according to variety, F = Fragrant
HEDGING: F = Formal, I = Informal, V = Varies, depending on variety

continued

CHARACTERISTICS AND GROWING INFORMATION FOR SELECTED SHRUBS AND CONIFERS (CONTINUED)

SHRUBS AND CONIFERS	CONDITIONS			CHARACTERISTICS											
	SUN OR SHADE	WATER REQMNTS	SOIL TYPE	FOLIAGE TYPE	HEIGHT	GROWTH HABIT	GROWTH RATE	FLOWER COLOR	FRUIT COLOR	AUTUMN COLOR	WINTER EFFECT	THORNS	HEDGING	HEDGE SPACING
Hydrangea macrophylla and cvs	S-PS	M	L	D	S-M	R	F	V	–	–	–	–	–	–
paniculata 'Grandiflora'	S-PS	M	L	D	L	U-R	F	W-Pk	–	–	*	–	I	30"
quercifolia	All	M	L	D	S-M	I-U	S-M	W-Pk	–	R-Pr	–	–	I	30"
Hypericum, most	S-PS	D-M	S-L	D	D	M	F	Y	–	–	–	–	I	15-18"
Ilex, broadleaf evergreen types	S-PS	M	L	E	V	V	S-M	–	–	Gn	*	–	F-I	24-30"
g.cv. 'Chamzin' P.P.6962-Nordic®	S-PS	M	L	E	D-S	R	S-M	–	–	–	*	–	F-I	24-30"
deciduous types	S-PS	M-V	V	D	S-M	V	S-M	–	V	Y-O	*	V	I	3'
Itea spp.	S-PS	M	S	D	D	V	F	W	–	R	–	–	I	3'
Juniperus, low types	S	D-M	All	E	D	M-Pr	M-F	–	Bu	V	*	–	I	2-3'
Juniperus chinensis 'Aquazam'-Aquarius®	S	D-M	All	E	R	M-F	–	–	–	–	*	–	F-I	2-3'
taller types	S	D-M	All	E	V	V	S-M	–	V	V	*	–	F-I	2-5'
Kalmia latifolia	All	M	L	E	M	M-R	S	V	Br	Gn	*	–	I	30-36"
Kerria japonica 'Pleniflora'	All	M	All	D	M	R	F	Y	–	–	*	*	I	3-4'
Kolkwitzia amabilis	S	D-M	All	D	M-L	U-R	F	Pk	Br	–	–	–	I	3-5'
Leucothoe, most	S-PS	M	S-L	E	D-S	M	F	W	–	V	*	–	I	15-24"

Key:

CONDITIONS
SUN OR SHADE: S = Sun, PS = Partial Shade, Sh = Shade, All = Sun through Shade
WATER REQUIREMENTS: D = Dry, M = Moist, but well drained, W = Wet, All = Dry through Wet
SOIL TYPE: S = Sand, L = Loam, All = Sand through Clay
CHARACTERISTICS
FOLIAGE TYPE: H = Herbaceous, D = Deciduous,

S = Semi-Evergreen, E = Evergreen, C = Coniferous
SHRUB HEIGHT: D = Dwarf (up to 3'), S = Small (3' to 6'), M = Medium (6' to 10'), L = Large (over 10')
GROWTH HABIT: I = Irregular, M = Mounding, O = Oval, Pr = Prostrate, Py = Pyramid, R = Round, U = Upright, W = Weeping, V = Varies, according to variety
GROWTH RATE: S = Slow, M = Medium, F = Fast

FLOWER, FRUIT, AUTUMN & WINTER COLORS IF SHOWY:
W = White, Pk = Pink, R = Red, O = Orange, Y = Yellow, Br = Brown, Bu = Blue, Bk = Black, Bz = Bronze, Gn = Green, Gy = Gray, Pr = Purple, L = Lavender, V = Varies, according to variety, F = Fragrant
HEDGING: F = Formal, I = Informal, V = Varies, depending on variety

continued

CHARACTERISTICS AND GROWING INFORMATION FOR SELECTED SHRUBS AND CONIFERS (CONTINUED)

SHRUBS AND CONIFERS	CONDITIONS			CHARACTERISTICS											
	SUN OR SHADE	WATER REQMNTS	SOIL TYPE	FOLIAGE TYPE	HEIGHT	GROWTH HABIT	GROWTH RATE	FLOWER COLOR	FRUIT COLOR	AUTUMN COLOR	WINTER EFFECT	THORNS	HEDGING	HEDGE SPACING
Ligustrum, most	V	D-M	All	D	V	V	F	W	Bk	Y	–	–	F-I	1-2'
Lindera benzoin	All	All	All	D	M-L	R	F	Y	R	–	–	–	–	–
Lonicera, shrubby types	All	M	All	D	V	I	F	V	R-Bk	–	–	–	I	18-30"
Magnolia, most	S-PS	M	L	D	M-L	V	M	V	O-R	–	*	–	I	30-36"
Mahonia aquifolium and cvs	All	M	S-L	S	S	M-U	M	Y	Bu	Bz	*	*	I	2-3'
Microbiota decussata	All	D-M	S-L	E	D	Pr	M	–	–	Bz	*	–	–	–
Myrica pensylvanica	S-PS	D-M	All	D	S-L	U-R	M-F	–	Gy	Gn-Bz	*	–	I	18-24"
Philadelphus virginalis and cvs	S-PS	M	L	D	M-L	U-R	M	F/W	–	–	–	–	I	24-30"
Photinia villosa	S-PS	M	L	D	L	I	M	W	R	R	–	–	I	4'
Physocarpus opulifolia and cvs	S-PS	D-M	All	D	M	U-R	M-F	W-Pk	R	V	–	–	I	24-30"
Picea, dwarf to small types	S	M	S-L	E	D-S	V	S-M	–	Br	V	*	–	–	–
Pieris japonica and cvs	S-PS	M	L	E	M	U	M	W	–	Gn	*	–	I	24-36"
Pinus mugo	S-PS	M	S-L	E	D-M	V	M	–	Br	Gn	*	–	I	30"
other small types	S	M	S-L	E	D-M	V	S-M	–	Br	V	*	–	–	–
Potentilla, most	S	M	S-L	D	D	V	M	V	–	–	–	–	I	15"

Key:

<u>CONDITIONS</u>
SUN OR SHADE: S = Sun, PS = Partial Shade, Sh = Shade, All = Sun through Shade
WATER REQUIREMENTS: D = Dry, M = Moist, but well drained, W = Wet, All = Dry through Wet
SOIL TYPE: S = Sand, L = Loam, All = Sand through Clay
<u>CHARACTERISTICS</u>
FOLIAGE TYPE: H = Herbaceous, D = Deciduous,

S = Semi-Evergreen, E = Evergreen, C = Coniferous
SHRUB HEIGHT: D = Dwarf (up to 3'), S = Small (3' to 6'), M = Medium (6' to 10'), L = Large (over 10')
GROWTH HABIT: I = Irregular, M = Mounding, O = Oval, Pr = Prostrate, Py = Pyramid, R = Round, U = Upright, W = Weeping, V = Varies, according to variety
GROWTH RATE: S = Slow, M = Medium, F = Fast

FLOWER, FRUIT, AUTUMN & WINTER COLORS IF SHOWY:
W = White, Pk = Pink, R = Red, O = Orange, Y = Yellow, Br = Brown, Bu = Blue, Bk = Black, Bz = Bronze, Gn = Green, Gy = Gray, Pr = Purple, L = Lavender, V = Varies, according to variety, F = Fragrant
HEDGING: F = Formal, I = Informal, V = Varies, depending on variety

continued

CHARACTERISTICS AND GROWING INFORMATION FOR SELECTED SHRUBS AND CONIFERS (CONTINUED)

SHRUBS AND CONIFERS	CONDITIONS			CHARACTERISTICS										
	SUN OR SHADE	WATER RQMNTS	SOIL TYPE	FOLIAGE TYPE	HEIGHT	GROWTH HABIT	GROWTH RATE	FLOWER COLOR	FRUIT COLOR	AUTUMN COLOR	WINTER EFFECT	THORNS	HEDGING	HEDGE SPACING
Prunus 'Cistena'	S	M	S-L	D	M	U-R	M	F/Pk	Bk-Pr	R-Pr	–	–	I	3'
glandulosa 'Rosea'	S	M	S-L	D	S	I	M	Pk	–	–	–	–	I	18-36"
Pyracantha, most	S-PS	D-M	All	S	M-L	I	F	W	O-R	Gn	*	*	F-I	2-5'
Pyracantha a.cv. 'Gnozam'-Gnome®	S-PS	D-M	All	S	M-L	I	F	W	O-R	Gn	*	*	F-I	2-5'
Rhamnus frangula 'Columnaris'	S-PS	M	L	D	L	U	M	W	R-Bk	Y	–	–	F-I	18-30"
Rhododendron, most	S-PS	M	L	E	V	V	S-M	V	–	Gn	*	–	I	24-36"
Rhodotypos scandens	All	All	All	D	S	M	M-F	W	Bk	–	–	–	I	24-36"
Rhus, most	S-PS	D-M	All	D	V	V	F	V	R	Y -O-R	–	–	I	2-4'
Ribes alpinum and cvs	All	D-M	All	D	S	R	M	Gn-Y	R	–	–	–	F-I	15 24"
Rosa, most	S	M	All	D	D-M	V	V	F/V	O-R	V	–	*	F-I	18-24"
Salix, small shrubby types	S	M-W	All	O	V	V	F	–	–	–	–	–	V	V
Sambucus canadensis	S-PS	D-M	All	D	M-L	R	M-R	W	R	Y	–	–	–	–
Shepherdia argenta	S-PS	D-M	All	D	M	R	M-F	Y-W	Y-R	–	–	*	–	–
Spiraea, most	S	D-M	All	D	D-S	V	M-F	W-Pk	–	V	–	–	I	1-2'
Stephanandra incisa 'Crispa'	S-PS	M	All	D	D	M-Pr	F	W	–	Y-O	–	–	I	1-3'
Symphoricarpos x chenaultii 'Hancock'	All	M	All	D	D	M-Pr	F	Pk	Pk	O	–	–	–	–
Syringa, French hybrids	S	M	S-L	D	M-L	I-U	M	F/V	–	Y	–	–	I	30"

Key:

CONDITIONS
SUN OR SHADE: S = Sun, PS = Partial Shade, Sh = Shade, All = Sun through Shade
WATER REQUIREMENTS: D = Dry, M = Moist, but well drained, W = Wet, All = Dry through Wet
SOIL TYPE: S = Sand, L = Loam, All = Sand through Clay
CHARACTERISTICS
FOLIAGE TYPE: H = Herbaceous, D = Deciduous,

S = Semi-Evergreen, E = Evergreen, C = Coniferous
SHRUB HEIGHT: D = Dwarf (up to 3'), S = Small (3' to 6'), M = Medium (6' to 10'), L = Large (over 10')
GROWTH HABIT: I = Irregular, M = Mounding, O = Oval, Pr = Prostrate, Py = Pyramid, R = Round, U = Upright, W = Weeping, V = Varies, according to variety
GROWTH RATE: S = Slow, M = Medium, F = Fast

FLOWER, FRUIT, AUTUMN & WINTER COLORS IF SHOWY:
W = White, Pk = Pink, R = Red, O = Orange, Y = Yellow, Br = Brown, Bu = Blue, Bk = Black, Bz = Bronze, Gn = Green, Gy = Gray, Pr = Purple, L = Lavender, V = Varies, according to variety, F = Fragrant
HEDGING: F = Formal, I = Informal, V = Varies, depending on variety

continued

SHRUBS AND CONIFERS	CONDITIONS			CHARACTERISTICS									
	SUN OR SHADE	WATER RQMNTS	SOIL TYPE	FOLIAGE TYPE	HEIGHT	GROWTH HABIT	GROWTH RATE	FLOWER COLOR	FRUIT COLOR	AUTUMN COLOR	WINTER EFFECT	THORNS	HEDGING	HEDGE SPACING
Late blooming hybrids	S	M	S-L	D	M-L	M-R	M-F	F/V	–	Y	–	–	I	30"
Taxus, most	S-PS	D-M	All	E	M	V	S-M	–	R	Gn	*	–	F-I	18-36"
Thuja occidentalis and cvs	S-PS	D-M	All	E	V	V	V	–	–	V	*	–	F-I	30 36"
Viburnum dentatum	S-PS	M-W	All	D	M-L	R	M	W	Bk	Y-O-R	–	–	I	2-4'
dilatatum and cvs	S-PS	M	L	D	M	U	S-M	W	R	R	*	–	I	2-4'
fragrant types	S-PS	M	L	D	M-L	V	S-M	F/W	V	Y-O-R	–	–	I	2-4'
lantana and cvs	S-PS	D-M	L	D	L	R	M	W	Y-R-Bk	R-O	–	–	I	2-4'
lentago	All	All	All	D	L	R	F	O	Bu-Bk	R-Pr	–	–	I	3'
opulus and cvs	S-PS	M-W	All	D	D-L	V	S-F	W	R	Y-O-R	–	–	I	2-4'
plicatum tomium and cvs	S-PS	M	S-L	D	M-L	R	M	W	R-Bk	R-Pr	–	–	I	2-4'
p.cv. Newzam-Newport®	S-PS	M	S-L	D	D	R	S-M	W	R-Bk	R-Pr	–	–	I	2'
prunifolium and cvs	All	D-M	All	D	L	R	S-M	W	Y-R-Bk	Pr	–	–	I	4'
x *rhytidophyllum* and cvs	S-PS	M	S-L	D-S	L	U-R	M	W	R-Bk	Gn-Bz	*	–	I	4'
sargentii and cvs	S-PS	M-W	All	D	L	U-R	M	W	R	Y-R	–	–	I	4'
setigerum	S-PS	D	S-L	D	M-L	U	M	W	R	O-R	–	–	I	2-4'
sieboldii	S-PS	M	L	D	L	U-O	M	W	R-Bk	R-Bk	–	–	I	4-6'
trilobum and cvs	S-PS	M	L	D	S-L	V	M	W	R	Y-O-R	–	–	I	2-4'
Weigela florida and cvs	S	M	S-L	D	M	R	M	V	–	–	–	–	F-I	2-3'
Yucca filamentosa and cvs	S	D-M	S-L	E	D	U-M	M	W	Br	V	*	–	I	2'

Key:

CONDITIONS
SUN OR SHADE: S = Sun, PS = Partial Shade, Sh = Shade, All = Sun through Shade
WATER REQUIREMENTS: D = Dry, M = Moist, but well drained, W = Wet, All = Dry through Wet
SOIL TYPE: S = Sand, L = Loam, All = Sand through Clay
CHARACTERISTICS
FOLIAGE TYPE: H = Herbaceous, D = Deciduous,

S = Semi-Evergreen, E = Evergreen, C = Coniferous
SHRUB HEIGHT: D = Dwarf (up to 3'), S = Small (3' to 6'), M = Medium (6' to 10'), L = Large (over 10')
GROWTH HABIT: I = Irregular, M = Mounding, O = Oval, Pr = Prostrate, Py = Pyramid, R = Round, U = Upright, W = Weeping, V = Varies, according to variety
GROWTH RATE: S = Slow, M = Medium, F = Fast

FLOWER, FRUIT, AUTUMN & WINTER COLORS IF SHOWY:
W = White, Pk = Pink, R = Red, O = Orange, Y = Yellow, Br = Brown, Bu = Blue, Bk = Black, Bz = Bronze, Gn = Green, Gy = Gray, Pr = Purple, L = Lavender, V = Varies, according to variety, F = Fragrant
HEDGING: F = Formal, I = Informal, V = Varies, depending on variety

SHRUBS FOR SMALL GARDENS

COMMON NAME	BOTANICAL NAME	LIGHT REQUIREMENTS	LEAF	HARDINESS ZONES*
Aucuba	*Aucuba japonica*	Shade	Evergreen	7
Azalea	*Rhododendron* spp.	Partial shade	Evergreen/Deciduous	2-9
Barberry	*Berberis* spp.	Sun	Evergreen/Deciduous	3-7
Boxwood	*Buxus* spp.	Sun/Shade	Evergreen	5-7
Camellia	*Camellia japonica*	Partial shade	Evergreen	7
Cotoneaster	*Cotoneaster* spp.	Sun	Evergreen/Deciduous	4-7
Cypress	*Cupressus* spp.	Sun	Evergreen	5-8
Euonymus	*Euonymus* spp.	Sun	Evergreen/Deciduous	3-6
Firethorn	*Pyracantha* spp.	Sun	Evergreen	6-8
Forsythia	*Forsythia* spp.	Sun	Deciduous	4-5
Heather	*Calluna, Erica* spp.	Sun	Evergreen	3-7
Heavenly bamboo	*Nandina domestica*	Sun/Partial shade	Evergreen	7
Hydrangea	*Hydrangea* spp.	Partial sun	Deciduous	4-7
Juniper	*Juniperus* spp.	Sun	Evergreen	2-7
Podocarpus	*Podocarpus* spp.	Sun/Shade	Evergreen	7-9
Privet	*Ligustrum* spp.	Sun	Evergreen/Deciduous	8
Rosemary	*Rosmarinus officinalis*	Sun	Evergreen	8

* Chart shows coldest hardiness zone tolerated by a species. Where a specific species is not named on the chart, look for a species appropriate to the hardiness range indicated.

Source: *The Able Gardener,* Kathleen Yeomans, R.N.

Fruiting Shrubs for Yard and Kitchen

NAME		DESCRIPTION	HEIGHT
American highbush cranberry	(Viburnum trilobum)	Sparkling red berries good for preserving are preceded in spring by clusters of showy hydrangea-like white flowers. Does well along shorelines, on slopes, in sun or shade. Plant 4 feet apart for hedge 8 feet apart for individual plants.	8-12 ft.
Autumn olive	(Elaeagnus umbellata)	Its dense silvery green hedge is covered with berries that make a piquant jelly. Is good for a windbreak planting.	6-10 ft.
Elderberry		Has large clusters of glistening black fruit. Is good for pies, wine, jelly, jams, and preserves. Attractive white flower clusters appear in June	5-6 ft.
European cranberry	(Viburnum opulus)	Rugged shrub with dark green maple-shaped leaves and bright scarlet berries. Berries are sour but can be used to make a jelly that is high in vitamin C.	6-8 ft.
Hansen's bush cherry	(Prunus besseyi)	An improved form of the Western bush cherry, it produces white flowers followed by deep crimson fruit. Its silvery leaves form a dense screen.	4-5 ft.
Hardy beach plum	(Prunus maritima)	Thrives well on poor soil, produces deep purple plums good for jam or jelly.	6 ft.
Juneberry	(Amelanchier canadensis)	Fruit is similar in taste to blueberry, but shrub can be grown more quickly. Is very hardy and not fussy about soil. Red berries turn blue are highly ornamental and make good pies.	10-12 ft.
Nanking cherry	(Prunus tomentosa)	Is very hardy. Showy white blossoms are followed by bright red fruit of true cherry flavor.	8-10 ft.
Prunus Japonica		A dwarf bush cherry that is good for hedge or specimen planting. White flowers are followed by red fruit that make good jam. Two are needed for pollination.	2-3 ft.
Purple leaf hazelnut	(Corylus)	Round leaves are a beautiful dull purple to brownish red. Is good for foliage contrast; produces edible nuts.	12-15 ft.
Rosa Rugosa		Has crimson-pink, semidouble roses; produces abundantly, blooms intermittently until frost. When planted 2 feet apart, makes a rose fence that keeps out intruders. Each blossom produces an orange-red rose hip – nature's richest source of vitamin C.	6 ft.
Scarlet flowering quince	(Chaenomeles speciosa or japonica)	Single blossoms of fiery scarlet bloom very early in spring, covering the branches. Leaves appear later with a dark, glossy green foliage. Fruit makes a tasty jelly.	3-5 ft.
Silver buffaloberry	(Shepherdia argentea)	Thorny shrub with silvery foliage is similar to Russian olive. Is very hardy. Orange-red fruit makes good jelly.	8-12 ft.
Western bush cherry	(Prunus besseyi)	Hardy shrub has silvery green foliage. White flowers bloom in May. Purple-black marble-sized sweet cherries are good for pies and preserves.	4-6 ft.
Wild black cherry	(Prunus serotina)	A real jelly tree! White blossoms in spring are followed by delicious black fruit in August. A hardy rapid grower that is useful for wind-breaks or as a specimen tree.	10-15 ft.

Source: *Successful Small Food Gardens,* Louise Riotte

PLANTS THAT ATTRACT BIRDS

COMMON NAME	BOTANICAL NAME	ZONES*/ PLANT TYPE	COMMON NAME	BOTANICAL NAME	ZONES*/ PLANT TYPE
FRUITS OF			FLOWERS OF		
Blackberry	*Rubus* spp.	3	Acacia	*Acacia* spp.	8-10
Cherry	*Prunus* spp.	1-9	Bee balm	*Monarda didyma*	4
Currants, gooseberries	*Ribes* spp.	2-5	Butterfly bush	*Buddleia* spp.	5-10
Fig	*Ficus* spp.	8-9	Ceanothus	*Ceanothus* spp.	4-8
Firethorn	*Pyracantha* spp.	5-7	Citrus	*Citrus* spp.	10
Grape	*Vitis* spp.	4-7	Fuchsia	*Fuchsia* spp.	5-10
Ivy	*Hedera* spp.	6-9	Honeysuckle	*Lonicera* spp.	4-5
Peach	*Prunus persica*	5	Impatiens	*Impatiens* spp.	TA
Persimmon	*Diospyros* spp.	5-6	Nicotiana	*Nicotiana* spp.	HHA
Plum	*Prunus* spp.	4-6	Penstemon	*Penstemon* spp.	3-7
Roses	*Rosa* spp.	3-8	Phlox	*Phlox* spp.	4-5
SEEDS OF					
Bachelor's-button	*Centaurea cyanus*	VHA	Marigold	*Tagetes* spp.	HHA
Birch	*Betula* spp.	3-5	Oak	*Quercus* spp.	3-8
Cosmos	*Cosmos* spp.	HHA	Pine	*Pinus* spp.	1-9
Elm	*Ulmus* spp.	2-5	Sunflower	*Helianthus* spp.	TA
Goldenrod	*Solidago* spp.	4	Zinnia	*Zinnia* spp.	TA
Most grasses					

continued

PLANTS THAT ATTRACT BIRDS (CONTINUED)

COMMON NAME	BOTANICAL NAME	ZONES*/ PLANT TYPE
SHELTER IN		
Abelia	*Abelia* spp.	5-8
Autumn olive	*Elaeagnus umbellata*	3
Bayberry	*Myrica pensylvanica*	4
Birch	*Betula* spp.	3-5
Blueberry	*Vaccinium* spp.	1-4
Bramble	*Rubus* spp.	3
Cedar	*Cedrus* spp.	6-7
Elderberry	*Sambucus* spp.	3-5
English ivy	*Hedera helix*	6
Grape	*Vitis* spp.	4-7
Holly	*Ilex* spp.	4-8
Honeysuckle	*Lonicera* spp.	4-5
Mulberry	*Morus* spp.	2-4
Oak	*Quercus* spp.	3-8
Privet	*Ligustrum* spp.	3-7
Trumpet vine	*Campsis radicans*	4
Viburnum	*Viburnum* spp.	4-8
Virginia creeper	*Parthenocissus quinquefolia*	4

PLANT TYPE: HHA = Half-hardy annual, TA = Tender annual, VHA = Very hardy annual.
* Chart shows coldest hardiness zone tolerated by a species. Where a specific species is not named on the chart, look for a species appropriate to the hardiness range indicated.

Source: *The Able Gardener,* Kathleen Yeomans, R.N.

Easy-Maintenance Deciduous Hedges

Acanthopanax	(five-leaf aralia)	The two-to-four clippings necessary each year are easily accomplished.
Acer campestre	(hedge maple)	Even though the foliage on this plant is large, it is attractive and easy to grow where climate permits.
Berberis	(barberry)	Choose the upright-growing kinds for the easiest maintenance – mentor, truehedge, and box barberry, for example.
Buxus microphylla var. *koreana*	(Korean boxwood)	This low-growing plant with fine foliage shears easily. With power clippers, large plantings can be beautifully maintained.
Carpinus	(hornbeam)	Both the native and European kinds make a tight, slow-growing, easy-to-maintain hedge that will grow fairly tall, if you wish.
Euonymus alata 'Compacta'	(winged spindle tree)	The dwarf size of this plant makes it easy to care for.
Euonymus fortunei	(wintercreeper)	A fast-growing, easy-care hedge plant. Many different kinds offer a variety of foliage.
Forsythia		The dwarf varieties make an easy-to-care-for, informal, blooming hedge.
Ligustrum	(privet)	Upright-growing kinds such as dwarf border privet are easy to care for, even though several prunings are needed during the summer.

Malus	(crab apple)	The various crab apples can be sheared into tight hedges that are easily maintained, although some additional care is needed to shape them. It is better not to use grafted varieties, because suckers are difficult to control.
Rhamnus frangula	(buckthorn)	The columnar varieties such as tallhedge are best, but careful early shearing is sometimes necessary to keep the plants tight at the bottom.
Viburnum		Sheared or unsheared, many of the viburnums make neat hedges. Some are dwarf naturally, so choosing the mature height you want will insure the least care and make berry production more certain.

Easy-Maintenance Evergreen Hedges

Ilex	(holly)	Upright-growing varieties need two or three relatively easy shearings each season.
Picea	(spruce)	Dwarf-growing varieties of Norway spruce, such as birdsnest, need only one easy shearing on the sides each year.
Taxus cuspidata 'Capitata'	(upright yew)	This variety and other upright-growing yews need one to three easy shearings each year.
Thuja occidentalis	(American arborvitae, white cedar)	One or two easy shearings will control this favorite in northern gardens.
Tsuga canadensis	(Canada hemlock)	One or two easy shearings will keep this beauty looking nice for years.

Source: *Pruning Simplified*, Lewis Hill

Source: *Pruning Simplified*, Lewis Hill

CHARACTERISTICS AND GROWING INFORMATION FOR SELECTED TREES

TREES	CONDITIONS				CHARACTERISTICS								
	SUN OR SHADE	WATER REQMNTS	SOIL TYPE	URBAN TOLERANCE	FOLIAGE TYPE	HEIGHT	GROWTH HABIT	GROWTH RATE	FLOWER COLOR	FRUIT COLOR	AUTUMN COLOR	WINTER EFFECT	STREET TREE USE
Acer campestre	S-PS	D-M	All	I	D	S	R	M	–	Br	Y	–	*
freemani cv. 'Celzam' P.P.7279 Celebration®	S-PS	M	L	R	D	M	O	M	R	–	Y	–	*
ginnala and cvs	S-PS	D-M	L	I	D	S	R	M	Y-W	Br	O-R	–	–
griseum	S-PS	M	S-L	I	D	S	O	S	Gn-Y	Br	O-R	*	–
palmatum and cvs	S-PS	D-M	L	I	D	S	R	S	Pr	R-Br	V	–	–
platanoides and cvs	S	D-M	L	I	D	M-L	V	M-F	Gn-Y	Br	Y-O	–	*
rubrum and cvs	S-PS	M-W	All	I	D	M-L	V	M-F	R	R-Br	Y-O-R	–	*
saccharinum	S	M	All	R	D	L	I	F	Y-R	Br	Y	–	–
saccharum and cvs	S-PS	D-M	L	S	D	L	O	M	Gn-Y	Br	Y-O-R	–	*
tataricum	S-PS	D-M	L	I	D	S	O	M	Gn-Y	R-Br	Y	–	–
Amelanchier spp. and cvs	S-PS	D-M	S-L	I	D	S	O-U	M	W	R-Pr	Y-O-R	–	*
Amelanchier c.cv. 'Sprizam'-Spring Glory®	S-PS	D-M	S-L	I	D	S	O-U	M	W	Pr-Bk	Y-O	–	*
Amelanchier c.cv. 'Trazam'-Tradition™	S-PS	D-M	S-L	I	D	S	O-U	M	W	Bu-Bk	R-Y-O	–	*
Betula jacquemontii	S-PS	D-M	L	I	D	S	Py	M	–	–	Y	*	–
Nigra	S-PS	All	All	I	D	M-L	O	M	–	–	Y	*	–
White-Barked spp., cvs	S-PS	D-M	L	S	D	M	O	M	–	–	Y	*	–

Key:

CONDITIONS
SUN OR SHADE: S = Sun, PS = Partial Shade, Sh = Shade, All = Sun through Shade
WATER REQUIREMENTS: D = Dry, M = Moist, but well drained, W = Wet, All = Dry through Wet
SOIL TYPE: S = Sand, L = Loam, All = Sand through Clay
URBAN TOLERANCE: S = Sensitive, I = Intermediate, R = Resistant

CHARACTERISTICS
FOLIAGE TYPE: H = Herbaceous, D = Deciduous, S = Semi-Evergreen, E = Evergreen, C = Coniferous
TREE HEIGHT: D = Dwarf (up to 15'), S = Small (15' to 30'), M = Medium (30' to 45'), L = Large (over 45')
GROWTH HABIT: I = Irregular, M = Mounding, O = Oval, Pr = Prostrate, Py = Pyramid, R = Round, U = Upright,

W = Weeping, V = Varies, according to variety
GROWTH RATE: S = Slow, M = Medium, F = Fast
FLOWER, FRUIT, AUTUMN & WINTER COLORS IF SHOWY:
W = White, Pk = Pink, R = Red, O = Orange, Y = Yellow, Br = Brown, Bu = Blue, Bk = Black, Bz = Bronze, Gn = Green, Gy = Gray, Pr = Purple, L = Lavender, V = Varies, according to variety, F = Fragrant

continued

CHARACTERISTICS AND GROWING INFORMATION FOR SELECTED TREES (CONTINUED)

TREES	CONDITIONS				CHARACTERISTICS									
	SUN OR SHADE	WATER REQMNTS	SOIL TYPE	URBAN TOLERANCE	FOLIAGE TYPE	HEIGHT	GROWTH HABIT	GROWTH RATE	FLOWER COLOR	FRUIT COLOR	AUTUMN COLOR	WINTER EFFECT	STREET TREE USE
Betula v cv. 'Avalzam'-Avalanche®	S-PS	D-M	L	I	D	L	O	M	–	–	Y	*	–
Carpinus betula 'Fastigata'	S-PS	M	L	S	D	M	Py-O	S	–	Gn-Br	Y-O	*	*
Celtis occidentalis	All	All	L	I	D	L	U-R	M-F	–	O-R	Y	–	*
Cercidiphyllum japonicum	S-PS	M	L	S	D	M	U-R	M	–	–	Y-R	–	–
Cercis canadensis	S-PS	D-M	L	S	D	S-M	R	S-M	Pr-Pk	Br	Y-O	–	–
Chamaecyparis nootkatensis and cvs	S	M	L	R	E	S-M	V	M	–	Y-Br	Gn	*	–
Cladrastus lutea	S-PS	D-M	S-L	S	D	M	R	M	W	–	–	–	–
Cornus alternifolia	S-PS	M	L	S	D	S	R	M	Y-W	Bu-Bk	R-Pr	*	–
florida and cvs	S-PS	M	L	S	D	S	R	M	W-P	R	R	–	–
kousa chinensis and cvs	S-PS	M	L	I	D	S	U	M	W	R	R	–	–
mas and cvs	S-PS	M	L	I	D	S	R	M	Y	R	–	–	–
Corylus colurna	S-PS	D-M	L	I	D	M-L	Py	M	–	Br	–	–	*
Crataegus spp. and cvs	S	D-M	All	R	D	S	O-R	M	W	R-O	Y-O-R	*	*
Crataegus c.i. cv. 'Cruzam'-Crusader®	S	D-M	All	R	D	S	R	M	W	R	Y-O-R	*	*
Elaeagnus angustifolia	S	D-M	All	R	D	S	I-R	F	F/W	–	–	–	–

Key:

CONDITIONS
SUN OR SHADE: S = Sun, PS = Partial Shade, Sh = Shade,
 All = Sun through Shade
WATER REQUIREMENTS: D = Dry, M = Moist, but well
 drained, W = Wet, All = Dry through Wet
SOIL TYPE: S = Sand, L = Loam, All = Sand through Clay
URBAN TOLERANCE: S = Sensitive, I = Intermediate,
 R = Resistant

CHARACTERISTICS
FOLIAGE TYPE: H = Herbaceous, D = Deciduous,
 S = Semi-Evergreen, E = Evergreen, C = Coniferous
TREE HEIGHT: D = Dwarf (up to 15'), S = Small (15' to 30'),
 M = Medium (30' to 45'), L = Large (over 45')
GROWTH HABIT: I = Irregular, M = Mounding, O = Oval,
 Pr = Prostrate, Py = Pyramid, R = Round, U = Upright,

W = Weeping, V = Varies, according to variety
GROWTH RATE: S = Slow, M = Medium, F = Fast
FLOWER, FRUIT, AUTUMN & WINTER COLORS IF SHOWY:
 W = White, Pk = Pink, R = Red, O = Orange, Y = Yellow,
 Br = Brown, Bu = Blue, Bk = Black, Bz = Bronze,
 Gn = Green, Gy = Gray, Pr = Purple, L = Lavender,
 V = Varies, according to variety, F = Fragrant

continued

TREES	CONDITIONS				CHARACTERISTICS									
	SUN OR SHADE	WATER REQMNTS	SOIL TYPE	URBAN TOLERANCE	FOLIAGE TYPE	HEIGHT	GROWTH HABIT	GROWTH RATE	FLOWER COLOR	FRUIT COLOR	AUTUMN COLOR	WINTER EFFECT	STREET TREE USE
Eucommia ulmoides	S	D-M	All	I	D	M	R	M	–	–	Gn	–	*
Fagus sylvatica and cvs	S-PS	D-M	S-L	I	D	L	V	S	–	Br	Bz	–	–
Fraxinus americana and cvs	S-PS	M	L	S	D	L	V	M	–	–	Pr	–	*
excelsior 'Hessei'	S	M	L	I	D	L	R	F	–	–	–	–	*
pennsylvanica and cvs	S	All	All	R	D	L	O	F	–	–	Y	–	*
Fraxinus pennsylvanica cv. 'Cimmzam' P.A.F. Cimmaron™	S-PS	All	All	R	D	L	O	F	–	–	R-Y-O	–	*
Ginkgo biloba and cvs	S	M	L	R	D	L	U-Py	S-M	Gn	–	Y	–	*
Gleditsia triacanthos inermis and cvs	S	All	All	R	D	M-L	I-R	F	–	Br	Y	–	*
Gymnocladus dioica	S	M-W	L	R	D	L	I-0	S-M	Y	Br	Y	*	–
Halesia carolina	S-PS	M	L	I	D	S	R	M	W	–	Y	*	–
Koelreuteria paniculata	S	D-M	All	R	D	M	R	M	Y	Br	Y	*	*
Laburnum × *watereri* 'Vossii'	S-PS	M	L	–	D	S	O-U	M	Y	Br	–	–	–
Larix kaempferi	S	M	L	I	D	L	Py	M-F	–	Br	Y	–	–
Liquidambar styraciflua and cvs	S	M	All	R	D	L	Py-V	M	–	Br	Y-R-Pr	–	*

Key:

CONDITIONS
SUN OR SHADE: S = Sun, PS = Partial Shade, Sh = Shade, All = Sun through Shade
WATER REQUIREMENTS: D = Dry, M = Moist, but well drained, W = Wet, All = Dry through Wet
SOIL TYPE: S = Sand, L = Loam, All = Sand through Clay
URBAN TOLERANCE: S = Sensitive, I = Intermediate, R = Resistant

CHARACTERISTICS
FOLIAGE TYPE: H = Herbaceous, D = Deciduous, S = Semi-Evergreen, E = Evergreen, C = Coniferous
TREE HEIGHT: D = Dwarf (up to 15'), S = Small (15' to 30'), M = Medium (30' to 45'), L = Large (over 45')
GROWTH HABIT: I = Irregular, M = Mounding, O = Oval, Pr = Prostrate, Py = Pyramid, R = Round, U = Upright,

W = Weeping, V = Varies, according to variety
GROWTH RATE: S = Slow, M = Medium, F = Fast
FLOWER, FRUIT, AUTUMN & WINTER COLORS IF SHOWY:
W = White, Pk = Pink, R = Red, O = Orange, Y = Yellow, Br = Brown, Bu = Blue, Bk = Black, Bz = Bronze, Gn = Green, Gy = Gray, Pr = Purple, L = Lavender, V = Varies, according to variety, F = Fragrant

continued

TREES	CONDITIONS				CHARACTERISTICS								
	SUN OR SHADE	WATER REQMNTS	SOIL TYPE	URBAN TOLERANCE	FOLIAGE TYPE	HEIGHT	GROWTH HABIT	GROWTH RATE	FLOWER COLOR	FRUIT COLOR	AUTUMN COLOR	WINTER EFFECT	STREET TREE USE
Liquidambar s.cv. 'Goduzam'-Gold Dust®	S	M	All	R	D	L	Py-R	M	–	Br	Y-R-O	–	*
Liriodendron tulipifera	S-PS	M	S-L	I	D	L	Py-O	M-F	Gn-Y	Br	Y	–	–
Malus spp. and cvs	S	M	All	R	D	S-M	V	V	V	V	V	V	*
Nyssa sylvatica	S-PS	All	L	I	D	M-L	O-Py	S	–	Bu	R	–	–
Ostrya virginiana	S-PS	D-M	All	S	D	M	O-Py	S	-	Br	Y	–	*
Oxydendrum arboreum	S-PS	M	S-L	I	D	S-M	O-Py	S	W	W-Br	R	–	–
Phellodendron amurense	S	D	All	I	D	M	R	M-F	–	Bk	Y	–	*
Photinia villosa	S-PS	M	S-L	I	D	D	U	M	W	R	Y-R-O	–	–
Picea spp. and cvs	S	M	All	R	E	V	V	V	Y-R	Br	V	*	–
Pinus spp. and cvs	S	D-M	S-L	V	E	V	V	V	Y-R	Br	V	*	–
Platanus x *acerifolia* 'Bloodgood'	S-PS	D-M	All	S	D	L	R	F	–	Br	–	*	*
Populus spp., hybrids, and cvs	S	D-M	All	R	D	M-L	V	F	–	–	–	–	–
Prunus, tree spp. and cvs	S	D-M	L	V	D	S-M	V	M	V	V	Y-O-R	–	*
Prunus x cv. 'Snofozam'-Snow Fountains®	S	D-M	L	I	D	S-M	W	M	W	Bk	Y-O-R	*	–

Key:

CONDITIONS
SUN OR SHADE: S = Sun, PS = Partial Shade, Sh = Shade,
   All = Sun through Shade
WATER REQUIREMENTS: D = Dry, M = Moist, but well
   drained, W = Wet, All = Dry through Wet
SOIL TYPE: S = Sand, L = Loam, All = Sand through Clay
URBAN TOLERANCE: S = Sensitive, I = Intermediate,
   R = Resistant

CHARACTERISTICS
FOLIAGE TYPE: H = Herbaceous, D = Deciduous,
   S = Semi-Evergreen, E = Evergreen, C = Coniferous
TREE HEIGHT: D = Dwarf (up to 15'), S = Small (15' to 30'),
   M = Medium (30' to 45'), L = Large (over 45')
GROWTH HABIT: I = Irregular, M = Mounding, O = Oval,
   Pr = Prostrate, Py = Pyramid, R = Round, U = Upright,

W = Weeping, V = Varies, according to variety
GROWTH RATE: S = Slow, M = Medium, F = Fast
FLOWER, FRUIT, AUTUMN & WINTER COLORS IF SHOWY:
   W = White, Pk = Pink, R = Red, O = Orange, Y = Yellow,
   Br = Brown, Bu = Blue, Bk = Black, Bz = Bronze,
   Gn = Green, Gy = Gray, Pr = Purple, L = Lavender,
   V = Varies, according to variety, F = Fragrant

continued

TREES	CONDITIONS				CHARACTERISTICS									
	SUN OR SHADE	WATER REQMNTS	SOIL TYPE	URBAN TOLERANCE	FOLIAGE TYPE	HEIGHT	GROWTH HABIT	GROWTH RATE	FLOWER COLOR	FRUIT COLOR	AUTUMN COLOR	WINTER EFFECT	STREET TREE USE
Pyrus calleryana and cvs	S	D-M	All	R	D	M	O-Py	M	W	V	Y-O-R	–	*
Pyrus c cv. 'Valzam'-Valiant	S	D-M	All	R	D	M	Py	M	W	–	R	–	*
salicifolia p cv. 'Silfrozam'-Silver Frost®	S	D-M	All	R	D	S	I	M	W	Gy-Gn	–	–	–
Quercus spp.	S	V	L	I	D	L	V	M	Y-Gn	Br	V	–	*
Salix, spp. and cvs	S	M-W	All	I	D	M-L	R	F	V	–	V	V	–
Salix x cv. 'Scarcuzam'-Scarlet Curls®	S	M-W	All	I	D	S-M	R	F	–	–	–	*	–
Sorbus spp. and cvs	S-PS	D-M	S-L	S	D	S-M	O	M-F	W	V	Y-O-R	V	–
Taxodium distichum	S	M-W	All	R	D	M-L	Py	M	Gn-W	Br	Bz	*	*
Tilia cordata and cvs	S	M	L	S	D	L	O-Py	M	F/Y	Br	Y	–	*
Tilia c cv. 'Corzam'-Corinthian®	S	M	L	R	D	L	Py	M	W	–	Y	–	*
Tsuga spp.	All	M	L	S	E	M-L	Py	S-M	–	Br	Gn	*	–
Ulmus spp. and cvs	S-PS	D-M	All	R	D	M-L	R-Py	M-F	–	–	Y	–	*
Zelkova serrata and cvs	S	M	All	S	D	M-L	V	M-F	–	–	Y-O-R	–	*

Key:

CONDITIONS
SUN OR SHADE: S = Sun, PS = Partial Shade, Sh = Shade, All = Sun through Shade
WATER REQUIREMENTS: D = Dry, M = Moist, but well drained, W = Wet, All = Dry through Wet
SOIL TYPE: S = Sand, L = Loam, All = Sand through Clay
URBAN TOLERANCE: S = Sensitive, I = Intermediate, R = Resistant

CHARACTERISTICS
FOLIAGE TYPE: H = Herbaceous, D = Deciduous, S = Semi-Evergreen, E = Evergreen, C = Coniferous
TREE HEIGHT: D = Dwarf (up to 15'), S = Small (15' to 30'), M = Medium (30' to 45'), L = Large (over 45')
GROWTH HABIT: I = Irregular, M = Mounding, O = Oval, Pr = Prostrate, Py = Pyramid, R = Round, U = Upright,

W = Weeping, V = Varies, according to variety
GROWTH RATE: S = Slow, M = Medium, F = Fast
FLOWER, FRUIT, AUTUMN & WINTER COLORS IF SHOWY:
W = White, Pk = Pink, R = Red, O = Orange, Y = Yellow, Br = Brown, Bu = Blue, Bk = Black, Bz = Bronze, Gn = Green, Gy = Gray, Pr = Purple, L = Lavender, V = Varies, according to variety, F = Fragrant

FRUITS

DWARF FRUIT TREES

VARIETY	RIPENING TIME	HARDINESS (ZONES)	FRUIT DESCRIPTION AND USES	COMMENTS
APPLE				
Beacon	Late summer/ early fall	3-4	Red, large; cooking	Vigorous grower, heavy bearer
Cortland	Mid-season	4-8	Red, large size, sweet, crunchy flesh; good keeper, white flesh resists browning when cut; eating, cooking, cider	Hardy, vigorous, heavy bearer
Cox Orange	Fall	5-8	Red-yellow; eating	
Duchess	Late summer	(2) 3-6	Red; cooking	Trees are long lived and fairly disease resistant
Empire	Late fall	5-7	Red (colors before fully ripe), juicy, flavorful flesh; good keeper, eating, cider	Hybrid between McIntosh & Delicious, self-fruitful, heavy bearer needs thinning
Golden Delicious	Early	(4) 5-8	Large, yellow skin, crisp juicy flesh; bruises easily; eating, cooking	Self fruitful
Granny Smith	Late fall	6-9	Large, green, tart, juicy, high quality; good keeper, eating, cooking	Heavy bearer, sometimes difficult in home orchards, needs long growing season
Gravenstein	Mid-season	5-8	Fragrant, orange-yellow skin with red stripes; crisp, juicy, yellowish flesh; eating, cooking	Vigorous, but sometimes difficult to grow in home orchards; best in areas with cool summers
Jonathan	Mid-to-late fall	5-7	Round, red fruit with juicy flesh; eating, cooking	Heavy bearer, self-fruitful but better with cross-pollinator, disease resistance depends on variety
Lodi	Summer	4-8	Yellow or green, crisp, juicy flesh; cooking	Heavy bearer, requires pollinator, resists apple scab
Macoun	Very late fall	3-4	Red skin, firm, juicy flesh; eating	Tends to bear fruit biennially, disease resistant, popular in the Northeast
McIntosh	Early & late selections available	(3) 4-7	Red; eating, cooking, does not keep well	Resistant to some disease problems

continued

VARIETY	RIPENING TIME	HARDINESS (ZONES)	FRUIT DESCRIPTION AND USES	COMMENTS
APPLE (continued)				
Melba	Early fall	3-4	Red, excellent flavor for eating, cooking, cider	
Northern (Red) Spy	Late fall	4-8	Green and red striped skin, firm, juicy, yellow flesh; good keeper, cooking, eating, storing	Heavy bearer, but slow to mature; good in northern states
Paulared	Summer/ early fall	5-8	Red; eating	
Quinto	Early fall	3-4	Red; eating	
Red Delicious	Late fall	5-8	Dark red, shiny skin, crisp, juicy flesh; eating	Many varieties productive and fast growing, self-sterile (needs cross-pollinator), disease resistant
Red Rome	Early and late selections available	5-8	Large, round, red fruit; tart, crunchy flesh; eating, cooking, cider	Vigorous, self-pollinating
Spartan	Early fall	4-7	Aromatic, deep red skin, firm white flesh; eating	Heavy bearer, disease resistant, self-fruitful but yields better if planted with Lodi; especially recommended for midwestern states
Wealthy	Late summer	4-7	Red skin; crisp flesh; eating, cooking	Very resistant to disease
Winesap	Mid-to-late summer	5-8	Deep red skin, tart, juicy, yellow flesh; good keeper, eating, cooking, cider	Attractive blossoms, disease resistant, needs pollinator, sometimes difficult in home orchards, best in mild climates
APRICOT				
Chinese (Mormon Chinese)	Mid-to-late summer	5-8	Yellow to orange fruits with good flavor; eating	Heavy bearer, trees produce fruit at an early age; late-flowering prevents damage from spring frosts
Early Golden	Mid-summer	5-8	Large, smooth orange-gold fruits with sweet, succulent flesh; eating, canning, cooking, drying	Self-fruitful, but better with cross-pollination; especially good in south and southwestern regions

continued

Dwarf Fruit Trees (continued)

VARIETY	RIPENING TIME	HARDINESS (ZONES)	FRUIT DESCRIPTION AND USES	COMMENTS
APRICOT (continued)				
Goldcot	Mid-summer	5-8	Golden yellow skin, firm, juicy, tangy, freestone flesh; eating, canning, freezing	Hardy, vigorous, heavy bearing (needs thinning), self-fruitful; late flowering prevents damage from spring frosts; especially good in northwestern region
Moongold	Mid-summer	4-9	Golden fruit with sweet, freestone flesh; eating, canning, preserves	Very hardy, disease resistant; needs Sungold variety for cross-pollination
Moorpark	Mid-summer	5-8	Large, orange fruits with red blush and juicy, aromatic flesh; eating, canning, drying	Natural dwarf, vigorous; attractive pinkish white blossoms; self-pollinating but better in pairs; especially good in southeast and west coast regions
Sungold	Mid-summer	4-9	Gold skin with orange blush; sweet, juicy, freestone flesh; eating, canning, preserves	Very hardy, heavy bearer, pink blossoms; best when cross-pollinated with Moongold variety

Apricots are very successfully grown in the West and in favorable situations may be quite satisfactory in other sections. It is important to remember that apricots bloom early when weather conditions may be unfavorable for pollination and fruit-setting. Blossoms are often destroyed by spring frosts and hence protected locations are essential for success, particularly in the northeast and middle-western areas.

VARIETY	RIPENING TIME	HARDINESS (ZONES)	FRUIT DESCRIPTION AND USES	COMMENTS
CHERRY				
Bing (sweet)	Early summer; fruit ripens all at once	5-8	Large, dark red, sweet fruit; eating	Thrives in relatively warm and dry regions; requires cross-pollination, with varieties other than Lambert or Napoleon
Black Tartarian (sweet)	Early summer	5-8	Dark, soft fruits with rich, sweet flavor; eating	Heavy bearing, very compatible as cross-pollinator
English Morello (sour)	Early summer	4-7	Dark, good quality fruits for cooking & preserving	
Lambert (sweet)	Early summer	5-7	Large, sweet, dark red fruit, but skin splits easily; eating	Does not cross-pollinate well with Bing or Napoleon varieties
Montmorency (sour)	Early summer	5-7	Bright red fruit with firm, yellow, tart flesh; cooking, preserving, freezing	Most common sour cherry; self-fruitful

continued

VARIETY	RIPENING TIME	HARDINESS (ZONES)	FRUIT DESCRIPTION AND USES	COMMENTS
CHERRY (continued)				
Napoleon, or Royal Anne (sweet)	Early summer	5-8	Large, high quality, yellow fruits with red blush and sweet, juicy flesh; eating, canning	Heavy bearer, standard tree grows 20-25' tall; does not cross-pollinate well with Bing or Lambert varieties
North Star (sour)	Early summer	4-8	Large, light red fruits with juicy, red flesh; canning, freezing, preserves	Naturally dwarf tree (grows 6-12' tall), self-fruitful, heavy bearer, disease resistant and very hardy
Stella (sweet)	Early summer	5-8	Heart-shaped, dark red fruit with sweet, juicy flesh; skin resists splitting; eating, cooking	Vigorous and hardy tree; good pollinator, self-fruitful, bears abundantly
NECTARINE				
Mericrest	Mid-summer	5-8	Dark red fruit with sweet, juicy, tangy, yellow, freestone flesh	Hardy and disease resistant, self-fruitful
Nectar Babe	Mid-summer	9	Large, red fruits with sweet, yellow, freestone flesh	Genetic dwarf (up to 6' tall), very productive but needs cross-pollinator (preferably Honey Babe variety)
Red Gold	Late summer	5-8	Mostly red skinned fruit with firm, yellow, juicy, freestone flesh and outstanding flavor	Vigorous, productive, self-fruitful, winter hardy, but susceptible to disease
Nectarine trees are very similar to peach trees. The fruits are smaller; the flavor is different, and the skin is smooth, like a plum.				
PEACH				
Elberta	Early and late selections available	5-8	Large, yellow, freestone fruits; eating, canning, freezing, jam	Hardy, productive, disease-resistant, and reliable bearers (some trees tend to drop mature fruits)
Golden Jubilee	Very early	5-8	Yellow with red blush, freestone; freezing, canning	Productive and vigorous tree
Halehaven	Mid-season	5-8	Yellow-skinned with red blush, large, oval-shaped fruits; firm, sweet, juicy flesh; canning, freezing	Abundant producer, vigorous, hardy

continued

VARIETY	RIPENING TIME	HARDINESS (ZONES)	FRUIT DESCRIPTION AND USES	COMMENTS
PEACH (continued)				
Honey Babe		6-9	Yellow skin with red blush; sweet, freestone, orange flesh; eating	Genetic dwarf (3-5' tall), dense foliage, self-fruitful; especially good in western states
Redhaven	Very early to mid-summer	5-8	Red, nearly fuzzless fruit with firm, yellow, freestone flesh; eating, canning, freezing	Hardy, self-pollinating, disease-resistant, reliable and heavy yield, needs thinning, does especially well in lower Midwest
Valiant	Very early	5-8	Good quality, round, yellow fruit with red blush and freestone flesh	Very productive
PEAR				
Anjou	Late fall	5-8	Large, light green skin, aromatic, dry flesh; good keeper, eating, canning, drying	Vigorous and hardy, needs Bosc or Bartlett for cross-pollination, somewhat disease resistant
Bartlett	Late summer	5-8	Large, golden fruit with red blush, sweet, juicy, white flesh; eating, canning, preserves	Vigorous and highly productive, long-lived, may be self-fruitful in dry or warm climates but needs cross-pollinator elsewhere
Bosc	Late fall to winter	5-8	Long, tapered, dark brown fruits with firm, rich, sweet, fragrant flesh; eating baking, drying	Slow-growing but productive; needs cross-pollinator, susceptible to disease in warm, moist areas
Clapp's Favorite	Late summer	5-8	Large, tapered, yellow fruit with sweet, fine-grained, white flesh; eating, canning	Hardy, vigorous tree but susceptible to blight
Duchess	Late fall	5-8	Large, good quality fruit; eating, preserves	Reliable bearer
Kieffer	Late fall	4-9	Large yellow fruits with red blush; crisp, juicy, white flesh; good keeper, baking, canning, preserves	Hardy, vigorous, long-lived, dependable bearer; tolerates heat but grows well in moist areas, disease resistant
Seckel	Early fall	(4) 5-8	Small, yellowish brown fruits with red blush; extremely sweet and juicy flesh; eating, canning, pickling, and spicing	Vigorous, healthy tree; heavy bearer, self-fruitful but better with cross-pollination; naturally grows only 15-20 feet (without dwarfing)
Tyson	Late summer	5-8	Sweet, juicy fruit; canning	Heavy bearer, fairly disease resistant

continued

VARIETY	RIPENING TIME	HARDINESS (ZONES)	FRUIT DESCRIPTION AND USES	COMMENTS
PLUM				
Burbank	Late summer	5-9	Large, purple fruits with juicy flesh; excellent sweet flavor; eating, canning	Japanese, naturally small tree (12-15' tall); sometimes difficult in home orchards
Damson	Early fall	5-9	Small to medium fruits; canning, preserves	European; heavy, regular bearer; yields early in life; not always available
Formosa	Mid-summer	5-9	Juicy, reddish yellow fruit; eating	One of the finest Japanese selections
Green Gage	Mid-summer		Yellow-green fruit with sweet, amber flesh; eating, canning, cooking, preserves	European, hardy, productive self-pollinating
Italian Prune	Mid- to late summer	5-9	Purple-black fruit with yellow flesh; canning	European, self-fruitful, but produces better with cross-pollination; sometimes difficult in home orchards
President	Late summer	5-9	Large, purple-black fruit with yellow flesh	Heavy bearer, self-fruitful, but better with cross-pollination; sometimes difficult in home orchards
Santa Rosa	Mid-summer	5-9	High quality, reddish purple fruit; eating, canning	Japanese, vigorous, productive; self-fruitful, but better if cross-pollinating with Japanese varieties; popular in the western states
Shiro	Mid-summer	5-9	Excellent quality, large, yellow fruits; sweet and very juicy; eating, canning, cooking, preserving	Japanese, reliable producer, needs cross-pollination
Stanley Prune	Early fall	5-7	Large, dark blue fruits with very sweet yellow-green flesh; eating, canning, cooking, drying, preserves	European, heavy bearer, will produce without cross-pollination, good pollinator for other varieties; does especially well in northern and midwestern regions
QUINCE				
Champion	Very late fall	6-8	Sour, cooking, preserves	Self-pollinating, ornamental
Orange	Very late fall	(5) 6-8	Sour, cooking, preserves	Self-pollinating, ornamental
Pineapple	Very late fall	6-8	Eating, cooking	Better in western regions

Quinces are used principally for preserves, jams, and jellies. However, the trees are considered as ornaments on many lawns. Trees known as flowering quince (*Chaenomeles japonica,* and *C. speciosa)* produce fruit of inferior quality and are cultivated primarily for ornament.

Source: *Planning and Planting Your Dwarf Fruit Orchard,* Editors of Gardening Way Publishing

Fruit Cultivars Suggested for Beginning Growers

ZONE 3	
Apple	Astrachan, Beacon, Connell, Dolgo Crab, Duchess, Lodi, Prairie Spy, Wealthy, Yellow Transparent
Cherry Plum	Compass, Sapalta
Peach	None
Pear	Golden Spice, Mendell, Parker, Patten
Plum	La Crescent, Pipestone, Redcoat, Waneta
Sour Cherry	Meteor, North Star, Richmond
Sweet Cherry	None
Nuts	Butternuts

ZONE 4	
Growers in this zone should be able to grow everything listed for zone 3, plus	
Apple	Freedom, Honeygold, Liberty, MacFree, Northwest Greening, Regent, Yellow Delicious
Peach	Reliance (in favored spots)
Pear	Flemish Beauty, Kieffer, Seckel
Plum	Green Gage, Monitor, Stanley
Sour Cherry	Richmond
Sweet Cherry	None
Nuts	Black walnuts, hardy filberts

ZONE 5	
Growers in zone 5 should be able to grow everything listed for zones 3, 4, plus	
Apple	Gravenstein, Prima, Priscilla, Rhode Island Greening
Peach	Stark Frost King, Stark Sure Crop, Sunapee
Plum	Burbank, Damson, Earliblue, Italian, Santa Rosa, Shiro
Sour Cherry	Montmorency
Sweet Cherry	Bing, the Dukes, Stella, Windsor
Nuts	Carpathian walnut, filbert, hickory

ZONE 6-8	
Some cultivars that will grow in the colder zones do not grow as well here, because they need a longer chilling period during the winter.	
Apple	Adina, Granny Smith, Grimes Golden, Stayman, Winesap
Cherry	All sweet and sour cherries should do well.
Peach	Candor, Elberta, Halehaven, Madison, Redhaven
Pear	Anjou, Bartlett, Bosc, Clapp's Favorite, Oriental kinds
Plum	All except American hybrids should do well.
Nuts	The chestnut hybrids, walnut, and the hardiest pecans

Source: *Fruits and Berries for the Home Garden,* Lewis Hill

FRUIT TREE PESTS

PEST	SUSCEPTIBLE TREES & DAMAGE	WHERE PEST OVERWINTERS & PREVENTIVE MEASURES	CONTROLS
Aphids (several species)	All fruit trees – Suck juices from leaves and fruit. Cause yellowing and tight curling of new leaves. Fruit discoloration can be caused by black sooty mold that grows on the honeydew secreted by aphids.	Eggs on twigs– Spray dormant oil during late dormancy as buds begin to swell but before any green shows. Apply only when temperatures are between 35°F and 85°F. Paint tree wounds to prevent feeding. Regularly loosen and cultivate soil 1-3" deep around trees to prevent root-feeding by woolly apple aphid. Aphids cause most damage in absence of beneficials.	Syrphid flies, green lacewings, ladybug larvae and predatory gall midges feed on aphids. Chalcid and braconid wasps parasitize. Tanglefoot spread in a band around each tree one foot above ground prevents ants from carrying aphids up trees. Safer's Insecticidal Soap or soapy water spray of 2 tablespoons dishwashing liquid/one gallon of water repels some aphids. Spray entire plants. Summer horticultural spray oil. Rotenone dust as a last resort.
Apple Maggot	Apples, plums, pears– Females begin laying eggs in fruit 30 days after petals fall. Larvae tunnel throughout fruit (versus codling moth larvae which tunnel from blossom end to center of fruit).	Pupae overwinter underground– Clean up dropped fruit. Remove nearby abandoned apple trees.	Monitor with red spheres smeared with Tanglefoot or use 4-6 spheres per tree to provide control in small orchard. Make bait traps to hang in trees: solution of 1 part molasses diluted with 9 parts water and little yeast; or 2 teaspoons of household ammonia and small amount of soap powder in 1 quart of water. Hang plastic cups of bait on sunny side of tree about 60" high. Renew bait after rain.
Borers (several species)	All fruit trees, especially peaches– Borers drill holes in trunk or branch tips, leaving piles of sawdust or excrement near hole. Trees weaken and die.	Larvae under bark– Remove broken, diseased, or dead wood and any infested branches. Treat all wounds promptly. Coat trunk and large lower limbs with whitewash or slurry of rotenone and diatomaceous earth to prevent egglaying in early spring, midsummer, and fall. Monitor peach tree borer with pheromone traps.	Kill borer by very carefully probing into holes with wire and paint over wound with wound healer. Paint bark with interior white latex paint. Wrap bottom 12"-18" of trunk with glossy magazine paper in April/May and remove and destroy in fall.
Codling Moth	Apples, pears, apricots, plums– Females begin laying eggs in leaves near fruit at petal fall. Grubs tunnel through apples from blossom end to center of fruit (versus apple maggot which tunnels throughout fruit), leaving excrement outside hole.	Larvae in cocoons under bark scales, debris or ground litter or at base of smooth-barked tree– Tie strips of burlap or corrugated cardboard around base of trunk and large limbs to trap larvae moving down tree to pupate. Then burn strips. Or cover strips with Tanglefoot. Tie paper bags around individual fruits after thinning in May or June. Carefully scrape loose bark from trees and remove ground litter. Larvae like to pupate in sweet clover stems so remove any nearby. Monitor with pheromone traps.	Mating disruption. Trichogramma wasps parasitize moth eggs. Dormant oil spray. Ryania, pyrethrum, Imidan.

continued

FRUIT TREE PESTS (CONTINUED)

PEST	SUSCEPTIBLE TREES & DAMAGE	WHERE PEST OVERWINTERS & PREVENTIVE MEASURES	CONTROLS
Green Fruitworms (several species)	Many fruits– Larvae eat leaves, make large holes in fruit causing drop. Fruits that mature are misshapen with corky areas.	Pupae or adults underground; eggs on twigs or leaves– Cultivate under trees 1-4" deep. Monitor with pheromone traps.	Trichogramma wasps, *Bt*, Imidan.
European Apple Sawfly	Apples– Females lay eggs in fruit from time buds turn pink to after bloom. Larvae burrow in fruit causing long curving russeted path on skin.	Larvae on ground– Remove ground litter.	Visual traps (white sticky rectangles). Summer horticultural spray oil.
Japanese Beetles*	Many fruits– Adults skeletonize leaves and devour fruits.	In soil– Pick ripe fruit; milky spore disease controls larvae, but it can take a season or two to work.	Lay tarp underneath tree in early morning when beetles are groggy and shake branches to dislodge beetles. Drown beetles in kerosene. Rotenone spray.
Mites*	Many fruits– Cause yellowing and stippling of leaves. Mites are so tiny, they are hard to detect, but their webs on leaf axils and undersides are more visible.	Plant debris– Remove debris. Don't plant marigolds nearby because they attract mites.	Spray with dormant oil when buds begin to open. Spray with insecticidal soap, soapy water, garlic/onion water, or buttermilk solution (½ cup buttermilk, 4 cups wheat flour, 5 gallons of water).
Oriental Fruit Moth	Favor peaches: also other fruits– Causes most damage in May. Larvae feeds inside twigs causing wilting, and on fruit causing black blotches.	Larvae in tree bark or ground litter– Plant early maturing varieties. Cultivate soil around trees 1"-4" deep 1-3 weeks before bloom. Monitor with pheromone traps.	Mating disruption. Dust impregnated with mineral oil (viscosity of 100): sulfur 60%, 300-mesh talc 35%, light grade mineral oil 5%; all percentages by weight. Apply at 5 day intervals 20 days before picking fruit.
Leaf Rollers (several species)	Many fruits– Larvae feed on buds, fruit, leaving holes and burrows in fruit and rolled leaves.	Larvae or eggs under bark or on twigs, or pupae in debris– Remove debris and loose bark. Monitor with pheromone traps.	Pick off old leaves and destroy larvae. Trichogramma and other parasitic wasps. *Bt*, dormant oil, ryania. Summer horticultural spray oil.
Pear Psyllas*	Pears– Cause defoliation and black, sooty secretions on leaves and fruit. Can ruin an entire crop	Under bark.	Horticultural dormant oil spray, summer oil spray, insecticidal soap.

continued

PEST	SUSCEPTIBLE TREES & DAMAGE	WHERE PEST OVERWINTERS & PREVENTIVE MEASURES	CONTROLS
Plum Curculio	Many fruits— Adults feed on fruit making crescent-shaped cuts: larvae tunnel in fruit and cause drop.	Adults overwinter in soil and other debris— Collect and destroy dropped fruit frequently to eliminate larvae. Chickens roaming beneath trees eat adults. Cultivate soil around trees in late spring/early summer to destroy larvae and pupae.	Lay tarp beneath tree and bang tree to dislodge and collect adults. Rotenone/pyrethrum, Imidan.
Rodents and Rabbits	All trees— Chew on bark; can girdle and kill tree.	Keep ground cover closely mowed beneath trees. Move mulch away from trunks in fall. Trunk guard made by wrapping tree with old window screening. Push into ground few inches. Will work when no snow on ground. When snow up to 18", use screening and also wrap with tar paper or newspaper above it. Place 6" of gravel or crushed stone around trunk, extending 12"-14" out from trunk. For rabbits: paint trunks and major branches up to 30" high trees with undiluted liquid lime sulfur. Paint late fall, early winter.	Vitamin D3 bait kills them.
Sawflies*	Many fruits— Cause circular raised ridges on the fruit.	Larvae in soil	Rotenone spray at petal fall, horticultural summer oil spray.
Scale*	Many fruits— Sucks plant sap from branches and twigs, causing them to weaken and eventually die. Their feeding leaves red spots on fruit.	On branches	Horticultural dormant oil spray.
Tarnished Plant Bug	Many fruits— Feed on developing buds shortly after new growth in spring. Damage terminal shoots and cause sunken areas on fruit.	Adults under leaf litter, stones, bark— Remove weeds beneath trees. Destroy infested fruit. Prune damaged twigs.	Visual traps (sticky white rectangles). Sabadilla.
Tent Caterpillars*	Many fruits— Their cobwebby masses are easily seen on leaves. Can defoliate entire tree.	Eggs on twigs	Horticultural dormant oil spray, summer oil spray.

Source: Reprinted with permission from Gardener's Supply, Burlington, VT.
* This information from *Fruits and Vegetables: 1001 Gardening Questions Answered,* Editors of Garden Way Publishing, and *Fruits and Berries for the Home Garden,* Lewis Hill

DISEASES OF FRUIT TREES

DISEASE	SUSCEPTIBLE TREES & DAMAGE	WHERE DISEASE OVERWINTERS & PREVENTIVE MEASURES
Apple Scab	Apples– Scab-like lesions on fruit and foliage. Deformed fruits, warped leaves, weakened trees. Worse during damp or rainy weather.	Fallen leaves– Resistant varieties. Clean up leaves under trees. Prune trees to open canopy and improve air circulation. Select site with good air drainage. Foliar feed with urea in fall to hasten leaf drop and decomposition and thus number of spores. Dormant oil. Sulfur or other fungicides. Lime-sulfur, Bordeaux mixture sprayed prior to rain.
Bitter Rot (Fungus or Bacteria?)*	Apples– Fruit rot.	Infected fruit and in bark– Remove infected fruit and fruit mummies. Scrape off loose bark. Prune dead and damaged limbs.
Black Knot (Fungus)	Peaches, plums, apricots, nectarines– Fruit rot, leaf spot, and cankers.	Cankers, old prunings and fruit, and on wild hosts– Remove and burn dead and infected branches. Dormant pruning can reduce susceptibility. Fungicides.
Brown Rot (Fungus)*	Stone fruits– Fruit rot.	Decaying fruit on ground– Harvest all fruit. Remove dead and diseased wood, fallen leaves, and dropped fruit. Apply dormant spray of Bordeaux mixture, copper, or sulfur.
Cankers (Virus and Bacteria)*	Many fruits– Wounds on branches and trunk.	Infected wounds– Avoid injuring trees when planting and cultivating. Cut out diseased wood and cover wound with tree-patching compound. Sterilize tools.
Cedar Apple and Quince Rusts (Fungi)	Apples, quinces, cedars– Orange or rust-colored leaf and fruit spots. Can cause defoliation and ruin fruit.	Cedar apple overwinters in galls on eastern red cedar. Quince overwinters on creeping junipers– Resistant varieties. Remove nearby junipers and red cedars. Fungicides.
Cherry Leaf Spot	Cherries– Leaf spots that can eventually defoliate tree. Worse in damp weather. Spread by wind.	Fallen leaves– Remove fallen leaves. Bordeaux mixture, sulfur, lime-sulfur, other fungicides.
Crown Gall (Bacteria)*	Many fruits– Large swellings on roots.	Soil– Avoid injuring trees when planting and cultivating. Plant disease resistant varieties in uninfected soil. Remove galls with disinfected knife and cover wound with tree-patching compound. Remove and burn heavily infected trees.

continued

Diseases of Fruit Trees (continued)

DISEASE	SUSCEPTIBLE TREES & DAMAGE	WHERE DISEASE OVERWINTERS & PREVENTIVE MEASURES
Fireblight	Apples, pears– Branches wither and turn black. Orange-brown pustules on trunk are signal. Worse in high humidity.	Cankers under bark– Resistant varieties. Remove suckers and infected branches during dormant season. Sterilize pruners. Seal new wounds. Lush growth is more susceptible so don't overfertilize. Remove alternate hosts, i.e., wild apples. hawthorns, mountain ash, cotoneaster. Control pear psylla, leafhoppers, and aphids which spread disease. Antibiotics. Copper sprays.
Peach Leaf Curl (Fungus)	Peaches– Curled, thickened leaves	Twigs– Cut out and burn infected parts. Sterilize pruners. Fungicides.
Powdery Mildew (Fungus)	Many fruits– Leaves distorted and covered with white powder. Infected blossoms don't set fruit. Causes russetted fruit.	Leaf and flower buds– Resistant varieties. Prune to open canopy and improve air circulation. Cut out and burn infected tips. Sterilize pruners. Sulfur and other fungicides.
Sooty Blotch and Fly Speck (Fungi)	Apples– Sooty blotch causes brownish green blotches on fruit that can be removed by rubbing. Fly speck causes black shiny dots on fruit. These diseases often occur together. Worse in high humidity.	Twigs– Prune to open canopy and improve air circulation. Sterilize pruners. Fungicides.
Wilts (Bacteria)	Many fruits– Leaves wilt and die. Can cause branch dieback. Symptoms can resemble those caused by drought and girdling, so confirm diagnosis.	Soil– Keep fruit trees far away from vegetable garden to reduce spread. Avoid planting new trees in soil that might harbor wilt bacteria. Avoid overfertilizing with nitrogen. Cut out and burn disease wood. Sterilize pruners.

Source: Reprinted with permission from Gardener's Supply, Burlington, VT.
* This information from *Fruits and Vegetables: 1001 Gardening Questions Answered,* Editors of Garden Way Publishing, and *Fruits and Berries for the Home Garden,* Lewis Hill

CONTAINER GARDENING

Growing Edibles in Containers/198

Growing Edibles in Containers

PLANT	SUGGESTED VARIETIES	GROWING TIPS	HIGH OR LOW LIGHT*
Beans	Bush: Romano, Royal Burgundy, Venture. Pole: Scarlet Runner	Soak seeds in water overnight to improve germination. Use trellis or support for pole beans.	High light
Beets	Detroit Dark Red, Early Wonder, Burpee's Golden, Cylindra, Boltardy	3-4" between plants if harvesting roots; 2" between plants if harvesting only tops. Plant any time indoors in sunny window. Avoid overcrowding.	Low light
Broccoli	Spartan, Italian Green Sprouting, DiCicco	1-3 plants per 5 gallon container. Continue fertilizing after first harvest to encourage secondary heads.	High light
Brussel Sprouts	Jade Cross Hybrid, Long Island Improved	2-3 plants per 5 gallon container. Sprouts must mature during cool temperatures. Stake when plants are 10-14" tall. Remove tops of plants if necessary to force sprout development. Will produce year-round in southern states. Mild frost improves flavor. Grow indoors in sunny window.	Low light
Cabbage	Earliana, Early Jersey Wakefield, Copenhagen Market, Red Ace, Ruby Ball Hybrid, Red Head Hybrid	2-3 plants per 5 gallon container. Don't plant in same container as cauliflower, brussel sprouts, broccoli, kohlrabi, chinese cabbage, kale, or collards because of disease spread. Maintain uniform moisture.	Low light
Carrots	Little Finger, Ox-Heart, Baby Finger, Royal Chantenay, Spartan Bonus, Nantes, Short N Sweet, Gold Pak	2" between plants. Use loose soil-less mix. Place plastic cover over container to improve germination. Grow indoors in sunny window.	Low light
Cauliflower	Early Snowball, Snow Crown Hybrid, Purple Head	1-2 plants per 5 gallon container. Avoid moisture stress during early growth or they'll form small heads. Tie large outer leaves together over developing head to prevent discoloration. Grow as winter crop if you have mild winters.	High light
Cucumbers	Burpee Hybrid, Bush Whopper, Salad Bush, Park's Burpless Bush, Pot Luck, Burpless Early Pik.	2 plants per 5 gallon container. Support maturing fruit in a sling tied to support or suspend dwarf varieties in hanging basket. Plant vine varieties in long rectangular planter box with trellis.	High light
Eggplant	Slim Jim, Ichiban, Black Beauty, Small Ruffled Red, Thai Green, Bambino	1 plant per 12-18" pot. Likes heat reflected from nearby wall or hang black plastic behind plant. Challenging to grow indoors but it will produce fruit under lights at 65-70°.	High light
Endive	Broadleaved Batavian, Salad King, Green Curled, White Curled	To improve flavor before harvesting, gather outer leaves and tie loosely with string for 2 weeks. Grow indoors in sunny window.	Low light
Garlic	Most varieties	Need 8" deep container. Plant cloves 2" deep and 5" apart. Water well during warm weather. Lift bulbs when foliage shrivels in late summer. Tie in bunches and dry in sun.	High light

continued

PLANT	SUGGESTED VARIETIES	GROWING TIPS	HIGH OR LOW LIGHT*
Herbs	Most varieties	Annual herbs can be brought indoors during cold weather. Perennials should be placed in cold frame or cool basement for winter. Repot once a year. Grow indoors in sunny window.	Light requirement depends on variety
Lettuce	Oak Leaf, Buttercrunch, Salad Bowl, Dark Green Boston, Ruby, Bibb, Little Gem	Can grow indoors year-round in sunny window. Leaf varieties are easiest. Fertilize weekly. Shield from intense sun.	Low light
Melons	Consult seed catalogs for best varieties.	6-8 plants in 1' x 4' box with trellis or support. Or 2 plants per 5 gallon container. Grow best against south facing wall. Make support out of galvanized, welded-wire, 2" x 4" screen. Support developing fruit with nylon sling attached to support. Reduce watering as melons near maturity.	High light
Peas	Sugar Snap, Snowbird, Alaska, Little Marvel, Frosty, Green Arrow, Burpee Sweet Pod	3-6 plants per 5 gallon container. Edible pods are easiest. Plant in long planter boxes with trellis. Yields are reduced in containers so plant a large crop.	High light
Peppers	Bell: Bell Boy, Keystone Resistant, California Wonder, New Ace, World-beater, Sweet Banana. Hot: Red Cherry, Long Red Cayenne, Jalapeño, Thai Hot	1 plant per 8-10" pot. Stake the plants in windy areas. Bring the pots inside when the outside temperature drops below 60° or above 90°.	High light
Potatoes	Chippewa, Sable, White Cobbler	Use a 30-gallon trash can with hole drilled in the bottom for drainage. Plant 3 seed potatoes in half soil/half compost in the bottom. When the potato sprouts are 6" high, cover them with soil/compost, leaving a few leaves showing. Continue to cover with more medium whenever the sprouts are 6" high until the medium reaches the top of the can. Water heavily and don't fertilize. At the end of the season, dump the can over or shovel out your harvest.	High light
Radishes	Cherry Belle, Scarlet Globe	Plant weekly for continuous harvest all summer. When days shorten in fall, bring indoors under lights to extend harvest. Plant in any container at least 8" deep. Grows well with carrots, lettuce, and beets in large planter. Grow indoors in sunny window.	Low light
Shallots/ Onions	Bulbs: White Sweet Spanish, Yellow Sweet Spanish, Southport White Globe, Southport Yellow Globe. Bunching: Evergreen, White Bunching, Kujo Green Multistalk	Outside, plant onion sets 2" apart in spring. Plant mature shallot bulbs 2-3" deep, 4-6" apart in early fall. Overwinter plants, protecting from freezing. Mature shallots can be harvested in summer. Don't let either plant dry out. Grow indoors under lights for 12 hours/day at 60-70°.	High light

continued

PLANT	SUGGESTED VARIETIES	GROWING TIPS	HIGH OR LOW LIGHT*
Spinach	Melody, Long Standing Bloomsdale, America, Avon Hybrid	Best grown in spring and fall. Indoors, keep temperatures between 50-65°. Grow indoors in sunny window.	Low light
Squash	Zucchini: Green Magic, Burpee Golden Zucchini, Burpee Hybrid Zucchini. Acorn: Table King, Cream of the Crop Hybrid. Butternut: Early Butternut, Burpee Butterbush	1-3 plants per 5 gallon container or 1 plant per 12" pot. Use trellis. Support fruit with nylon sling tied to trellis.	High light
Swiss Chard	Fordhook Giant, Burpee's Rhubarb Chard	1 plant per 12" pot or 2-3 per 5 gallon container. Outside, plants will die back in winter and resume growth the following spring. Grow indoors year-round in sunny window.	Low light
Tomatoes	Standard size: Early Girl, Better Boy VFN. Dwarf Determinates: Patio, Pixie, Red Robin, Sugar Lump	Dwarf determinates (patio or cherry types) grow 8" to 3' tall. Dwarf indeterminates grow 3-5' tall and produce larger, more standard size fruit. They are easily supported with a short stake. 1 plant of standard variety per 5 gallon container. Dwarf varieties can be planted in smaller pots or hanging baskets. Need consistent watering. Grow indoors under lights in warm location.	High light
Fruit Trees	Apple: Garden Delicious, Starspur Compact Mac. Apricot: Stark Goldenglo, Goldcot. Cherry: Compact Lambert, North Star. Nectarine: Nectar Babe, Stark Honeyglo. Peach: Honey Babe, Stark Sensation. Naval orange: Washington. Grapefruit: Oro Blanco. Avocado: Mexicola. Banana: Dwarf. Fig: Dwarf	Plant early spring. Buy disease resistant varieties. Need at least 8 hours sun/day. Move to protected area during winter where tree can go dormant without soil freezing. If outdoors, mulch container with straw or newspapers and cover with large appliance box. Water well in early winter and not again until spring. Can train trees as espaliers, with branches growing flat against trellis.	High light
Fruits, Small	Blueberries: Berkeley, Bluecrop, Blueray, Earliblue, Jersey. Choose 2-3 year-old certified plants 1-3 feet tall. Plant bare-root stock in early spring. Strawberries: Alexandria, Baron Solemacher, Blakemore, Surecrop, Solana, Tioga. Raspberries: Allen, Brandywine, Bristol, Latham. Blackberries: Darrow, Oregon Thornless, Thornfree.	For strawberries, use strawberry pots or commercially available strawberry barrels. Some fruits, like blueberries, require 2 different varieties for pollination. Blueberries do especially well in containers because it's easy to keep soil acid enough. During the winter, move all fruits to an unheated garage or basement, mulch the soil, and cover with a protective cover such as GardenQuilt.	High light

* High light is more than 6 hours per day; low light is less than 6 hours per day.

Source: Reprinted with permission from Gardener's Supply, Burlington, VT.

PART III:
INDOOR PLANTS

HOUSEPLANTS

NAME	PROPAGATION BY SEED	VEGETATIVE PROPAGATION	GROWING CONDITIONS	COMMENTS
Abutilon (flowering maple) *Malvaceae hybridum* A. *magapotamicum* (trailing)	Seedlings will not be identical to parents. Sow in February (60-70°F) for autumn flower. In July for spring flowers.	* Take 3-4" tip cuttings (60-65°F). Pot into 3" pots when rooted.	55-75°F (min 50°F). Full sun. Water moderately, keep nearly dry in winter. Don't overfertilize.	Can grow to 5 feet. Prune by ⅓" in March. Discard after 2-3 years. Look out for scale and whitefly.
African violets, see Gesneriads.				
Aralia, see Fatsia				
Asparagus Fern *Liliaceae* *Asparagus plumosus* A. *sprengeri*	Sow seed in April or May (60-70°F). Soaking for 48 hours helps germination, which may take up to 2 months.	* Divide plants in spring.	55-70°F (min 50°F). Good indirect light. Keep moist except in winter.	Attractive, feathery foliage. New stems often bare at first.
Azalea *Ericaceae* *Rhododendron indicum, syn R. simsii* and others	Sow seed in early spring on moist peat, sprinkling sand over top (55-60°F). Keep shaded and moist.	* Take 2-3" cuttings in spring or summer, inserting in 1 peat/2 sand (60°F). Takes 2-3 months to root. Layer by making small slit in young stem and burying 2" deep. Sever after 2 years.	45-55°F (min 35°F, max 70°F). Partial sun. Does well in all-peat mixture. Keep thoroughly moist, avoid hard water.	Likes acid soil, moisture, semi-shade and cool conditions. Prefers to be somewhat potbound. Spray daily when buds form, and keep atmosphere humid. Put outdoors in shade and keep moist in summer.
Begonia (fibrous rooted) *Begoniaceae* *Begonia semperflorens* ("wax-leaved") and others	Sow seed in early spring (60-70°F) on surface of soil in good light. Sprouts in 2-3 weeks. Blooms in 4-6 months. Or sow in August for winter.	* Take 3-4" cuttings any time. Root in peat-sand or water (60-70°F). Flowers in 2 months.	60-70°F (min 50°F). Good indirect light. Add extra peat or leaf mold. Do not firm the soil.	Very easy to grow. Prefers warmth and indirect light, but very tolerant. Water well. Pinch back for bush plants. Some tall species have dramatic stems and foliage. Look out for powdery mildew.
Begonia (rhizomatous) *Begoniaceae* *Begonia rex,* and others	Sow seed in early spring on surface of soil. (65-70°F).	Divide plants in April. * Take leaf cuttings with 1" stalk in spring (65-70°F). For *B.rex,* nick underside of main veins and place flat on peat-sand mix; will root from each wound. When 2 or 3 leaves each, separate seedlings and pot. Take 2-3" stem cuttings of rhizomes.	60-70°F (min 50°F). Good indirect light.	Easy to grow. Culture as for fibrous-rooted begonias.

continued

NAME	PROPAGATION BY SEED	VEGETATIVE PROPAGATION	GROWING CONDITIONS	COMMENTS
Begonia (tuberous) *Begoniaceae* *Begonia cheimantha* (Lorraine) *B. heimalis* *B. tuberhybrida,* and others	Sow seed on surface of soil in February (65-70°F). Blooms in 4-5 months.	Divide tubers in March, one shoot per section. Take stem cuttings in early summer in peat-sand mix (65°F). Pinch back and remove buds until November, then treat as ordinary tubers.	60-65°F (45°F in winter). 50-60°F for Lorraine and B. heimalis varieties when flowering. Good indirect light. Add extra peat or leaf mold or use all-peat mix. Use high potash feed. Plant tubers concave side up, half their depth in soil.	When leaves die back naturally, overwinter tubers at 45°F giving little water. Can store tubers in damp peat over winter. In March increase heat to 60°F and increase watering to start growth. Keep atmosphere moist and avoid drafts. Stake large flowers. Some varieties become only semi-dormant and retain leaves. *B. Heimalis* and Lorraine are winter-blooming.
Beloperone (shrimp plant) *Acanthaceae* *Beloperone guttata*		* 2-3" tip cuttings in spring (65°F). Pot 3-4 cuttings together when rooted.	60-70°F (min 50°F). Partial sun. Water moderately. Add extra peat. 6" pot.	Flowers over long period. Pinch regularly. Prune by ⅓ in March and pot.
Bougainvillea (paper flower) *Nyctaginaceae* *Bougainvillea* x *buttiana* hybrids *B. glabra* Other varieties take several years to flower.		* 3-6" cuttings in spring or summer, with bottom heat (70-75°F). Or 6" cuttings of dormant shoots in January (55°F).	60-70°F (50°F in winter). Full sun. Water moderately; keep nearly dry in winter. 6-8" pot or deep bed.	Colorful bracts around insignificant flowers. Usually loses leaves in winter. Can get very large; prune by ⅓ in early spring.
Bromeliads *Bromeliaceae* *ananas* (pineapple) *Billbergia* and others	Sow fresh seed on surface in 2 peat/1 sand (80°F). Germinates quickly, but takes many years to reach flowering size.	* Offsets produced after flowering; should be potted when leaves are 3-4" and have formed a rosette. Cut close to parent. Best done in early spring.	60-75°F for most. High humidity; mist in warm weather. Full sun in winter, partial shade in summer. Thin-leaved varieties need less sun. Use half loam and half coarse leaf mold for soil mix. Avoid lime. Use rainwater if possible.	Most have watertight reservoir at base of leaves from which they absorb food, therefore need relatively small pots. Ethylene gas from ripe apples or banana skins will induce flowering. Most plants die after flowering.

continued

NAME	PROPAGATION BY SEED	VEGETATIVE PROPAGATION	GROWING CONDITIONS	COMMENTS
Brunfelsia (yesterday, today, and tomorrow) *Solanaceae Brunfelsia paucifolra calycina*	Sow in summer	* Take 3-5" tip cuttings in spring or summer (70°F). When rooted, fertilize weakly, but do not pot for 3 months.	60-80°F. If you want the plant to rest, then keep nearly dry at 50-55°F (min 40°F) in winter. Partial shade in summer; full sun in winter. Maintain high humidity. 5-6" pot.	Flowers change color with age from purple to lavender to white; sometimes fragrant. Flowers better when rootbound. Replace soil in early spring without increasing pot size. Prune by ⅓ to ½ in early spring and pinch growing tips during summer.
Cactus (except epiphytes) *Cactaceae*	Sow fresh seed on surface of soil (70-80°F). Sprouts in about 1 month. Transplant when ½" (may take a year). Some bloom in 3 years, some take much longer.	Divide varieties which produce offshoots in spring. Take cuttings in late spring or early summer. Cut at joint or 4" from tip. Dry for 24 hours then pot in sand or peat-sand mix.	55-70°F (45°F in winter) (min 35°F). Full sun. Water moderately in summer, keep nearly dry in winter. Add extra grit for drainage. Feed only when in bud and flower; use high potash feed.	Likes well-drained soil and lots of light. Do not overpot. Make a paper collar to hold spiney plants with when repotting. Do not firm the compost, just tap the pot to settle it into place. Avoid repotting in winter. Needs very little plant food. Best outdoors in summer. Look out for soft rotting spots which must be cut away completely.
Cactus, epiphytic *Cactaceae Schlumbergera (Christmas cactus) Epiphyllum (Orchid cactus)* and others		Take cuttings at joints in spring or summer. Dry for 24 hours, then pot in ordinary cactus mix.	60-70°F, night 55°F (min 50°F). Partial sun in summer, full sun in winter. Add extra grit. Keep moist and maintain humid atmosphere when in bud and flower. Decrease water after flowering, but do not allow to dry out completely. Avoid hard water and excess nitrogen. 4-5" pot.	Tropical jungle plants with spectacular flowers. Good in hanging baskets when large. Can place outdoors in semishade in summer. Christmas cactus need long nights to set buds; beware of electric lights. A cold period at the end of summer will encourage bud formation of all epiphytic cacti. Do not turn plants in bud, as buds may drop off in effort to turn towards light.
Camellia *Theaceae Camellia japonica C. reticulata C. williamsii* and many hybrids		* Leafbud cuttings or 3-4" cuttings of side shoots in summer (55-60°F).	40-60°F (min 25°F; max 65°F). Partial sun. Maintain humidity. Water well, but keep nearly dry for 6 weeks after flowering. Use lime-free soil, and add extra peat or leaf mold. 8-12" pots or deep bed.	Shiny, evergreen leaves with showy flowers. Early varieties will flower in winter. Will survive freezing, but buds may be damaged. Can grow to 12 feet. Trim if necessary in April. Look out for scale insects.

continued

NAME	PROPAGATION BY SEED	VEGETATIVE PROPAGATION	GROWING CONDITIONS	COMMENTS
Capsicum, see Solanum				
Carnations & Pinks *Caryophyllaceae* *Dianthus*	Sow carnation seed in late winter (65°F until it sprouts, then 50°F). Sow pinks seed in spring or in August for winter flowers (65-70°F). Blooms in 4 months.	* Take 3" cuttings of perpetual carnations in winter (though will root anytime). Insert in sand (65°F reducing to 50°F when begin to grow). Take 3-4" cuttings of pinks in summer. Pot in 1 peat/1 loam/1 sand mix. Keep in partial shade. Cuttings bloom in 4-8 months. Layer side shoots of pinks, border, and annual carnations in midsummer. Sever after 6 weeks, transplant 1 month later.	60°F, night 50°F summer 5°F higher (min 45°F for perpetual carnations, others are frosthardy). Full sun.	Pinch young plants at least once (except for border and annual carnations) to ensure many flowers and bushy plants. Remove all but one bud on each stem if you want large flowers. Support stems with canes or string. Ventilate freely.
Chrysanthemum *Compositae* *Chrysanthemum frutescens* *C. morifolium*	Sow seed shallowly (55-60°F). Sprouts in about 2 weeks.	Divide perennial species in early spring. * Take 2-4" cuttings and pot shallowly in sand or peat-sand mix (55-60°F). Roots in 1-3 weeks. Blooms in 6 months.	50-65°F (min 45°F). Partial to full sun. Buds form only if continuous darkness for 10 hours daily. Maintain humidity. Give good ventilation. Water thoroughly, but allow to dry out between waterings.	Plant shallowly and support large plants with canes. Pinch out the growing tip for more flowers and bushier plant. Or, on standard mums, remove all but one main bud to produce a single enormous flower. Do not grow too close together or few flowers will appear. Time of flowering (2 months from beginning of 10-hour nights) can be accurately controlled by lengthening dark period in summer or giving extra light in fall. Outdoor plants are often lifted in fall to bloom indoors after frost.
Cineraria *Compositae* *Senicio cruentus* hybrids	* Sow April to July (55°F) for flowers January to May. Prick out and grow outdoors over summer, avoiding hot sun.		45-50°F until buds form, then 50-60°F (65°F max). Water well, but don't let them get waterlogged. 6-7" pots.	Usually bought in winter and discarded after flowering. Keep cool and humid. Look out for aphids and whitefly.

continued

NAME	PROPAGATION BY SEED	VEGETATIVE PROPAGATION	GROWING CONDITIONS	COMMENTS
Cissus and Rhoicissus (kangaroo vine, grape ivy, etc.) *Vitaceae* *Cissus antartica* *C. rhombifolia* *Rhoicissus kapensus*		* 3-6" tip cuttings or layered stems	60-70°F (55°F in winter). Indirect light. Water moderately; keep barely moist in winter. 8-10" pots.	Easy foliage plants, will climb or trail. Can grow to 10 feet. Pinch often. Can prune hard in spring. Look out for spider mites.
Clivia *Amaryllidaceae* *Clivia miniata*		* Remove 8-10" tall offsets after plant flowers. Insert in 4" pot of peat-sand (60-65°F). Water sparingly. Flowers in 1-2 years. Old plants can be divided with a knife. Try to avoid damaging roots.	60-70°F (45-50°F in winter). Partial shade. Water and feed well in summer. Keep nearly dry in winter til buds appear. 8-10" pot.	Spectacular flowers in early spring. Prefers being pot bound. Replace top few inches of soil annually in late winter. Repot after flowering every 2-3 years. Remove fruits as flowers fade. For maximum effect do not remove offsets.
Coleus (flamenettle) *Labiatae* *Coleus blumei*	Sow seeds in late winter on surface of soil in good light (70-75°F). Sprouts in 2-3 weeks.	* Take 2-3" cuttings in late summer or early spring (60-65°F).	55-70°F (not over 60°F in winter). Good indirect light. Keep moist in summer, fairly dry in winter.	Brilliantly colored, fast-growing foliage plants. Pinch back for bushiness and remove any flowers which form. Best to start new plants from cuttings or seed each year.
Crassula *Crassulaceae* *Crassula argentea* (jade tree) *C. falcata* (propeller plant) *C. rupestris* (rosary vine) and others		* 2-3" stem cuttings or single leaf cuttings in spring (70°F).	55-75°F (45-55°F in winter). Partial sun. Water moderately; keep nearly dry in winter. Add sharp sand to potting mix. 6-10" pots.	Succulents with unusual leaf forms. Need rest period in winter.
Crown of Thorns *Euphorbiaceae* *Euphorbia milii, syn.* *E. splendens*		* 3-4" tip cuttings. Dip in powdered charcoal and allow to dry for a day. Insert in barely moist peat-sand. Do not overwater.	65-80°F (min 55°F). Full sun. Water moderately; less if below 60°F. Add extra sand to soil mix and pack in firmly.	Very spiny plant with red or yellow bracts over a long period. Lower leaves eventually fall, leaving bare spiny stem.

Episcia, see Gesneriads

Euphorbia, see Crown of Thorns and Poinsettia

continued

NAME	PROPAGATION BY SEED	VEGETATIVE PROPAGATION	GROWING CONDITIONS	COMMENTS
Fatshedera and Fatsia *Araliaceae* *Fatshedera lizei* *Fatsia japonica*	Sow fresh fatsia seed 1" deep in April (55-60°F).	* 3-4" tip or lower stem cuttings (60-70°F).	Fatshedera 55-75°F. Fatsia 45-65°F. Both 40-50°F in winter (min 35°F except variegated – 60°F). Water moderately, less in winter if cold. Extra peat. 8-10" pots.	Easy, nearly hardy, foliage plants. Fatshederas climb or trail. Fatsias make rounded bushes. Can prune hard in spring and will sprout from below. Will survive some freezing, but may be damaged.
Felicia compositae *Felicia amelloides* *F. pappei*		* 2-3" cuttings. June for winter bloom, August for spring and summer.	45-65°F (min 35°F). 5" pots.	Sky-blue daisies all winter. Pinch twice before set buds. Remove flowers as they fade.
Ferns many genera and species	Reproduce by spores that produce prothalli that in turn produce little ferns.	* Some species can be divided. Best done in early spring. Take 2" tip cutting of above-ground rhizomes.	Tropical species, 65-70°F. Temperate species, 55-65°F. Medium indirect light. Maintain humid atmosphere. Spray with fine mist hot weather. Keep soil moist, except in cold weather. Avoid cold or hard water. Use humusy soil (add extra peat or leaf mold) and do not overpot. Apply weak liquid feed. Wide pots better than deep ones.	Avoid direct sunlight. Many ferns are sensitive to pollution in either air or water and to chemical insecticides. Most become dormant below 50°F.
Ficus (fig) *Moraceae* *Ficus Benjamina* *F. elastica* (rubber plant) *F. pumila* (creeping fig) *F. sagittata* and others		*F. pumila* and *F. sagittata* 4-6" cuttings in spring (60-65°F). Larger ficuses are better air layered.	60-70°F (min 50°F for *F. Benjamina* and *F. sagittata* min 35°F for *F. pumila*). Indirect light. Water moderately (except *F. pumila*, keep moist).	An enormous range of foliage plants from trees to creepers. Shiny-leaved ficuses must be kept clean. To encourage branching of rubber plants, cut off tips and sprinkle with powdered charcoal to stop flow of latex sap. Variegated ficuses need more light.
Fuchsia *Onagraceae* *Fuchsia*	Sow seeds in spring (60°F).	Take 3-4" cuttings. Pinch at 3".	50-65°F (40-50°F in winter) (min 35°F, max 70°F) Partial sun. Feed well. 5" pots.	Pot lightly. Keep moist, but water less in winter. Too much heat will cause buds to drop, so give partial shade in hot weather. Cut back in fall or late winter. Keep cold and dry over winter. Will lose leaves. Standards need a little more heat to be sure the head is not damaged. Look out for whitefly.

continued

GROWING POPULAR HOUSEPLANTS (CONTINUED)

NAME	PROPAGATION BY SEED	VEGETATIVE PROPAGATION	GROWING CONDITIONS	COMMENTS
Geranium *Geraniaceae* *Pelargonium domesticum* (regal pelargonium or Martha Washington geranium) *P. hortorum* (zonal or ordinary geranium) *P. peltatum* (ivyleaf geranium) and many scented-leaf geraniums	Sow seeds in early spring (60-65°F). Flowers in 5-9 months.	* Take 3-4" cuttings in late summer or early spring, in sand or peat-sand mix (60-65°F). Flowers in 6-8 months (3-4 months if taken in spring). Summer cuttings bloom all winter if not too cold.	60-70°F (winter 45-50°F) (min 35°F). Full sun. Water thoroughly but allow to dry out between waterings. Keep almost dry in winter. Use high potash feed.	Shade only if necessary to prevent overheating in summer. Will stop flowering if too hot. Does well out of doors in summer. Cut back in fall before taking in. Pinch tips of young plants, except regals. Regals give best show of bloom but have briefer season and should be kept fairly dry for 2 months after flowering.
Gesneriads *Gesneriacea* *Episcia* (flameviolet) *Saintpaulia* (African violet) *Streptocarpus* (Cape primrose)	Sow seed on surface of peat-sand mix (70°F) in good light. Sprouts in about 3 weeks. Blooms in 6-10 months.	Take African violet leaf cuttings (70°F). Blooms in about 1 year. Cut *Streptocarpus* leaves in 3" sections; insert top end up. Blooms in 6-9 months. Pot rooted *Episcia* plantlets at end of stolons. Divide mature plants in early spring.	60-75°F (min 55°F). Good indirect light. Maintain humidity. Water from below to prevent splash marks on leaves and possible rotting. Keep moist but not sodden, and use tepid water. A light, free draining, humusy soil is essential. Does well in all-peat mixture. Give very weak feed at every watering. 5-6" pots.	Does well under fluorescents. Likes warm nights. Pull off any damaged leaves; do not cut. Look out for aphids and mealybugs.
Hibiscus *Malvaceae* *Hibiscus rosa-sinenis*		* 3-4" cuttings, with heel if possible, in spring or summer (65°F). Give weak feed for a month or two after rooting before transplanting.	60-70°F (45-55°F in winter). Partial sun. Water moderately when in growth, keep nearly dry in winter. 8-12" pots.	Big flowers on big plants. Pinch young plants. Can grow to 6 feet plus. Prune hard in early spring.
Hoya see Wax Plant				
Impatiens (Busy Lizzie) *Balsaminaceae* *Impatiens sultanii,* syn *I. wallerana*	Sow seed in spring or summer on surface of soil in good light (65-75°F). Sprouts in 2-3 weeks. Blooms in 3-4 months.	* Take 3" cuttings any time. Root in water or peat-sand mix (60°F). Flowers in 1-2 months. 3 cuttings in a pot quickly makes a bushy plant.	60-75°F (min 50°F, 55°F to flower). Good indirect light. Keep moist, but water less if below 55°F. 5" pots.	Can bloom all year. Pinch back young plants. Prune old plants hard in early spring. Look out for spider mites and aphids.

continued

NAME	PROPAGATION BY SEED	VEGETATIVE PROPAGATION	GROWING CONDITIONS	COMMENTS
Ivy *Araliaceae* *Hedera, Helix,* and others		Take 3-4" cuttings in summer. Root in water or peat-sand mix.	45-65°F (50°F in the winter) (min 30°F). Keep only just moist in winter.	Will climb or trail. Wide variety of leaf shape and variegation. Look out for spider mites.
Jasmine *Oleaceae* *Jasminum officinale* *J. polyanthum*	Sow seeds in fall.	3-5" tip cuttings or heel cuttings after flowering (40-50°F). Pinch 10". Will flower the following winter. Layer shoots in early fall; sever a year later.	5-6" post. 40-60°F (min 30°F; *J. officinale* min 20°F). Full sun. Keep moist, especially in summer. Ventilate well. 8-10" pots, or better in deep bed.	Fragrant climber. *J. polyanthum* winter blooming. Train up wires or canes. Can be set outdoors in summer. Very vigorous. Can grow to 15 feet. Prune after flowering. For small plants, replace every 3 years.
Kalanchoe *Crassulaceae* *Kalanchoe* *blossfeldiana*	Sow on surface in light (70°F). Sow February for winter bloom. May for early spring. Difficult.	3" tip cuttings in May.	55-70°F (min 50°F). Full sun in winter. Water moderately, less after flowering. 5" pots.	Bright red, orange, or yellow winter flowers with shiny succulent leaves. Usually bought in bud and discarded. Need long nights then short nights to flower. Look out for mealybugs and spider mites.
Lantana *Verbaenaceae* *Lantana camara*	Sow February (60°F) for summer.	3" stem cutting in August (60-65°F).	60-70°F (winter 50°F) (min 45°F). Partial to full sun. Maintain humidity. Keep moist in summer, nearly dry in winter. 6-8" pots (up to 12" for standards).	Bright colored, fragrant summer flowers. Can grow as annuals. Pinch overwintered cuttings in late winter. Prune old plants hard in February. Look out for whitefly.
Monstera (Swiss cheese plant) *Araceae* *Monstera deliciosa*		Tip cutting in April or May (75-80°F) or air layers.	65-70°F (min 45°F). Good indirect light. Water sparingly and maintain humidity. Add leaf mold to soil. 10-12" pots.	Large, shiny leaves that develop holes with age. Can grow to 15 feet, but needs staking. Train aerial roots around damp moss-covered pole if possible. If not, let them root in pot.

continued

NAME	PROPAGATION BY SEED	VEGETATIVE PROPAGATION	GROWING CONDITIONS	COMMENTS
Orchid *Orchidaceae*	Propagation by seed is a difficult, highly specialized business.	Mature plants can be divided. Each piece of rhizome should have at least 1, preferably 2 or 3, pseudobulbs attached.	Temperature depends on species. Full sun in winter. Partial shade or good indirect light in summer. Terrestial orchids – 1 coarse peat/1 loam/1 sand/1 sphagnum moss. Epiphytic orchids – 2 osmunda fiber or shredded bark/1 sphagnum moss, or 1 coarse peat/1 perlite/1 sphagnum moss. Allow soil nearly to dry between watering, then soak well. Needs little plant food. A foliar feed once a month should be enough.	Avoid stagnant air. Most species like a lot of heat if there is sufficient humidity (from 70% up to 100% for tropical species). Remove damaged roots and pack soil in firmly when repotting. Do not water newly planted orchids, mist daily for 3-4 weeks. Many orchids have a dormant period in fall or winter when they require very little water. Epiphytic orchids grow naturally on trees and suffer greatly if their roots are kept wet. Grow them on a piece of bark, a wooden basket or special perforated pot for sufficient aeration.
Orchid Cactus, See Cactus, epiphytic				
Palm *Palmae* *Howea, syn Kentia* *Washington* and others	Sow seed in February (80°F). May take months to sprout.		55-70°F. Partial shade in summer, partial sun in winter.	Water well in summer, keep fairly dry in winter. Keep atmosphere moist in spring and summer. Dislikes drafts. Difficult to propagate, easiest to buy small plants. Look out for scale insects.
Passiflora (Passion flower) *Passifloraceae* *Passiflora caerulea* *P. edulis*	* Sow in spring (65-70°F).	* 3-4" stem cuttings in summer (60-65°F). When rooted give weak feed till winter, then keep fairly dry. Pot in early spring.	60-70°F (winter 50°F) (min 40°F). Partial sun. Keep moist in summer, nearly dry in winter. Maintain humidity. 8" pot.	Extraordinary flowers, thought to represent the Passion of Christ. *P. edulis* has more attractive leaves and delicious fruits like pale green eggs. Fast-growing climbers. Prune hard in early spring, cut side shoots to 2-3". If frosted, plant will often send up new shoots from base. Look out for spider mites.
Pelargonium, see Geranium				
Philodendron *Araceae* *Philodendron*	Nonclimbing varieties can be propagated by seed. Sown in April (75°F).	3-6" cuttings in June or October (70°F). Some species can be divided.	55-65°F (min 50°F). Good indirect light. Add extra peat to soil. 10-12" pot.	Keep soil and atmosphere moist, especially in summer. Most need staking; damp moss on stake will encourage aerial roots.

continued

NAME	PROPAGATION BY SEED	VEGETATIVE PROPAGATION	GROWING CONDITIONS	COMMENTS
Pinks, see Carnations				
Plumbago *Plumbaginaceae* *Plumbago capensis,* *syn P. auriculata*		* 3-4" heel cuttings in June (60-65°F). When rooted, feed weakly till 12" high then pinch and pot.	55-75°F (winter 45-50°F) (min 35°F). Partial sun. Water well in summer; keep nearly dry in winter. 8-10" pot (better in ground bed).	Pale blue or white flowering climber. Must be tied to support. Will survive, but loses leaves at 30°F. Can grow to 15ft. Prune new growth by ⅔ in February.
Poinsettia *Euphorbia* *Pulcherrima*		Take 3-6" cuttings in spring; dip in powdered charcoal (60-65°F). Keep fairly dry until well-rooted, then water young plants freely.	Winter 55-50°F, rest of year 60-75°F. Full sun in winter, partial sun in summer. Allow soil to dry between waterings, then water well.	Not really worth keeping for a second year, but if you want to try, keep just moist in winter; gradually dry off after flowering. Cut back to 2" from base. Start watering again in April. Keep humid atmosphere when growing. Can be put out of doors in summer. Needs long nights to flower. Provide 2 hours extra darkness from October on to produce flowers by Christmas. Commercial growers use dwarfing hormones to keep plants short.
Salvias *Labitae* *Salvia argentea* *S. fulgens* *S. patens* *S. rutilans*	Sow seeds in March (65°F).	3" cuttings April or September (55-60°F).	50-60°F (min 35°F). Water well in summer; keep nearly dry in winter. 6-8" pots.	Brilliantly colored red or blue flowers. Can be made to bloom indoors in winter, or grown for summer garden. Pinch. Prune to 4-6" in February. Look out for spider mites.
Schefflera *Araliaceae* *Schefflera* *actinophylla, syn.* *Brassaia* *actinophylla*	Sow fresh seed with bottom heat (70-75°F).	Air layer.	60-70°F (min 55°F). Good indirect light. Water moderately; keep nearly dry in winter. Maintain humidity. 8-10" pots.	Shiny leaves and attractive structure. Keep leaves clean. Can grow to 6 feet. Difficult to propagate, easiest to buy small plants.

continued

NAME	PROPAGATION BY SEED	VEGETATIVE PROPAGATION	GROWING CONDITIONS	COMMENTS
Solanums and Capsicums *Solanceae* *S. capsicastrum* (winter cherry) *S. pseudocapsicum* (Jerusalem cherry) *C. frutescens* (ornamental pepper)	Sow shallowly in March (60-65°F). Pinch.		70-80°F (55-60°F in winter) (min 50°F). Full sun. Water well. Maintain humidity. 4-6" pots.	Ornamental fruits in winter. Will fruit again if pruned hard, potted, and put outside for the summer. Keep fairly dry to rest in spring. Mist plants while flowering to encourage fruit set. Look out for spider mites and whitefly.
Sparmannia (room lime or zimmer linden) *Tiliaceae* *Sparmannia africana*		3-6" cuttings in April (60-65°F). Pinch.	55-65°F (45°F in winter). Good indirect light or partial sun. Keep humid if over 60°F. Water well in summer; keep barely dry in winter. 6" pot (10" for 6 foot plant).	Fast growing, bush plants with large leaves and white flowers. Can grow to 10 feet. Prune hard in March. Replace overgrown plants with cutting.
Spider plant *Liliaceae* *Chlorophytum* *Elatum variegatum*		Set small plants on surface of soil in separate pots. Sever when well rooted. Divide large plants in spring.	50-60°F (min 45°F). Partial shade. Good in hanging baskets.	Easy trailer. Keep moist in spring and summer, somewhat drier in fall and winter. Avoid drafts. Invasive, will root in other plants' pots.
Streptocarpus see Gesneriads				
Wandering Jew *Commelinaceae* *Callisia* *Setcreasea* *Tradescantia* *Zebrina Purpusii*		Take 3" cuttings in summer. Root in peat-sand mix or just water (60-65°F). Three in a pot will quickly produce a bushy plant.	60-75°F (min 50°F). 4-6" pots.	Hard to keep for more than a few years, but easy to propagate. Pinch young plants to promote bushiness. Remove any nonvariegated shoots. Water freely in summer, less in winter.
Wax Plant *Asclepiadaceae* *Hoya camosa* *H. bella* (miniature)		Take 3-4" cuttings of mature stems in summer. Root in peat-sand mix (60-65°F). Layer shoots in spring.	60-70°F (winter 55-65°F) (min 45°F). Full sun in winter, partial shade in summer. Maintain humidity. 6-10" pots.	Fragrant flowers drip sweet nectar. Pinch back young plants, but do not prune older ones. Keep moist in summer, cooler and drier in fall and winter. Dislikes root disturbance.

* preferred method of propagation

Source: *Sunspaces,* Peter Clegg and Derry Watkins

INDOOR PLANT PESTS

PEST	DESCRIPTION	SYMPTOM	CURE
Aphids or plant lice	(3 mm): White, red, green, or black, these small, softbodied insects suck plant juices and carry fungus and disease.	Foliage deformation. Sticky, curled, or yellowed leaves. Sometimes a sooty mold.	Remove aphids with an alcohol-dipped cotton swab. Rinse plant in a soapy solution and then in lukewarm water. Spray with pyrethrin, if necessary.
Mealybugs	(6 mm): These white, oval, hairy-looking insects with a cottony appearance suck plant juices.	Pale foliage. Leaf drop. Stunted growth.	Remove mealybugs with an alcohol-dipped cotton swab. Wash with soapy water. Spray only if necessary.
Mites	(7 mm): Very hard to see without a magnifying glass, mites suck plant juices.	Leaf curl. Leaf drop. Stunted growth. Blackened buds. Grayish, dusty look to the plant. Webs on the underside of the plant.	Very difficult to eradicate. Try soapy water. Remove from the rest of your plants. Spray with insecticide. Put plant outside. High humidity sometimes helps.
Scales	(3 mm): Hard-shelled lumps on stems and leaves attach so tightly they sometimes look like part of the plant.	Yellowed foliage. Dropping leaves.	Scrub off with alcohol-soaked swab. Rinse in soapy water. Spray as necessary. Very difficult to eradicate if the infestation is heavy.
Whiteflies	(1.60 mm): White, wedge-shaped winged insects that suck plant juices and spread diseases, especially viruses.	Yellowing leaves. Dropping leaves. Swarms when plant is disturbed.	Wish with strong water spray. Difficult to eradicate. Sometimes a hot pepper spray solution helps. Quarantine the plant.

Source: *The Able Gardener*, Kathleen Yeomans, R.N.

INDOOR PLANT DISEASES

DISEASE	SYMPTOM	CURE
Bacterial infection	Graying and yellowing leaves. Crown rot.	Use antifungal spray. Water from the bottom.
Botrytis blight	Gray mold on all parts of the plant.	Avoid overcrowding, overfeeding, and overwatering. Provide good air circulation. Spray with antifungals. Dispose of infected plants.
Edema	Plants rapidly absorb water, but transpiration is slow and cells burst. Swelling on leaves and corky ridges.	Increase temperature and lower humidity. Allow soil to dry out before watering.
Fungal diseases	Stem and root rot.	Increase air circulation. Decrease humidity.
Powdery mildew	Leaves covered with white powder.	Use antifungal spray. Let dry between waterings. Usually can't be saved.
Virus	Mottled, yellowing leaves. Leaf curl. Spotted flowers. Stunted growth.	Remove and destroy infected plant promptly. Watch out for the insects that spread these diseases!

Source: *The Able Gardener*, Kathleen Yeomans, R.N.

NOTES

NOTES

NOTES